Robert Harley, Puritan Politician

Portrait of Robert Harley in the possession of Christopher Harley

Robert Harley, Puritan Politician

by Angus McInnes

VICTOR GOLLANCZ LTD · LONDON · 1970

ISBN 0 575 00521 1

The frontispiece is reproduced by
kind permission of Christopher Harley

PRINTED IN GREAT BRITAIN
BY EBENEZER BAYLIS AND SON LTD.
THE TRINITY PRESS, WORCESTER, AND LONDON

To my parents

To my parents

The tradition of all the dead generations weighs like a mountain upon the brain of the living.

KARL MARX

But most men seek the place where they were born.

ALUN LEWIS

Preface

THIS BOOK IS not, in the conventional sense, a life of Robert Harley, nor even a political biography. It is, rather, an attempt to elucidate Harley's political personality. In other words, its central purpose is not to tell a tale, but to explain what happened.

Since the aim of the study is, in this way, to analyse rather than describe it has not been felt necessary, or even desirable, to recount in detail all Harley's political doings. Throughout, the treatment is selective in its emphases. To illustrate each theme a competent number of examples has been singled out for detailed exposition. Other material has been passed over more lightly. To have given this equal attention would have been to clog the argument and make the book unnecessarily long.

All this is important to emphasise because it has implications for the balance of the study. The brief ministry of 1701, for example, is more lightly treated here than might otherwise have been the case in a more orthodox approach. The reason for this is that Harley's record as Court Politician can be more adequately illustrated by an examination of the much longer and better documented Triumvirate administration. By contrast, Harley's fall in 1708 and his collapse in 1714 have both been dissected in detail since these two events reveal more clearly than anything else the Herefordshire man's lingering Country mentality. However, precisely because the treatment is selective rather than enumerative in character it has been deemed wise to back up statements with very full and, at times, discursive footnotes.

Many people have helped me to write this book. I recall with particular pleasure the gifted teaching of Professor S. H. F. Johnston of Aberystwyth. It was Professor Johnston who first fired my interest in the period, and who encouraged me to

1*

tackle Harley. Since then I have benefited from conversations with Mr. Andrew Compton, Mr. J. A. Garrard, and Mr. Cedric Parry. The Marquess of Bath, the Marquess of Cholmondeley, the Earl of Dartmouth, the Duke of Devonshire and the Chatsworth Trustees, the Marquess of Downshire, Colonel James Hanbury, Mr. Christopher Harley, the Duke of Marlborough, the Duke of Portland, the Warden and Fellows of All Souls College, Oxford, and the Trustees of the Dr. Williams's Library were all kind enough to allow me to use manuscripts in their possession, and to them I am most grateful. I have also had a great deal of help from librarians and archivists up and down the country. In particular I should like to thank the library assistants at the University College of Wales, Aberystwyth, the National Library of Wales, and the University of Keele. One's deepest obligations are, of course, of a personal nature not proper to be recorded in public. One of them, however, is hinted at on another page.

A.M.

DECEMBER, 1969.

B.M.	British Museum.
Bodl.	Bodleian Library, Oxford.
Bol. Corr.	G. Parke (ed.) *Letters and Correspondence Public and Private of the Right Honourable Henry St. John, Lord Viscount Bolingbroke* (London, 1798).
Coxe.	W. Coxe, *Memoirs of John Duke of Marlborough, with his original Correspondence* (London, 1820).
Defoe Letters.	G. H. Healey (ed.), *The Letters of Daniel Defoe* (Oxford, 1955).
H.M.C.	*Report of the Historical Manuscripts Commission.*
Luttrell.	N. Luttrell, *A Brief Historical Relation of State Affairs from September 1678 to April 1714.* (Oxford, 1857).
N.L.W.	National Library of Wales.
N.U.L.	Nottingham University Library.
P.R.O.	Public Record Office.
Ranke.	L. von Ranke, *A History of England, Principally in the Seventeenth Century* (Oxford, 1875).
R.O.	Record Office.
Sarah Corr.	*Private Correspondence of Sarah, Duchess of Marlborough* (London, 1838).
Somers Tracts.	W. Scott (ed.) *A Collection of scarce and valuable Tracts selected from . . . the Royal, Cotton, Sion and other . . . Libraries, particularly that of the late Lord Somers* (London, 1809–15).
Swift Corr.	F. Elrington Ball (ed.), *The Correspondence of Jonathan Swift* (London, 1910–14).
Vernon Corr.	G. P. R. James (ed.), *Letters Illustrative of the Reign of William III from 1696 to 1708 Addressed to the Duke of Shrewsbury, by James Vernon* (London, 1841).
W.S.L.	William Salt Library, Stafford.

Note on Dates and Style

Unless otherwise stated all dates in this book are Old Style. In every case, however, the year is reckoned as beginning on 1 January not 25 March.

In transcripts from manuscript material spelling and punctuation have been modernised.

Contents

Robert Harley, Puritan Politician

1 Background of a Politician

HIGH UP THE Teme valley, ten miles to the west of Ludlow, lies the village of Brampton Bryan, nestling beneath the hills and sheepwalks of Radnorshire. Here, in a niche cut into the south wall of the village church, rests a stone figure, worn with age. It is, or rather was, the effigy of Margaret, the last of the Bramptons. In 1309 Margaret took in marriage the Shropshire knight Robert de Harley, and thus first brought the Harleys to these remote western parts of Herefordshire. At some subsequent date, it is believed in the latter half of the fourteenth century, Brampton Bryan became the main seat of Harley power, and throughout the ensuing centuries of turbulence the family succeeded in preserving and consolidating its estate in this region. By the mid-seventeenth century the Harleys' income from land totalled about £1,500 per annum.[1] In other words they ranked among what Professor Habakkuk has termed "the substantial squires".[2]

Up to this point, however, the family had been of local importance only. It is true that from time to time a Harley had flitted briefly across the broader page of English history. Sir William, for example, had accompanied Godfrey de Bouillon to the Holy Land. Sir Richard had assisted in Roger Mortimer's rescue of the captive Prince Edward from Hereford, while, at a later date, Richard's younger brother Malcolm was made Edward's Chaplain and King's Escheator South of the Trent. In the fourteenth century a Harley had fought with the Black Prince; another had defended Montgomery and Dolverin castles against Glyn Dŵr. Still later, in Tudor days, John Harley had become Chaplain to Edward VI and Bishop of Hereford. But such appearances were fleeting and individually of no great

[1] The Brampton Bryan rent roll for 1655 ran to £1,423 18s. 7d. B.M. Portland Loan, 53(2).
[2] H. J. Habakkuk, "English Landownership, 1680–1740", *Economic History Review*, vol. X (1939–40), pp. 2–17.

moment. Throughout the Middle Ages the Harleys were considerably outshone by their powerful Wigmore neighbours, the Mortimers. As with so many other families it was the seventeenth century dispute between Crown and Parliament which swept them on to the national stage. The first man to perform in this more exalted atmosphere was Sir Robert Harley (1579–1656). His son, and Robert Harley's father, Sir Edward (1624–1700), was the second.[3]

An analysis of the careers of these two men shows that both were vigorous Puritans. In the sixteen twenties and thirties Sir Robert made Brampton Bryan the home of early Welsh Puritanism, the sanctuary of men like Morgan Llwyd and Vavasour Powell.[4] When, later on, England dissolved into civil war, his religious convictions led him to embrace the Puritan cause without hesitation. He himself fought as an officer in the Roundhead armies, and at the same time he lent plate and money to boost rebel finances. But perhaps most noteworthy of all were the thoroughness and relish with which he performed his iconoclastic duties as a member of the Commons Committee for the Destruction of Idolatrous Relics, to the chair of which he was elected in 1644. A series of matter-of-fact bills and receipts preserved among the Harley papers[5] vividly documents the havoc wrought:

1644, November 26—Receipt by Thomas Gastaway of £2 6s. from Sir Robert Harley for taking down the organ and organ case at Greenwich, and for making a scaffold to cut out the Resurrection where the Kings and Queens stand in the Abbey of Westminster, and for planing out seven pictures.

1645, June 10—Receipt by Robert Hicks of £4 from Sir

[3] The chief sources for the early history of the Harley family are: the family notes and pedigrees in Longleat, Portland MSS., X, ff. 167–80, B.M. Additional MSS., 5,834, B.M. Harleian MSS., 1,545, and B.M. Stowe MSS., 597; the Harley Letters in Hereford City Library; the correspondence in *H.M.C. Portland MSS.*, III; Edward Harley's "Memoirs of the Harley Family", *ibid.* V, pp. 641–69; and A. Collins, *Historical Collections of Cavendish, Holles, Vere, Harley and Ogle* (London, 1752.)
[4] T. Froysell, *The Beloved Disciple* (London, 1658); G. F. Nuttall, *The Welsh Saints, 1640–60* (Cardiff, 1957), pp. 1–17, and *passim*; T. Richards, *Piwritaniaeth a Pholitics, 1689–1719* (Wrecsam, 1927), p. 65. Sir Robert's tutor at Oriel College, Oxford, it is worth noting, was Cadwallader Owen a member of a famous Welsh Puritan Family.
[5] *H.M.C. Portland MSS.*, III, pp. 132–4.

Robert Harley for new white glass in St. Margaret's Church, including thirty five feet of new glass on the north side of the chancel where the holy lambs were, forty feet of new glass in the window at the east end of the gallery, where the Virgin Mary was, and sixty feet of new glass in the window by the gallery stairs.

1645, June 14—Receipt by Richard Culmer of £8 11s. 2d. from Sir Robert Harley being the proceeds of the burning of embroidery called the Glory, belonging to the high altar of Canterbury Cathedral, delivered to Sir Robert Harley by the appointment of Mr. John Lade, Mayor of Canterbury.

All over the capital, thanks to Sir Robert's zeal, altars were pulled down, pictures defaced, copes and mitres removed, stained glass broken, communion tables displaced, crosses and statuary smashed, and priceless vestments consigned to the flames.

Sir Edward was built in a similar mould. Educated at Magdalen Hall, Oxford, at that time a hotbed of Puritanism, he too carved out for himself a successful career in the parliamentary armies. His servitor at Oxford had been George Griffiths, a Montgomeryshire man, who was later to become a leader among the Sectaries in England,[6] and the influence of men like this never left him. Throughout his life he made a practice of "constant reading of the Scriptures".[7] Although he conformed to the Established Church at the Restoration, it is clear that he was very much on the left wing of Anglicanism, and, in fact, on more than one occasion he was represented to Charles II as a "Presbyterian rogue".[8] Throughout these years he continued to attend chapel as well as church, and he remained on the closest terms with Nonconformist leaders like Edmund Calamy and the "incomparable" Richard Baxter.[9] All attempts to persecute the Dissenters he regarded as "a national sin". "It grieves me", he wrote on one occasion, "the

[6] Nuttall, op. cit., p. 9.
[7] Edward Harley's "Memoirs", H.M.C. Portland MSS., V, p. 643.
[8] E.g. Sir Edward Harley to the Earl of Clarendon, 12 Dec. 1665, H.M.C. Portland MSS., III, p. 294, and Sir Robert Harley to Sir Edward Harley, 4 Jan. 1668, ibid., p. 306.
[9] Edward Harley's "Memoirs", ibid. V, p. 643. "I am greatly grieved for the loss of incomparable Mr. Baxter". Sir Edward Harley to Robert Harley, 14 Dec. 1691, B.M. Portland Loan, 142(6).

poor Dissenters who preach and live poor in this world, rich in faith, must be engaged to the punishment of paying out of nothing". He vigorously opposed the Test Act, and he took an equally firm stand against the catholicising policy of James II. He did his best, for instance, to dissuade Herbert Croft, Bishop of Hereford, from reading out James's Declaration of Indulgence. Always Sir Edward acted, in his own words, as "a child of God" who "hath his conversation in heaven". For him, as for Bunyan's Pilgrim, life was a journey through "this valley of the shadow of death" towards "that unchangeable state to which every moment hastens".[10]

It was not just in their religious convictions, however, that father and son were alike. In their attitude to the great public causes of the day, too, they steered a similar course. Politically both of them were essentially moderate, middle-way men. It is true of course, that they hated Charles I's system implacably, and were prepared to fight it tooth and nail. Sir Robert in particular bayed as loud as anyone for Strafford's blood. Nonetheless, the fact remains that they were as suspicious of Cromwell's "sober, regular army" as of Charles and his minions. Their real ideal was neither royal absolutism nor army rule, but limited monarchy. To the end they hoped for an accommodation with the King,[11] and when the axe fell they withdrew their support from the rebel regime, Sir Robert preferring to forfeit his lucrative post as Master of the Mint rather than coin money for a regicide government.[12] For their pains both men were expelled from the Commons, and for the rest of the Protectorate period they lived under a cloud. When Sir Edward attempted to get back into Parliament in 1659 he was excluded. So too was his brother.[13]

[10] Edward Harley's "Memoirs", *H.M.C. Portland MSS.*, V, pp. 642–3; Sir Edward Harley to Robert Harley, 25 Feb. 1691, B.M. Portland Loan, 141(1); same to same, 22 Dec. 1691, *ibid.*, 141(5); same to same, 22 Jan. 1692, *ibid.*, 141(5); same to same, 9 Feb. 1692, *ibid.*, 141(6).

[11] Sir Harbottle Grimstone to Sir Robert Harley, 21 Oct. 1648, *H.M.C. Portland MSS.*, III, p. 165; Edward Harley's "Memoirs", *ibid.*, V, p. 641; C. H. Firth (ed.), *The Memoirs of Edmund Ludlow* (Oxford, 1894), Vol. I, pp. 149–52.

[12] Edward Harley's "Memoirs", *H.M.C. Portland MSS.*, V, p. 641; *Calendar of State Papers Domestic, 1649–50*, p. 142. The salary of the Master of the Mint seems to have been £500 p.a. *ibid*, 1625–6, p. 469.

[13] Edward Harley's "Memoirs", *H.M.C. Portland MSS.*, V, p. 641; Viscount Conway to Sir Edward Harley, 25 Feb. 1660, *ibid.*, III, p. 218; *Memoirs of Edmund Ludlow*, vol. II, p. 232.

Sir Robert Harley died in 1656 when the family fortunes were at their nadir. But at the Restoration the Harleys again came into their own, and honours were showered upon his son. He was elected to the Council of State, made Governor of Dunkirk, and dubbed a Knight of the Bath.[14] However, neither such preferential treatment nor the discrimination shown against him under Cromwellian rule altered his basic political outlook. He remained what he always had been, a qualified and critical royalist, ready to pounce at the slightest hint of tyrannical behaviour. When news of the Popish Plot broke, for example, all the old suspicions welled up once more, and from that moment on he became an ardent supporter of Exclusion.[15] After Charles II had succeeded in routing the Whigs at the Oxford Parliament, Sir Edward found himself peremptorily bundled out of the commission of the peace along with Shaftesbury and his lieutenants. In 1685 the government felt it wise to take the Herefordshire man into custody lest he should join Monmouth's rebellion. Although in the balmy days of 1660 the exiled Stuarts smiled on Sir Edward, they quickly came to realise that they were dealing with the same man who had taken up arms against the Crown in the sixteen forties.[16]

One more point of comparison may perhaps profitably be drawn between Sir Robert and his son. Both men had a deep sense of public spirit and of fair play. From his correspondence Sir Robert emerges as a sombre figure, obsessed with questions of right and wrong. He willingly devoted toilsome hours of his time both as member of Parliament and as J.P. in the performance of what he saw to be his bounden duty. Sir Edward was a man of the same stamp. Gentle, humane and generous, he was far

[14] *Journals of the House of Commons*, VII, p. 849; Edward Harley's "Memoirs", *H.M.C. Portland MSS.*, V, p. 641; paper entitled "remembrances for my equipage for Knight of the Bath", *ibid.*, III, p. 249.

[15] Sir Edward voted for the first Exclusion Bill in 1679. (A. Browning and D. J. Milne, "An Exclusion Bill Division List", *Bulletin of the Institute of Historical Research*, vol. XXIII (1950), pp. 205–25). Two years later the prospect of barring James's accession still sent him into ecstasy. "The Lord reigns", he exclaimed, when the Oxford Parliament resolved to press Exclusion, "let the earth rejoice". (Sir Edward Harley to Lady Harley, 26 March 1681, B.M. Portland Loan, 183). See generally Sir Edward's family correspondence in the 1679–81 period in *ibid.*

[16] Sir Edward's confinement in 1685 drew forth a veritable deluge of biblical moralising. See the papers in Sir Edward's hand variously dated between 18 June and 15 July 1685, *ibid.* These papers are noted in *H.M.C. Portland MSS.*, III, pp. 384–5, but not printed in full.

removed from the typical grasping political aspirant with which Sir Lewis Namier has familiarised us in the eighteenth century. As Governor of Dunkirk he was meticulous and unbribable.[17] He financed out of his own pocket the rebuilding of Brampton Bryan church which had been destroyed in the civil wars. He augmented the livings of neighbouring parishes.[18] He and his family had endured great loss in the civil wars.[19] His mother's health had been shattered by the siege of Brampton Bryan. Yet he was not embittered or vengeful. When the estate of the royalist commander Sir Henry Lingen, one of the leaders of the siege of Brampton Bryan, was taken from him and given to the Harleys in reparation for their sufferings, Edward gave it back, relinquishing all claim to the property. He was not interested in the spoils of victory. "I pray God", he wrote, almost half a century later, "heal the divisions of His people".[20]

Possibly the most revealing of all Sir Edward's actions came at the time of the Glorious Revolution. When the Protestant wind began to blow, the old man, now in his middle sixties, gathered together a troop of horse and marched on Worcester, determined to hold it for the Prince of Orange. His second son, Edward, recorded:

[17] Of Sir Edward's work as Governor Auditor Harley writes: "King Charles II often expressed his great esteem for him for having saved above ten thousand pounds in the contingencies and other extraordinaries of the garrison, which was entirely under his own management; he paid the same into the Exchequer, which I have often heard the old Earl of Macclesfield mention as a very bad precedent for commanding officers". Edward Harley's "Memoirs", *ibid.*, V, p. 642. Sir Edward opposed the sale of Dunkirk to the French and is reputed to have refused a bribe of £10,000 to remain silent on the matter. Collins, *op. cit.*, p. 302.

[18] Edward Harley's "Memoirs", *H.M.C. Portland MSS.*, V, p. 642. Edward speaks of his father "giving yearly out of his estate about £180 for augmenting the vicarages and rectories of Brampton, Leintwardine, Wigmore, Leinthall, Lingen, Knighton, and Stow".

[19] In 1646 Sir Robert's losses in Herefordshire were estimated at £12,990. (Samuel Shelton's paper, 23 July 1646, Harley Letters, Hereford City Library). Auditor Harley states that his father's estate was "laid waste to the value of sixty thousand pounds". Edward Harley's "Memoirs", *H.M.C. Portland MSS.*, V, p. 641.

[20] *Ibid.*, p. 642; Sir Edward Harley to Robert Harley, Dec. 1692, B.M. Portland Loan, 142(1). For the siege itself see R. W. Banks, "An Account of the Siege of Brampton Bryan Castle", *Archaeologia Cambrensis*, 3rd series, vol X (1864), pp. 232–243, and J. D. La Touche, "Brampton Bryan Castle: its Sieges and Demolition", *Transactions of the Woolhope Club* (1882), pp. 189–97. There is a sketch of Sir Edward's mother, Brilliana, in W. Notestein, *English Folk* (London, 1938), pp. 271–308. Transcripts of many of Brilliana's letters may be found among the Harley Letters in Hereford City Library.

By his great care and prudence that very populous city was kept in absolute quiet, which perhaps was the only one throughout the kingdom that did not feel the shocks of this consternation.

It is all there—the courage, the sense of duty, the dislike of tyranny, the willingness to hazard personal fortune. Even religion crept in. Edward records how his father commanded the soldiers to give back all their plunder: all, that is, "except a blasphemous image of the Holy Trinity which he ordered to be broken to pieces in the open street".[21]

Into this atmosphere—puritannical, public spirited, anti-authoritarian—Robert Harley was born on 5 December 1661.

---

[21] Edward Harley's "Memoirs", *H.M.C. Portland MSS.*, V, pp. 643-4.

2 Court Whigs and Country Whigs

"BETH FYDD Y bachgen hwn?" What shall this child be? The question posed by Lloyd George's cobbler uncle would have been less poignantly applicable to Robert Harley. From childhood he was destined to a public life. Both as the heir of a leading family of country gentry and as the descendant of a politically active line, he was, in Sir Lewis Namier's phrase, "an inevitable Parliament man". However, if Harley's fortunes were in a measure irretrievably fixed, the wheels of destiny nonetheless ground slowly. It was not until 1689, his twenty-eighth year, that he made his parliamentary debut. In April of that year he was at length returned to the Commons as a member for the Cornish borough of Tregony. The author of "this dispensation" was Hugh Boscawen, the death of whose brother, the previous member, had brought about the vacancy. Harley had been recommended to Boscawen as a suitable successor by his father-in-law Thomas Foley by Thomas's brother Paul, and by their kinsman John Hampden.[1]

From the outset it must have been crystal clear to all that Harley was entering political life "on a Revolution bottom". The group whose protégé he was—the connexion headed by his father and the two Foley brothers—was unashamedly Whig in sentiment. Unlike the Harley clan the Foleys were not a long-established landed family. On the contrary their swift rise bore all the stigmata of the *nouveau riche*.[2] As iron masters in Stourbridge they succeeded during the course of the seventeenth century in piling up an enormous fortune. Then, having

---

[1] Sir Edward Harley to Robert Harley, 30 March 1689, *H.M.C. Portland MSS.*, III, pp. 435–6; T. Foley to Robert Harley, 13 April 1689, B.M. Portland Loan, 136.
[2] For the rise of the Foleys see B. L. C. Johnson, "The Foley Partnerships: the Iron Industry at the End of the Charcoal Era", *Economic History Review*, 2nd series, vol. IV (1951–2), pp. 322–40.

acquired the sinews of political power, they took steps to obtain
the necessary badge of prestige by buying up estates in Worcestershire, Herefordshire and Staffordshire. Even so, although in
their social origins the two families differed so markedly, in
their political and religious outlook they were identical. Like
Sir Edward the Foley brothers were sombre Puritans; like him
too they were deeply suspicious of the Crown's authority.
Throughout the Convention Paul Foley's conduct was a model
of Whig orthodoxy. He spoke against the Lords' conciliatory
amendments to the Bill for abrogating the old oaths of suprem-
acy and allegiance and substituting new ones. He clamoured for
the reversal of the judgement against Titus Oates. Repeatedly
he called for the punishment and proscription of James II's
former henchmen. "It is impossible the King and kingdom
should be safe", he told the Commons on one occasion "as long
as persons are in Council that have sat in King James's
Council". His especial venom was reserved for the judges.
"Some of his predecessors", he thundered at the unfortunate Sir
Thomas Jenner, who had unwisely participated in James's
purge of Magdalen College, Oxford, "have been hanged for less
crimes". Later in the session he returned once more to the
iniquities of the legal fraternity, roundly declaring that "things
will never be well till some of that profession be made examples".
The activities of Judge Jeffreys and his crew had clearly cut him
to the quick, and he had no intention of forgetting or forgiving.[3]

Thus, in linking up with the Foley group Harley was throwing in his lot with the "angry men" who were bent on "severe
revenges".[4] But he was not simply a Whig by association. He
too joined the fray. Already before his election he had committed himself by joining Sir Edward in his march on Worcester.
Then, with the city secured, he dashed southwards, determined
to be among the first of "the unspotted gentry" to compliment
William.[5] Once in Parliament he pursued the same steady
course. His first recorded speeches to the Commons were on the

[3] W. Cobbett, *Parliamentary History of England* (London, 1806–12), vol. V, pp. 107,
161, 167, 221, 252, 264, 271, 295, 300, 434, 466, 473, 480, 493, 506, 514.
[4] G. Burnet, *History of My Own Time* (Oxford, 1823), vol. IV, pp. 26–7.
[5] "The Prince", Harley recorded, "received me very graciously". Robert
Harley to Elizabeth Harley, 15 Dec. 1688, B.M. Loan, 164(1). The "unspotted
gentry of the nation" is Auditor Harley's phrase. See Edward Harley to Sir Edward
Harley, 11 March 1690, *H.M.C. Portland MSS.*, III, p. 445.

Indemnity Bill. In them he adopted the standard Whig line, maintaining that any exceptions to the general indemnity should be determined by categories of crimes rather than by selecting individuals.[6] Like the Foleys he smelt the foul influence of Jacobitism everywhere. "It is plain now", he wrote to his wife on 1 June 1689, "there is a party setting up to play the old game, the same that was in King Charles's and James's time. But I trust God will defeat them". Carmarthen he seems to have viewed with particular distaste, curtly dismissing him on one occasion as "a great monster of state". When in January 1690 the Ultra-Whig demagogue William Sacheverell introduced into the Commons his persecuting clause, designed to incapacitate all those who had been connected with the surrender of borough charters in the two previous reigns, Harley eagerly voted for it. By this time, indeed, many of the Tories were rapidly coming to regard the Herefordshire man as the *enfant terrible* of the Whig cause. Accordingly, when, in the spring of 1690, the Convention was dissolved, both Harley and his father were blacklisted as "Commonwealth's men" and declared to be mortal enemies of the Church. It was partly as a consequence of this clerical crusade that Sir Edward was unseated in Herefordshire.[7]

Harley, then, set out into the political world as an unrepentant Whig. However, in 1689 "Whig" was something of a portmanteau word. It is, of course, a commonplace that the Revolution destroyed the rationale of the Tory political faith and with it Tory unity. The passions generated by words like "abdicated" and "deserted" during the great constitutional debates of the Convention, together with the hair-splitting disputes between Regency Tories and *De Facto* Tories, Jacobites and Non-Jurors, afford ample illustration of this fact. What it is also important to remember is that the Whigs too suffered from internal division. Oppressed by James II's ill-advised extremism, all Whigs spoke with a single voice. But once the Catholic

---

[6] Cobbett, *op. cit.*, vol. V, pp. 257 and 532.
[7] Robert Harley to Elizabeth Harley, 1 June 1689, B.M. Portland Loan, 164(2); same to same, 4 June 1689, *ibid.*; J. Oldmixon, *The History of England During the Reigns of King William and Queen Mary, Queen Anne, King George I* (London, 1735), p. 36; Edward Harley to Sir Edward Harley, 22 Feb. 1690. *H.M.C. Portland MSS.*, III, p. 444; same to same, 11 March 1690, *ibid.*, p. 445.

King had been removed, cracks in the amalgam began slowly to appear.

Far and away the most serious fissure to open up in Whig ranks after 1689 was the split between Court and Country. Prior to the Revolution the role of the Whigs had, in essence, been a simple one. The sworn critics of royal power, they condemned theories of divine right and passive obedience, and pushed instead the claims of Parliament and of contractual monarchy. After the flight of James II, however, Whig society was faced with a dilemma. Were the Whigs to befriend the new monarch, the saviour of the Whig cause and their surest bulwark against the return of a vengeance-seeking Roman Catholic Stuart? Or, on the other hand, were they to retain their anti-royal prejudice?

Inevitably, perhaps, opinion was divided. Many Whigs, awkwardly at first and with much heart searching, gradually warmed to William. Like the Whig spokesmen in 1710 at the impeachment of Dr. Henry Sacheverell, the High Church champion, they laid stress on the Revolution as a solid achievement rather than as a prelude to further change. Divine hereditary right had been made ridiculous, parliamentary monarchy established. The important thing now was to concentrate on the war with Louis XIV, the protector of the exiled Stuarts and the enemy of all that the Whigs held dear. These, the Court Whigs, were led and directed by a group of extraordinarily able politicians, soon to become known collectively as the Junto.[8] In William's reign the Junto comprised four men: "Honest Tom" Wharton; Edward Russell, victor of La Hogue; Charles Montagu; and the gifted Worcestershire lawyer John Somers. In the following reign a fifth member, Marlborough's son-in-law Charles Spencer, third Earl of Sunderland, was added to their number. The Junto lords were to render William sterling service in the middle years of his reign. Their political flair lent a welcome degree of stability to the government, while it was the financial genius of Charles Montagu, the godfather of the Bank of England and of the system of deficit finance which

[8] For an excellent modern study of the Junto see E. L. Ellis, "The Whig Junto in Relation to the Development of Party Politics and Party Organization, from its Inception to 1714" (D.Phil. Thesis, Oxford University, 1962).

grew up after the Revolution, which made it possible for the King to meet his military commitments. Of course, relations between King and Junto were not always of the honeymoon type. As often as not they were at odds. Even in the hey-day of their liaison—the 1694–1697 period—Court Whig behaviour was at times all but unbearable. In December 1694, for instance, Wharton lent his support to an opposition amendment to the Triennial Bill, which, much to William's annoyance, aimed at bringing forward the date of the first compulsory dissolution of Parliament from 1 November 1696 to 1 November 1695. "Honest Tom" followed this up in the spring of 1695 by joining in a blistering back-bench attack on Henry Guy and Sir John Trevor, two of the most useful Commons lieutenants of the King's confidant Sunderland.[9] But manoeuvres of this kind should not be misunderstood. They were tactical rather than ideological in character. Their chief purpose was to impress on William the Junto's indispensability, not to forward "the good old cause".

The Court Whig reaction to the new political scene, however, forms only half the story. Another wing of the Party, the Country Whigs, resolutely refused to move with the times. From the days of Shaftesbury onwards they and their fathers had fought a relentless battle against the encroachment of the executive. They now saw no cause for change. William, after all, made no secret of his contempt for English institutions. He deliberately kept Parliament and even his ministers woefully ignorant of foreign affairs. During the Ryswick negotiations Shrewsbury, the English Secretary of State, "a stranger to all proceedings", was forced to write to Viscount Villiers to beg a few crumbs of information.[10] During the Convention William tried repeatedly to steamroller through the Indemnity Bill. He

[9] Bonnet's report, 11/21 Dec. 1694, Ranke, vol. VI, p. 256; Cobbett, op. cit. vol. V, p. 881 et seq.

[10] See Shrewsbury's appeals in W. Coxe (ed.), Private and Original Correspondence of Charles Talbot, Duke of Shrewsbury (London, 1821), pp. 169–71 and 319–21. The quotation is from Shrewsbury to Lexington, 8 Jan. 1695, H. Manners Sutton (ed.), The Lexington Papers (London, 1851), p. 40. Cf. G. Davies, "The Control of British Foreign Policy by William III", Essays on the Later Stuarts (San Marino, 1958), pp. 91–122. At times even Court Whigs were critical of William's high handedness. Burnet, for example, warned Halifax that it was "dangerous to give too much power to King William" since "he was inclined to give too arbitrary". Chatsworth MSS., Devonshire House Notebook, sub Salisbury.

made it patently obvious that he regarded the members' concern for constitutional issues as a tiresome irrelevance. His only aim was to end domestic strife and get on with the war. Moreover, the architects of Stuart despotism, men like Carmarthen and Sunderland, still thronged the Court unpunished. On top of this, since the Revolution a new threat had appeared. The enormous demands of war with France led to a rapid expansion in the size of government offices, in the army and navy, and in the numerous service departments. All this meant that the number of places at the executive's disposal rose dramatically. Hideous spectres now floated before the eyes of many members of a House of Commons packed with compliant yes-men each eager for his "snack of the booty".[11] Nerves were still further frayed by the financial scandals which broke with the regularity of winter over each successive session of Parliament. The army, the navy, Ireland, the East India Company, the Treasury—all seemed to be riddled with corruption and financial abuse of one sort or another. In 1699 Morgan Whitley, a local tax official in North Wales, was found to owe the government £43,000. Two years before this a major scandal had come to light in the office of Guy Palmes, Teller of the Exchequer. Upon investigation the accounts were shown to be £27,000 in the red, and although evidence was forthcoming of incompetence, forgery and even downright stealing on the part of the Teller's subordinates, Palmes kept his job. In 1689 naval supply was subject to such gross mismanagement that the Commons felt obliged to order the arrest of the entire Victualling Board.[12] Confronted with such a prospect, the Country Whigs chose to remain aloof from the new regime, determined to preserve intact their wary, questioning role as "physicians of the state".[13] It was to this Country Whig group that Harley gave his unqualified support.

The cleavage in Whig ranks, it should perhaps be noted, did not appear overnight. In the Convention there was very little sign of Whig division. All Whigs pressed for Toleration and for

[11] C. Davenant, *The True Picture of a Modern Whig* (London, 1701), p. 24.
[12] W. R. Ward, *The English Land Tax in the Eighteenth Century* (London, 1953), pp. 49–52; S B. Baxter, *The Development of the Treasury, 1660–1702* (London, 1957), pp. 157–66; J. H. Plumb, *The Growth of Political Stability in England, 1675–1725* (London, 1967), pp. 138–9.
[13] Robert Harley to Elizabeth Harley, 12 Nov. 1689. B.M. Portland Loan, 164(3).

the Bill of Rights. In the various votes on Indemnity, Whartons and Foleys, Harleys and Trenchards were all to be found rubbing shoulders in the same lobby. Even after this, Whig disintegration was a protracted affair. The first major clash did not come until the autumn of 1691. When in November of that year the Commons turned to consider the estimates, Harley led a spirited Country attack on the ministry's demands, and managed, in the teeth of Court Whig opposition, to get naval supply cut back by close on £300,000.[14] Other scuffles quickly followed. Wharton leapt to his feet to defend the memory of his now dead companion William Jephson when the latter's good name was called in question in a Country-inspired investigation into bribery.[15] Shortly afterwards, in December, more trouble blew up over the Trials for Treason Bill. Howe and Sedley spoke in favour of a Lords' amendment weakening royal control of peerage trial procedure. They were opposed by the Court Whigs led by Treby and Somers.[16] From then on things moved inexorably to their climax. In subsequent sessions the area of dispute widened and deepened. With the Junto's capture of the ministry in the spring of 1694 the final cord of unity was snapped. By accepting office the Court Whigs had made their peace with monarchy; the Country Whigs notoriously had not.[17]

Even so, although the break-up of the Whigs was gradual, it is crucial to realise that it was a complete breach. That this was clearly recognised by contemporaries is shown by the conduct of the leaders on both sides. After 1694 Wharton lumped Harley and his entourage indiscriminately together with his worst enemies. Nothing was too bad for the Country Whigs. Honest

[14] Bonnet's reports, 6/16 Nov. 20/30 Nov., Ranke, vol. VI, pp. 162–9; *Journals of the House of Commons*, X, pp. 546, 549 and 555; Edward Harley to Sir Edward Harley, 10 Nov. 1691, *H.M.C. Portland MSS*, III, p. 481; Robert Harley to Sir Edward Harley, 10 Nov. 1691, and same to same, 14 Nov. 1691, *ibid.*, pp. 481–2. The actual cut was from £1,855,054 to £1,575,890.

[15] Luttrell's Parliamentary Journal, All Souls MSS., 158a, f. 108.

[16] Cobbett, *op. cit.*, vol. V, pp. 675–89, 691–706; Luttrell's Parliamentary Journal, All Souls MSS., 158a, ff. 131–2.

[17] Practically all subsequent Country Whig apologies pin-point the Junto's acceptance of office as the great parting of the ways. As one "Old Whig" put it: "like the Roundheads in the Oliverian time, they were no sooner got into power but their former zeal for the public turned all into words and professions". S. Clement, "Faults on Both Sides" (1710), *Somers Tracts*, XII, p. 686. Cf. C. Davenant, *The True Picture of a Modern Whig* (London, 1701), and R. Harley, "Plain English to All who are Honest or would be so if they knew how" (1708), B.M. Portland Loan, 10(1).

Tom was prepared to descend even to barefaced lying in order to embarrass them. In 1695, for example, one of his pre-election tricks was to ferment trouble by disseminating the apparently quite unfounded story that William was determined to proscribe Harley and "keep him out of anything that should ever be in his power to give".[18] For their part the Country Whigs fully reciprocated Wharton's hostility. In the summer of 1695 we find Henry Guy excitedly reporting to Portland that Paul Foley had declared "a wonderful aversion" to Montagu and that the two men were at daggers drawn.[19] Harley's own hatred of the Junto lords became so intensely bitter that he was willing to believe them guilty not only of political crookedness but also of every form of spiritual laxity.[20]

What made the Whig split so decisive was a contemporaneous political development of which it was part cause and part consequence. As the Country Whigs drifted apart from the Junto they came into increasingly close contact with a group of dissident Tories—men like Thomas Clarges, Francis Gwyn, Christopher Musgrave, and the West Country magnate Sir Edward Seymour. In the Convention this back-bench Tory element had for most of the time been at the throats of Harley and his associates. Clarges and Musgrave, for instance, were stout advocates of Regency. Again, when, in November 1689, the news spread that Colonel Edmund Ludlow, one of the judges at Charles I's trial, had returned to England, Seymour rose in the Commons and delivered an impassioned speech saturated with the cult of Charles the Martyr. All three men vigorously opposed the Commons' vote on "vacancy", and each felt his gorge rise at the repeated Whig attempts to block the Indemnity Bill. [21] After the elections of 1690, however, the two groups, hitherto so diametrically opposed, began to move

[18] Guy to Portland, 18 June, and 5 July, 1695, N.U.L., Portland MSS., PWA, 504 and 506.
[19] Guy Portland, 31 May, 14 June, and 6 Aug. 1695, *ibid.*, PWA 502, 503 and 511.
[20] E.g. Harley to Tenison, 11 Aug. 1701, *H.M.C. Bath MSS.*, I, p. 52; Harley to Carstares, 12 Sep. 1709, J. McCormick (ed.), *State Papers and Letters Addressed to William Carstares* (Edinburgh, 1774), p. 775; and Harley to Daniel Williams, 5 Aug. 1710, Herefordshire R. O., Harley Papers, C. 64.
[21] Cobbett, *op. cit.*, vol. V, p. 34 *et seq.*, *passim*; A. Boyer, *The Reign of King William III* (London, 1702–3), vol. II, pp. 150–1. Cf. K. G. Feiling, *A History of the Tory Party, 1640–1714* (Oxford, 1924), pp. 245–72, *passim*, and pp. 292–3.

closer and closer together. That the gulf between them should narrow was indeed quite natural, for the desire of the Tory back benchers to harass the Dutch usurper forced them to take up a Country stance closely similar to that adopted by the Harley-Foley group.

Of course, it took time to patch up old quarrels, and on a number of occasions in the first twelve months after the dissolution of the Convention one can detect Country Whigs and Country Tories busily rubbing salt into each other's wounds. When, for instance, on 24 April 1690 Clarges moved to thank William for his care of the Church and noted specifically the recent removal of Whigs from the London Lieutenancy which the King had sanctioned, Foley was furious and denounced the new men as timeservers many of whom had "had their hands in blood several times over".[22] By 1691, however, teething troubles were largely over. From that year we may date Harley's unsullied friendship with Clarges and Francis Gwyn. 1691 also saw the beginnings of the long and intimate correspondence between Harley and Christopher Musgrave. Throughout the summer the two men were exchanging ideas on all current issues of national importance. They deplored the Irish abuses, poured scorn on pensions in general and Carmarthen's in particular, and expressed deep concern for the conduct of the war. "A line with your name", wrote Musgrave on 15 June, "is the best entertainment I can have". A year later he reiterated his affection for Harley in still more fulsome terms: "You have so accustomed me to receive the favour of yours that the want of them makes me fear it's from some indisposition, which gives me much trouble, having a real esteem for you".[23] When in the autumn of 1691 Parliament reassembled, the two wings of the Country opposition moved into action in unison. Both Clarges and Musgrave lent powerful support to Harley's successful bid to retrench naval supply.[24] On the army estimates it was the

[22] Burnet, *op. cit.*, vol. IV, p. 76; Cobbett, *op. cit.*, vol. V. pp. 590–94.
[23] Musgrave to Harley, 15 June 1691, and same to same, 25 July 1692, B.M. Portland Loan, 312. Box 312 contains a considerable number of Musgrave's letters to Harley. See also boxes 130, 151 and 313, and *H.M.C. Portland MSS.*, III, pp. 458–640, *passim*.
[24] Luttrell's Parliamentary Journal, All Souls MSS., 158a, ff. 2–42; Bonnet's reports, 6/16 Nov. to 20/30 Nov., Ranke, vol. VI, pp. 162–9; Cobbett, *op. cit.*, vol. V, pp. 656–7; French newsletter, 6/16 Nov., *H.M.C. Seventh Report*, p. 205.

same story. In his speech from the throne William had asked for 65,000 troops for the following year. Now Harley, Clarges, Foley and Musgrave all strove to get this number reduced, and when it became clear that the House was not with them, they tried hard to have it recognised that 65,000 was an all inclusive figure, comprehending officers as well as men.[25] On top of these questions of supply came the first report of the Public Accounts Commission. The most swingeing attack on the executive to be produced this session, it too was the joint product of the leaders of the Harley-Foley group and the Clarges Tories.[26] By the time Parliament rose for the Christmas recess few could have been in any doubt that old rivalries had by now been quietly buried. Country Whigs and Country Tories had ceased to exist as clearly separate political units. As Edward Harley put it on 23 December, "Sir Thomas Clarges and Sir C. Musgrave have got the character of Commonwealth men".[27] A new, integrated Country Party had been born.

For the rest of William's reign this refurbished Country opposition pursued a vigorous attacking policy. A great deal of its programme was strongly traditional in character. Part of its platform, for instance, involved the time-honoured fear of standing armies. After the signing of the Treaty of Ryswick in 1697 this fear was allowed full vent in the various Country motions designed to prune England's military establishment to a merely nominal level. But even before peace came, dislike of standing armies was made abundantly clear in the Country Party's oft-repeated preference for naval rather than continental war. "The sea", Harley told the Commons in November 1692, "must be our first care",[28] and his sentiments were echoed time and again in the utterances of Clarges, Foley, Musgrave, Thompson, and other Country leaders. Equally traditional was Country xenophobia. In Charles II's reign Shaftesbury had entertained an almost unbalanced hatred of the French. Countrymen in

[25] Cobbett, *op. cit.*, vol. V, pp. 655 and 660–6; Luttrell's Parliamentary Journal, All Souls MSS., 158a, ff. 49–55, 67–74, and 82–7.

[26] The Report is printed in full in *H.M.C. House of Lords MSS., 1690–1*, pp. 356–434. Nearly half of its thirty one observations were attacks on the executive. See also Cobbett, *op. cit.*, vol. V. p. 666 *et seq.*

[27] Edward Harley to Sir Edward Harley, 23 Dec. 1691, *H.M.C. Portland MSS.*, III, p. 485.

[28] Cobbett, *op. cit.*, vol. V, p. 725.

William's day felt much the same way about the Dutch. They suspected the King because of his continental origins; they despised his shabby blue-coated Dutch guards; above all they loathed William's confidential Dutch advisers. In 1695 all this pent-up little-England feeling boiled over in a frenzied attack upon the King's Dutch favourite William Bentinck, Earl of Portland, who had been granted the Lordships of Denbigh, Bromfield and Yale by his royal master. The assault was directed by a group of Welsh M.P.s headed by Harley's friend Robert Price, member for Weobley. Price's speech was one of the most histrionic performances to which any of William's Parliaments were ever subjected.[29] Claiming to speak with "the approbation of thousands" he warned the King in measured tones that previous grants of the lands in question had proved "very fatal" to both giver and receiver: "the one either lost his Crown or the other his head". He then drew a picture of Willam as a monarch criminally ignorant of English law, a puppet king in the clutches of evil counsellors, all of them bent on inducing him to trick the Welsh and "tear up the Bill of Rights and Liberties by the roots". Again and again he returned to the iniquities of Dutchmen of Portland's ilk:

> We see our good coin all gone, and our confederates openly coining base money, of Dutch alloy, for us. We see most places of power and profit given to foreigners. We see our confederates in conjunction with the Scots to ruin our English trade. We see the revenues of the Crown daily given to one or other, who make sale of them, and transmit their estates elsewhere. We do not find any of them buy lands or estates amongst us: but what they can get from us they secure in their own country. How can we hope for happy days in England when this great man, and others (though naturalized) are in the English and also in the Dutch councils?. . . . I foresee, when we are reduced to extreme poverty, as now we are very near it, we are to be supplanted by our neighbours and become a colony of the Dutch.

[29] The speech is printed in Cobbett, *op. cit.*, vol. V, pp. 979–85. For another version entitled "Gloria Cambria: Or the Speech of a Bold Briton in Parliament against a Dutch Prince of Wales" see *Somers Tracts*, XI, pp. 387–91. The assault on Portland had evidently been threatening for some time. See Guy to Portland, 5 July and 13 July 1695, N.U.L., Portland MSS., PWA, 506 and 509.

Fired by Price's oratory, the Commons unanimously voted to address the King to revoke Portland's grant. William, sensing the strength of the tide, gracefully gave way. [30]

Many other examples of Country conservatism could be listed—the dislike of high taxation, the concern over hallowed statutes like the Habeas Corpus Act, and so on. Enough has been said, however, to illustrate the point. What it is also interesting to note is that in William's reign the Country Party had in addition a more modern side. Usually this up-to-date aspect of the Country programme was a question of emphasis. Although since the days of Shaftesbury and Russell, for instance, Country politicians had viewed the metropolitan sophistication of the City with suspicion, the system of war finance evolved by Montagu in the course of the 1690s greatly intensified this hostility. The result was the flowering of a whole crop of new financial ideas on the opposition benches. Perhaps the most interesting of all these schemes was Harley's Land Bank project. In essence the Land Bank was rather like a modern building society. Its object was to raise capital and advance loans on the security of mortgages. A further aspect of the scheme was to set up Banks in many different parts of the country. Both these ideas appealed strongly to the provincial gentry and they were clearly designed to break the City Dissenters' near monopoly of high finance, and, if possible, to wreck the infant Whig Bank of England. Montagu saw the political motive behind the Land Bank from the start, and was livid. "I believe", he wrote bitterly to Blathwayt, "there never was any transaction in any place or in any age wherein there was more artifice or less sincerity showed than has appeared in this affair of the Land Bank. But I hope our master will make just reflections on the whole, and he will discern the authors of this disappointment".[31] But fume as he might Montagu could not disguise the fact that it was his own financial

<hr>

[30] Cobbett, *op. cit.*, vol. V, pp. 985–6.
[31] Montagu to Blathwayt, 17 July 1696, B.M. Additional MSS., 34,355, f.14. See also J. Clapham, *The Bank of England* (London, 1945), vol. I, p. 33; J. K. Horsefield, *British Monetary Experiments 1650–1710* (London, 1960), pp. 196–210; and L. Ming-Hsun, "The Great Recoinage" (Ph.D. Thesis, London University, 1940), p. 83. W. A. Shaw's analysis of the Land Bank project contains useful facts and figures but is excessively idiosyncratic. See *Calendar of Treasury Books; Introduction to Vol. XI–XVII*, pp. xli–lxxiii.

work which had stimulated a similar inventiveness among his opponents.

Just as the financial developments which followed the Revolution produced new thinking on the opposition benches, so too did the multiplication of patronage. Country concern over the number of King's men in the Commons can be traced back at least as far as the Long Parliament of Charles II. However, the enormous increase in the amount of largesse at the executive's disposal in the 1690s swept the concern for the purity of Parliament from the periphery to the very heart of the Country programme. The Country Party of William's reign was obsessed by place and financial corruption as by nothing else. Until the successful passage of the Triennial Act in 1694 virtually every session brought vociferous back-bench cries for frequent, if possible annual, Parliaments. Place Bills were introduced with similar regularity, and generated the same kind of heat. When William vetoed the Bill introduced in the autumn of 1693, members of the Commons were beside themselves with fury. Whipped up by Harley, they threatened to tack the Bill to supply, and resolved that those who had advised the King on this occasion were enemies "to their majesties and the kingdom".[32] Jack Howe led a campaign for a Land Qualification Bill, the effect of which would have been to confine membership of the Commons to independent men of property, while in 1696 two measures designed to secure freer elections actually reached the statute book. Fear of increasing government patronage also made many Country politicians oppose the introduction of a general excise. As Paul Foley observed in September 1692, many gentlemen would willingly have given six shillings in the pound on land rather than submit to such a tax.[33] But the most dramatic and the most original of all the opposition moves called forth by the growing strength of the executive in these years was the Commission for examining and taking the Public Accounts. Indeed, so significant was this development that it has been thought wise to accord the

[32] Cobbett, *op. cit.*, vol. V, pp. 829–33.
[33] Paul Foley to Robert Harley, 17 Sep. 1692, B.M. Portland Loan, 135(7). Cf. J. H. Plumb, *op. cit.* In chapters 4 and 5 of this work Professor Plumb discusses, among other things, the growth in place-holders after 1689 and the impact of this on party alignment.

Commission separate and extended treatment in the next chapter.

It will now be apparent why the Whig rift of the early 1690s proved so intractable. The quarrel was not simply a dispute within the Whig Party itself. It was part of something much broader. After the dissolution of the Convention the entire body politic underwent a profound change. The great issues which had hitherto divided Whig from Tory—things like religion, and the nature of William's title to the throne— faded into the background. They were replaced by the more immediate and more pressing problems of war, finance, and governing through Parliament. Hence inside the Commons the Whig-Tory cleavage gave way to a conflict between Court and Country. This pattern held good for the rest of the reign. Sometimes pressing the traditional elements in its programme, at other times giving its ideas a more contemporary look, the Country Party found ample material to fill each successive parliamentary session with its din and clamour. The spate of political pamphlets which appeared towards the close of William's period of rule, tracts like Charles Davenant's *True Picture of a Modern Whig* and John Toland's *Art of Governing by Parties*,[34] all took it as axiomatic that the real political conflict was between Court and Country. Only in the early 1700s, with the revival of the succession issue, with the growing concern of Churchmen over the practice of Occasional Communion, and above all with the accession to the throne of a High-Church Queen, did the former Whig-Tory division come back into prominence. All this, of course, left its mark on the Whig and Tory Parties themselves. Because so many Tories joined the Country Party in William's reign it meant that under Anne when the old political pattern was reassembled they carried back with them into their Toryism a strong Country streak. On the other hand, the Junto's long sojourn at Court enabled the Whig party to avoid being riven so deeply by back-bench independent attitudes. However, from our point of view, the really important thing about the new political scene in the 1690's is not its effect upon party but rather its significance for Harley personally. Although, as we have seen, it is indisputably true that Harley began political life as an

[34] Both these pamphlets were published in London in 1701.

orthodox Whig, the reshaping of politics after the Revolution renders it impossible satisfactorily to study his work under William in terms of Whig versus Tory. Harley in the 1690s must be judged not as a Whig partisan but as a Country politician.

3 Country Politician

IN HIS COUNTRY rôle Harley proved a spectacular success. By 1701, indeed, his stature in the Commons had become so considerable that William deemed it prudent to select him as Court candidate for the Speaker's chair and to show him "great civilities".[1]

Harley's climb to such eminence was smooth and steady. It also began very early. Already in the Convention it is apparent he had caught the public eye. In the elections which followed, for example, Seymour's brother-in-law, Sir Joseph Tredenham, was at pains to warn his Cornish electors at St. Mawes that although there was little harm in Mr. Foley "only as to his votes" with Harley it was a different matter, for "he was notable and made speeches and so was a dangerous person".[2] Admittedly one must take Tredenham with a grain of salt. At this stage he feared that Harley might challenge his candidature; hence he was out to fling as much mud as possible. Nonetheless, the fact that he could without patent absurdity depict Harley as a rising man is revealing. In any case another and more convincing proof of Harley's early impact was soon to follow. In December 1690 he was elected to the Public Accounts Commission.[3]

The Commission for examining and taking the Public Accounts was a small and very select body, composed initially of nine and subsequently of seven members all balloted for by the House of Commons. It was first set up in 1690, and enjoyed an uninterrupted existence for the next half dozen years. The job of the Commission was to probe government spending, and to report back its findings to the Lower House. Unfortunately

[1] Lord Raby's "Caracteres de plusieurs Ministres", J. J. Cartwright (ed.), *The Wentworth Papers, 1705–39* (London, 1883), p. 132.
[2] Anne, Lady Clinton to Sir Edward Harley, 17 April 1690, B.M. Portland Loan, 74(2).
[3] *Journals of the House of Commons*, X, p. 528.

2*

the whole project has had a rather bad press. In his celebrated introductions to the *Calendar of Treasury Books* Dr. W. A. Shaw subjected it to scalding criticism. He was prepared to admit that in theory the Commission had a good deal to recommend it. But practice was a very different matter. With biting irony Shaw launched a brutal attack on what he regarded as the commission's evil genius—the "sinister, unpractical brain" of Robert Harley. It was Harley's malignant influence, Shaw argued, which turned what might have been a useful means of co-operation between Parliament and Treasury into a tool of party warfare. A most promising administrative development was thereby irretrievably wrecked.[4]

Although written with superb assurance Shaw's strictures are both inaccurate and unfair. Harley in no way distorted the Accounts Commission. Obsessed with administrative tidiness Shaw failed to see that from the outset the Commission was designed by the Country Party as a means of clipping the executive's wings. The Commissioners' first report[5] makes this perfectly obvious. Nearly half of their thirty one observations were direct criticisms of the government. Profiteering, venality, incompetence, every form of financial malpractice came in for censure. In the stormy debate which followed the Commissioners elaborated their criticisms into a huge symphony of discontent. The whole affair culminated in the drafting of four strongly worded anti-Court resolutions.[6] Their tone neatly encapsulates the spirit of the Accounts Commission's early activities:

> *Ordered*, that the Commissioners appointed for taking the Public Accounts do lay before this House a list of all such persons who have salaries and have made the King pay the charge of passing their patents and their accounts as also the taxes upon their offices.

[4] *Calendar of Treasury Books, 1689–1692*, vol. IX, part I, pp. cli–clxxiv; *ibid.*, *Introduction to Vols. XI–XVII*, pp. clv–clxxxvi. The quotation is from p. 1 of the latter volume.

[5] *H.M.C. House of Lords MSS., 1690–1*, pp. 356–434.

[6] 3 Dec. 1691, *Journals of the House of Commons*, X, p. 572. Cf. the similar orders of 12 Dec., *ibid.*, p. 583. For the debate on 3 Dec. see Cobbett, *op. cit.*, vol. V, pp. 666–72 and Luttrell's Parliamentary Journal, All Souls MSS., 158a, ff. 103–8 Cf. the debate of 12 Dec. *ibid*; ff. 134–6, and Cobbett *op. cit.*, vol, V, pp. 681–2.

Ordered, that the said Commissioners do lay before this House a list of those that have great salaries and have upon slight pretences got them increased and who have had extraordinary bills of incident charges easily allowed.

Ordered, that the said Commissioners do lay before the House a list of the salaries which were granted upon special reasons and which are still continued though the reasons are ceased.

Ordered, that the said Commissioners do lay before this House a list of excessive fees that are exacted and taken by officers that have great salaries allowed them for execution of their places and for which no legal precedent appears to justify the same.

When, shortly afterwards, the Commission came up for renewal, government supporters in the Lords "desirous to get a bridle out of their mouths" made a spirited attempt to kill it. Their tactic was to load the renewing bill with amendments which they knew would be unacceptable to the Lower Chamber. But the Court's "supervisors" were not so easily disposed of. The Commons quickly countered the Upper House's move by tacking its cherished measure to the Poll Bill. Faced with the alternative of allowing the Commission to continue or of jeopardizing supply their Lordships meekly capitulated.[7]

Right from its inception, then, the Public Accounts Commission was looked on by both Court and Country not as part of the estimates machinery but as an opposition political weapon. Moreover, as such it was an extremely effective instrument. Its investigations always produced uneasiness on the government benches, and at times utter panic. One of the Commission's greatest triumphs came in the spring of 1695. As a result of various financial probings set in motion by the Commissioners it was discovered that the Speaker, Sir John Trevor, had accepted a bribe from the City of London. Petrified, poor Trevor was at first censured by the Commons, and then, four days later, expelled from the House altogether. Success was made all the sweeter for the opposition when, much to the King's ire, Trevor

[7] *Journals of the House of Commons*, X, pp. 605, 606, 612, 618, 620, 633, 645–7, 653–4, 666–70, and 693. The quotation is from Robert Harley to Sir Edward Harley, 2 Feb. 1692, B.M. Portland Loan, 79(2). See also same to same, 9 Feb. 1692, *H.M.C. Portland MSS.*, III, p. 490.

was replaced as Speaker not by the Court nominee Sir Thomas Littleton, but by Paul Foley the Country candidate.[8] It was sparkling victories of this sort that encouraged the Country Party in the latter part of William's reign to seek to extend the Commission system beyond finance into other spheres. 1695, for example, saw an abortive attempt to set up a parliamentary Council of Trade,[9] while four years later an Irish Land Commission actually materialised.[10] The Court, fully alive to the threatening nature of these moves, branded all such developments as "an encroachment upon the prerogative of the Crown".[11]

But the Accounts Commission was much more than a stick with which to beat the government. It represented nothing less than the front bench of the Country Party.[12] The Commissioners did not simply take upon themselves the task of delving into government finance. They directed opposition tactics in general. Even those debates in the Commons with which the Commission had no formal connection were dominated by Public Accounts men. Time and time again, on every conceivable variety of topic, Foley, Clarges and Harley headed the list of anti-Court Speakers. It is highly instructive to note that just as Cabinet ministers on the government sides were recompensed for their services, the Accounts Commissioners too received their reward. From the very beginning the House voted each Commissioner a salary of £500 per annum.[13] In fact, one of the aims of rank and file M.P.s in setting up the Commission was to provide "a competent number of good employments" to "reward their most useful and deserving members".[14] All too often in the past back-benchers had had the bitter experience of seeing their most promising leaders bought off by the Court. The Public

---

[8] Cobbett, *op. cit.*, vol. V. p. 881 *et seq.*
[9] *Ibid.*, pp. 977–8. Cf. R. M. Lees, "Parliament and the Proposal for a Council of Trade, 1695–6", *English Historical Review*, vol. LIV (1939), pp. 38–66.
[10] Cobbett, *op. cit.*, vol. V, pp. 1198–9.
[11] "Faults on Both Sides", *Somers Tracts*, XII, p. 689.
[12] Thus one Herefordshire gentleman described the chairmanship of the Commission as "the highest place of honour" to which an opposition member could aspire. Robert Harley to Sir Edward Harley, 23 Jan. 1692, B.M. Portland Loan, 79(2).
[13] Dr. Williams's Library, Roger Morrice's MS. Entering Books, III, f. 224; *Calendar of Treasury Books, 1689–1692*, vol. IX, part III, pp. 1149 and 1151.
[14] "Faults on Both Sides", *Somers Tracts*, XII, p. 689.

Accounts Commission was an attempt to arrest this process. It was the Country Party's bid to keep its top men.

The meaning of Harley's 1690 appointment will now be clear. His election to the Accounts Commission symbolised in un-impeachable fashion his political arrival. Less than two years after first setting foot in the Commons he was, with measured deliberation, being advanced by Country members to the select company of their "head and speaking men".[15] Indeed his achievement was more impressive than even this might suggest, for he was compelled to spend a good deal of these first two years outside Parliament. When, after the dissolution of the Convention in February 1690, he stood as candidate for New Radnor, he was defeated by Colonel Birch's nominee Rowland Gwynne. As a result he had to mount a protracted election peti-tion, and it was only in the following November that Gwynne was at length unseated.[16]

Obviously such story book success calls for explanation. How did Harley do it? What enabled him to make a mark so sharply and so soon? One factor which helped him forward was un-doubtedly his sincerity. In a recent study of later Stuart politics Professor J. H. Plumb speaks of Harley exploiting back-bench beliefs "in order to influence party politics to the advantage of himself and his friends".[17] In a sense this is misleading. Harley did not consciously exploit Country attitudes at all: he believed them. It is impossible to pick out any dividing line between his public and his private utterances in these early years. His letters to his friends and to his family strike the same note as do his harangues in the Commons. Phrases like "the ancient liberties of England", "the good of this poor nation", "the dangers to the very constitution" stud both indiscriminately. Harley had been bred in a Country tradition, and he breathed back-bench politics throughout his youth. It was psychologi-cally impossible for him to shake off a life time's experience

[15] A. Boyer, op. cit., vol. II, p. 174.
[16] For the disputed election: B.M. Harleian MSS., 6846, f. 294. For the success-ful petition: Journals of the House of Commons, X, pp. 469 and 470; Robert Harley to Sir Edward Harley, 25 Oct., 4 Nov., and 13 Nov. 1690, H.M.C. Portland MSS., III, pp. 450 and 452; Edward Harley to Sir Edward Harley, 8 Nov. 1690, ibid., p. 451; Robert Harley to Elizabeth Harley, 8 Nov. 1690, B.M. Portland Loan, 164(5).
[17] Plumb, op. cit., p. 127. In fairness it must be stressed that Professor Plumb is willing to concede that Harley "half believed" what he preached.

overnight. Countrymen in Parliament saw and understood this. They had had their fill of men like Wharton, cynics and sharpers who would butter them up one day and then rat on them the next. When they saw a man who meant what he said they warmed to him immediately. Harley was already half way to success among Country M.P.s simply because of the opinions he held.

However, sincerity on its own is not sufficient to explain Harley's swift ascent. Many a bone-headed squire who sat mute and unnoticed on the back-benches throughout his parliamentary career was a passionate believer in the Country cause. Success demanded aptitude as well as conviction. The thing which above all else distinguished Harley from the normal backbencher was his professionalism. Most of the M.P.s who flocked to the Country Party banner were landowners first and politicians a very poor second. It took much to drag them from their estates and their hunting at the beginning of each session, or to keep them cooped up in town when the heats of summer came. Their priorities were nicely delineated by Lord Hervey in 1711. In the spring of that year the Marlboroughs were pressing him to come up to London to cast his vote in a crucial election for Directors of the Bank of England. Hervey brushed aside their entreaties with the flimsiest of excuses, preferring, as he readily admitted, the pleasures of Newmarket and his own rolling acres to the bustle of the metropolis, for at home one might see "all the pride of nature opening itself day by day".[18] Harley's attitude was poles apart from this. He was as fond as the next man of his cornfields and his bowling green. But first things came first. From the start he threw himself heart and soul into politics. His early letters home hum with activity. Life in town, he explained

---

[18] Lady Hervey to John Hervey, 7 April and 10 April 1711, *The Letter-Books of John Hervey, First Earl of Bristol* (Wells, 1894), vol. I, pp. 287–90; John Hervey to Lady Hervey 9 April and 10 April 1711, *ibid*. Cf. the Leicestershire squire Sir Thomas Cave whose idea of a "return to paradise" was to quit "stinking London" and hurry back to his hounds and horses at Stanford Hall. Sir Thomas Cave to Ralph Verney, 17 May 1704, Margaret Maria, Lady Verney (ed.), *Verney Letters of the Eighteenth Century from the MSS. at Claydon House* (London, 1930), vol. I, p. 216; Cave to Lord Fermanagh, 27 April 1714, *ibid*., p. 247. At the eleventh hour Hervey seems to have repented. An entry in his diary for this period runs: "I travelled all night between the 11 and 12 of April from Newmarket to London to choose Governors and Directors of the Bank at the earnest request of the Duchess of Marlborough". *The Diary of John Hervey, First Earl of Bristol* (Wells, 1894), p. 53.

to his wife Elizabeth in January 1690, was little more than "Parliament, eat and sleep". His London cousins were lucky if they caught sight of him at all when the Commons was in session, while he rarely managed to snatch more than a month's break at Brampton Bryan in summer, if that. Soon his avid attachment to the wearisome demands of the political world became a by-word among his friends. In August 1692 we find Thomas Foley trying to work out ways of enticing him out of "that ingenuous Town, that Town of news, that admiring Town for a little health to be had in the country which you never much cared for". Another of his cronies, Francis Gwyn, scolded him with equal gentleness for spending late nights at his desk and being "always about town".[19]

Harley's keenness paid handsome dividends. He was soon thoroughly at home at Westminster, and his knowledge of men and measures rapidly outstripped that of the average M.P. His particular forte was constitutional history and parliamentary precedent. Rumour had it that for much of William's reign up to half his income went on clerks whose job it was to copy out extracts from political records and papers for their employers' subsequent perusal.[20] Whatever the truth of this rather extravagant tale, it is incontestable that Harley quickly came to know parliamentary procedure backwards. It was not only his brother Edward who stressed his "perfect knowledge of the orders of the House". Even the blatantly hostile Gilbert Burnet felt bound to admit that his "great industry and application" made him "very eminently learned" in both the "forms and the records of Parliament".[21] Harley admittedly was no orator.[22] But his grasp of the constitution gave a peculiar edge and authority to his pronouncements in debate. When, for instance, William

[19] Robert Harley to Elizabeth Harley, 17 Jan. 1690, B.M. Portland Loan, 164(4); Thomas Foley to Robert Harley, 29 Aug. 1692, *ibid.*, 136; Francis Gwyn to Robert Harley, 30 June 1694, *ibid.*, 137; same to same, 4 May 1696, *H.M.C. Portland MSS.*, III, p. 575.

[20] Lord Raby's "Caracteres de plusieurs Ministres", *Wentworth Papers*, p. 132.

[21] Edward Harley's "Memoirs", *H.M.C. Portland MSS.*, V, p. 647; Burnet, *op. cit.*, vol. IV, p. 191.

[22] One of the few contemporaries to praise Harley for eloquence was John Macky. See *Memoirs of the Secret Service of John Macky* (London, 1733), p. 116. Significantly Swift noted in the margin of his copy "a great lie". H. Davis (ed.), *Jonathan Swift: Miscellaneous and Autobiographical Pieces, Fragments and Marginalia* (Oxford, 1962), p. 262.

vetoed the Triennial Bill in 1693, Harley adroitly countered by endeavouring to persuade the Commons to "declare" annual elections to be legal under an unrepealed statute of Edward III. In the previous session a government attempt to paint the call for triennial Parliaments as an improper invasion of the prerogative produced an equally neat response. Harley rose to his feet, drew from his pocket a copy of William's Declaration, and proceeded to read out the King's own promise to accept any measures Parliament might think necessary for preventing a recurrence of arbitrary rule.[23] Sallies like this did not only delight the bucolic sensibilities of the back-bench squires. They also caused considerable flutterings among the more urbane dovecotes of the ministry. As Lord Raby put it, when Harley entered the Chamber "Mr. Blathwayt and others of the King's people were almost afraid to speak before him".[24]

It was, then, the somewhat eccentric combination of Country beliefs and hard work which swept Harley to the fore. And once inside the charmed circle of the Country Party's directing group he never looked back. Each successive year brought a growth in stature. The various enquiries of the Accounts Commission provided him with opportunities of studying the workings of government machinery second only to those enjoyed by the King's own ministers. He learnt much by pooling his ideas and discussing things with his colleagues. He became accustomed, too, to rubbing shoulders with leading men on the Court side. But the greatest of all his assets was his youth. In William's reign the leaders of the Country Party were, for the most part, ageing men, survivors of a previous generation. Sacheverell had seen his hey-day at the time of the Exclusion Crisis, Colonel Birch even earlier. The career of Harley's own father, Sir Edward, offers a nice illustration of the Party's plight. At the time of the Revolution, as we have seen, Sir Edward had en-

---

[23] Cobbett, *op. cit.*, vol. V, pp. 760–1, and 787.
[24] Lord Raby's "Caracteres de plusieurs Ministres", *Wentworth Papers*, p. 132. Harley himself, it should be noted, was as acutely aware as anyone of the political value of his intimate knowledge of legal and constitutional history. In his "Advice to a Son", penned in the reign of Anne, he counselled the youth of England to avoid games and "dog language" and concentrate instead on the acquisition of a "knowledge of the laws and constitutions" of their country. Furnished with such knowledge the young patriot need have no fear of "the birds of prey" hovering above or "the trumpets of sedition" sounding in his ears. "Advice to a Son", 27 Aug. 1705, N.U.L., Harley MSS., PW2, HY, Secretary of State's box, folder (1).

gaged in a flurry of activity. He followed this up in the Convention by leading a successful campaign for the abolition of that "intolerable grievance" the Council of the Marches and Wales.[25] But then the tide turned. In 1690 he was defeated at the polls, and although he returned to the Commons three years later he was no longer the same man. He never again spoke in Parliament, and his attention to public affairs gradually became more and more sporadic. Finally, in 1698 he retired from politics altogether. This slow winding down of energies was characteristic of the Party leadership as a whole. Indeed the years 1691 to 1700 saw the death of no less than eighteen prominent Country politicians.[26] Clarges went in 1695, Paul Foley in 1699. A year later Sir Edward himself was dead. Country leadership was unquestionably in decay.

Aided in this way by the ravages of time, Harley steadily climbed the remaining rungs of the Country Party ladder. One indication of his rising status came in the spring of 1694 when he topped the ballot for the Accounts Commission, beating even Foley. The following year he did it again with an increased majority.[27] There were also other straws in the wind. In October 1693 the ever astute Halifax was quite abnormally excited by the prospect of a liaison with Harley. "I make haste to congratulate your return to town", he wrote on the fifteenth. "I am now little less impatient than a lover would be to meet his mistress; therefore let me know whether you can come to my lodging at Whitehall, or if you had rather, at Somerset House". A still more interesting series of negotiations took place a year later. On this occasion it was a tripartite affair, with Shrewsbury, Harley and Foley the parties involved. Shrewsbury seems to have been making some kind of bid for Country co-operation in the coming parliamentary session. The real fascination of the talks, however, lies not so much in their content as in their form. When, in mid-October, Harley left London for a brief holiday

[25] Edward Harley's "Memoirs", *H.M.C. Portland MSS.*, V, p. 644; Oldmixon, *op. cit.*, p. 14.

[26] John Birch, Hugh Boscawen, Sir Thomas Clarges, William Garroway, John Hampden, Richard Hampden, William Harbord, Sir Edward Harley, Sir Robert Howard, William Jephson, Sir Thomas Lee, Sir William Leveson-Gower, Henry Powle, William Sacheverell, Sir Richard Temple, Sir John Trenchard, William Waller and Sir Francis Winnington.

[27] *Journals of the House of Commons*, XI, pp. 158 and 279.

at Brampton Bryan, everything ground to a halt. Shrewsbury could see no point in negotiating with Foley alone. It was only with Harley's return, early in November, that the threads were again picked up. On the sixth Shrewsbury was busily arranging a discussion with both men at Godolphin's house for the following evening, and sometime later the Secretary met Harley on his own to talk over matters of "immediate consideration".[28] The trend of the evidence is unmistakable. From 1693 onwards Harley was slowly but surely beginning to outpace his colleagues; and with the death of Clarges in October 1695 things at length swung decisively in his favour. From now on, as even Foley generously admitted,[29] Harley was supreme. Hitherto the Country Party's fortunes had been directed corporately from the Accounts Commission by its General Staff. Now, for the first time, it had a single, undisputed Commander-in-Chief.

As Party Captain-General Harley was soon to prove a most accomplished performer. In a way he was greatly helped by the fact that he took over command at an hour of terrible crisis for the Country cause. On the surface, it is true, things looked healthy enough. In the summer of 1695, for example, the Party had gained a useful accession of strength in the shape of Sir Edward Seymour and his Cornish following.[30] Bolstered up in this way the opposition won a series of eye-catching victories

[28] Halifax to Harley, 15 Oct. 1693, *H.M.C. Portland MSS.*, III, p. 544. Cf. same to same, 16 Oct. and 19 Oct., *ibid.*, pp. 544 and 547. Shrewsbury to Harley, 4 Oct., 6 Nov., and 20 Nov. 1694. *H.M.C. Bath MSS.* I, pp. 51–2; Robert Harley to Sir Edward Harley, 20 Nov. 1694, *H.M.C. Portland MSS.* III, p. 560.

[29] "All things stand still till he [Robert Harley] comes". Paul Foley to Sir Edward Harley, 5 Nov. 1695, *ibid.*, p. 573.

[30] In March 1692 Seymour had been bought off by the ministry. He was admitted to the Privy Council, made a Treasury Commissioner, and specifically recommended to the Queen by William "as a person fit for her Majesty to take advice of in his absence". (Boyer, *op. cit.*, vol. II, pp. 321–2; Luttrell, II, pp. 372 and 375). In April 1694, however, Seymour lost his post at the Treasury, and during and after the ensuing parliamentary session he was cautiously approached by several of Harley's friends at meetings of the "Thirty Club" at Lindsay House. (W. E. Buckley (ed.), *Memoirs of Thomas Bruce, Second Earl of Ailesbury, written by himself* (Westminster, 1890), vol. I, p. 359; J. Verney to Viscount Hatton, 24 April 1695, E. M. Thompson (ed.), *Correspondence of the Family of Hatton* (London, 1878), vol. II, p. 218). By the time the new Parliament opened in November 1695 the old warrior's reconversion was complete. By then he was vigorously denouncing Sir Thomas Littleton, the Court's preference for the Speaker's chair, and advocating instead the claims of "my friend Paul"—i.e. the Country nominee, Foley. (Seymour to Harley, 13 Nov. 1695, B.M. Portland Loan, 156).

when Parliament assembled in the autumn.[31] But then disaster struck. In February 1696 news suddenly broke of a Jacobite conspiracy to murder the King. The political scene was transformed overnight. Somers and his Junto colleagues, seizing their opportunity superbly, immediately produced an "Association", a paper which asserted that William was "rightful and lawful King of these realms" and vowed vengeance on his would-be assassins. Members of the House were then asked to subscribe to the document. The result for the Country Party was little short of catastrophic. Foley, Harley, and the old Country Whig section of the Party signed without too much misgiving. But Seymour, Granville, Musgrave, Bromley, and the rest of the Country Tories could not bring themselves to swear fealty to the Dutch usurper in such unqualified terms. Only when signing was made compulsory did they comply, and only then after Harley had begged them almost on his knees.[32] By raising the Whig/Tory issue, dormant since 1690, the Junto had succeeded in splitting the Country amalgam down the middle like a log.

With its unity thus shattered, the divided Country Party was now driven reeling backwards by the Court forces, splendidly managed and led by Charles Montagu. All the Party's most cherished projects seemed doomed. The Land Bank, undermined by an atmosphere bitterly hostile to many of its Tory backers, tottered and fell. The parliamentary Council of Trade, of which old Sir Edward Harley had entertained such high hopes, was swept aside to be replaced by a Court sponsored institution. Spurred on by the turn of events William blithely vetoed Howe's beloved Land Qualification Bill. A backbench attempt to censure him for blocking the measure was

---

[31] Not only was Foley unanimously re-elected Speaker, but an election petition at East Grinstead went against the Court by no less than 93 votes (*Journals of the House of Commons*, XI, p. 384). In addition Portland's grant of Welsh estates was revoked, a land Qualification Bill was carried in the teeth of Court opposition, and the celebrated Trials for Treason Bill at length reached the statute book. By February, much to Wharton's indignation, the House was well on the way to setting up a Country controlled Council of Trade. For the relevant debates see Cobbett, *op. cit.*, vol. V, p. 965 *et seq.*,

[32] *Ibid.*, p. 987 *et seq.*; Oldmixon, *op. cit.*, p. 139; Vernon to Lexington, 17 March 1696, *Lexington Papers*, p. 192; Harley to Bromley, 28 April 1696, *H.M.C. Portland MSS.*, III, p. 575; Francis Gwyn to Robert Harley, 4, 11, and 27 May 1696, *ibid.*, pp. 575–6. See also the signed copies of the Association, *ibid.*, p. 574, and the carefully edited lists in A. Browning, *Thomas Osborne, Earl of Danby* (Glasgow, 1944–51), vol. III, pp. 187–213.

contemptuously voted down by 219 to 70.[33] Then, in February 1697, came the saddest blow of all. Montagu, in alliance with the newly constituted Rose Club, succeeded in annihilating the Public Accounts Commission, for so long the Country Party's pride and joy. James Vernon thought he had never seen a Parliament so meekly compliant to royal wishes. Everything the Court tried, it seemed, "went on smoothly".[34]

It was this scene of desolation and defeat which gave Harley his chance to prove his worth as Country leader. His first priority was clearly desperate defence. He was acquainted with the Court Whigs of old. In the Convention he had himself been a party to their proscriptive schemes. He knew that in concocting the Association they were not playing games. Their aim was not just to discomfit the Country Party, but to destroy it. Indeed, within a short while the Junto's true colours were plain for all to see. Upon declining to set their names to the document both Seymour and Sir William Williams were summarily ejected from the Privy Council. Then, a full scale purge of non-subscribing J.P.s was set in train. Worse still, in April 1696 a Bill "for the better Security of His Majesty's Person and Government" was rushed through its various stages. This made the signing of the Association obligatory on all office holders and M.P.s. In view of the fact that over 90 members of the Lower House had withheld their signatures, the threat to the opposition in this last piece of Junto cunning can scarcely be exaggerated. Harley saw its punitive intent at once, and he moved might and main in the ensuing weeks to persuade the Country Tories to subscribe. Nothing, he argued, could aid their enemies more than continued resistance. At the very least such conduct would lead to a new election, followed by its inevitable corollary

---

[33] Burnet, *op. cit.*, vol. IV, pp. 287–9; *H.M.C. House of Lords MSS, 1695–7* pp. 415–19; Cobbett, *op. cit.*, vol. V, pp. 993–4; *Journals of the House of Commons*, XI, p. 556.

[34] Vernon to Shrewsbury, 27 Oct. 1696, *Vernon Corr.*, I, p. 30. For the Rose Club —a group of forty or so M.P.s, led by Sir Henry Hobart—and its alliance with the government see: Sunderland to William III, 30 April 1697, N.U.L., Portland MSS., PWA 1256, and Vernon to Shrewsbury, 8 Dec. 1696, *Vernon Corr.*, I, p. 112. The tactic adopted by the ministry's supporters was to get their men elected to the Commission, thus destroying its Country flavour. (*Journals of the House of Commons*, XI, p. 703). This forced the Country Party to scuttle the Bill as a whole. (Price to Beaufort, February 1697, Bodl. Carte MSS., 130, f. 381; *Journals of the House of Commons*, XI, p. 705).

—a rampant Whig majority in Parliament. They had, he continued, already made their protest by refusing to sign when signing was voluntary. If they signed now that the law compelled them to do so it would be "understood no other ways but in a legal sense". On this Bishop Sanderson, Grotius, and many other authorities were agreed. "I hope", he urged Bromley, "we shall be preserved by you from having stripes by scourges cut out of our own skins". Eventually, Harley's persuasions, backed up by invaluable help from Musgrave, carried the day. By midsummer all but a handful of the Country Tories had added their signatures to the offending document.[35]

With the Party now safe from immediate destruction Harley turned to the problem of rebuilding it once more into an effective political machine. Although Bromley's following had been successfully hustled into line over the Association, this could not hide the fact that the two wings of the Country opposition were still sadly divided. Many Country Tories believed that had Harley stood firm he could have smothered the Association in infancy.[36] They were also deeply suspicious of the Harley-Foley group's dealings with Whig magnates like Shrewsbury and with the arch political fixer Sunderland. Tory hatred of Sunderland, indeed, knew no bounds. Lord Norris expressed the general sentiment when in a speech "universally well received" he castigated the apostate Earl "as a man whose actions had been so scandalous during his whole life that he never had any way to excuse one crime but by accusing himself of another".[37] Sullen and resentful, many of the more extreme elements were beginning to branch out on their own in the Commons in wild, undisciplined manoeuvres. In January 1697, for instance, a group of Country Tories tried to tack the Land Qualification Bill to supply. The Harley-Foley section, aghast at the irresponsibility of such a move, was compelled to stamp on it. Vernon gleefully reported the scene to Shrewsbury:

[35] Browning, *op. cit.*, vol III, p. 198; Vernon to Lexington, 17 March 1696, *Lexington Papers*, p. 192; Cobbett, *op. cit.*, vol. V, p. 993; Harley to Bromley, 28 April 1696, *H.M.C. Portland MSS.*, III, p. 575; Francis Gwyn to Robert Harley, 4, 11 and 27 May 1696, *ibid.*, pp. 575–6; signed copies of the Association, *ibid.*, p. 574; Feiling, *op. cit.*, pp. 319–21.
[36] E.g. note the undertone of censure in Francis Gwyn's letters to Harley of 4, 11 and 27 May 1696, *H.M.C. Portland MSS.*, III, pp. 575–6.
[37] Burnet, *op. cit.*, vol. IV, p. 369, Dartmouth's note.

Paul Foley did very good service to-day in opposing the tacking clause, which they made sure to carry, having laboured at it ever since the Lords rejected the Bill of Elections, and mustered all their strength, among those who favoured the Bill before. By their first cry I thought they had overwhelmed us, but Mr. Foley, under pretence of speaking to order, answered all their precedents, and declared the like never was in Parliament.[38]

Unedifying divisions of this sort, publicly paraded, must have been as deeply distressing and demoralising to the Country leadership as they were gratifying to the King's ministers.

As soon as he could Harley stepped in to rectify the situation. His formula was to stage a number of spectacular set pieces in the Lower House. The first of these came over the Fenwick case. Sir John Fenwick, a notorious Jacobite, had been involved in the plot to kill William. Unfortunately for the Court he had made a confession which implicated certain members of the administration. Alarmed, the government produced a Bill of Attainder in order to remove him from the scene as rapidly as possible. Harley, quick to appreciate that the dubious character of such proceedings provided excellent ground for a fight, pounced on the opportunity. An elaborate debate was staged in which all the Country leaders, both Whig and Tory, spoke against Attainder. Harley himself made a most impressive contribution tearing to shreds the government case. Exposed to such blistering attack, many of the ministry's supporters began to waver in their allegiance. When the final count was taken the government got home by only 33 votes, Court Whigs like Thomas Pelham and Attorney-General Trevor siding with opposition.[39] Other boosts to Country morale soon followed. The administration got a particularly nasty fright on 10 December 1697, when a moderate and astutely worded motion, brought in by Harley, to reduce the military establishment to its 1680 level was triumphantly carried in the face of strong Court disapproval. A government attempt next day to get the matter re-committed

[38] Vernon to Shrewsbury, 26 Jan. 1967, *Vernon Corr.*, I, p. 189.
[39] Cobbett, *op. cit.*, vol. V, p. 1006 *et seq.*; *Vernon Corr.*, vol. I, pp. 48–83, *passim*; Burnet, *op. cit.*, vol. IV, pp. 324–35; Boyer, *op. cit.*, vol. III, pp. 204–37; Oldmixon, *op. cit.*, pp. 152–60.

failed dismally. Even a surprise effort to reopen the issue a month or so later proved unavailing. After eight hours furious debate the decision went against the Court by 24 votes.[40]

One should not exaggerate the significance of such successes. On most issues Montagu still ruled the roost in the Commons. In fact, if anything, the mauling he took over the army stung him into new life. At any rate, in the closing stages of the 1697–8 session he rounded on his enemies and beat them down brilliantly. When, for example, Charles Duncombe, one of Sunderland's creatures, began sniping at the Whig financier, he was not only accused of fraud but found himself confronted with a Bill of Pains and Penalties lopping off half of his estate.[41] What, however, Harley's nicely selected and deftly executed set pieces did achieve was to put heart back into the opposition. With the smell of success again in their nostrils, Country M.P.s gradually recovered their former cohesion and self-respect. By the time William's third Parliament broke up in the early summer of 1698, and members' coaches began to rumble homeward across England, Harley could well feel satisfied. The Country Party was once more in fighting trim.

Harley's career as Country leader now entered its third and final phase. This was the stage of all out attack. 1698 proved a bad year for the ministry. Apart from Montagu's successes in the Commons there was very little to show on the credit side. The feud between the Junto and Sunderland, which had long been smouldering, had at last burst into open flame. When in December 1697 rumours of Tory plans to impeach Sunderland spread abroad, the Junto lords refused to come to his aid, and, in a fit of panic, he resigned. William, deeply offended by the Junto's part in the quarrel, withdrew almost completely into his own shell, peevishly refusing to co-operate with his government.[42] Then, in summer, came the elections, when, "tired out with

[40] *Journals of the House of Commons*, XII, pp. 5 and 37; William III to Heinsius, 10/20 Dec. 1697, Ranke, vol. VI, p. 332; L'Hermitage's report, 10/20 Dec. 1697, B.M. Additional MSS., 17,677 RR, f. 526; Edward Harley to Sir Edward Harley, 8 Jan. 1698, *H.M.C. Portland MSS.*, III, p. 595. For an account drawing on the unpublished reports of Friedrich Bonnet, the Prussian resident in London, see Ranke, vol. V, pp. 173–4.
[41] Cobbett, *op. cit.*, vol. V, pp. 1170–1; Montagu to Shrewsbury, 18 Jan. and 1 Feb. 1698, *Private and Original Correspondence of Shrewsbury*, pp. 528–9 and 531–4.
[42] Feiling, *op. cit.*, pp. 322–9; J. P. Kenyon, *Robert Spencer, Earl of Sunderland* (London, 1958), pp. 293–307.

taxes",[43] the country gentry sent back a stiff anti-Court majority. Observing the happy turn of events Harley must have smacked his lips in anticipation. Immediately Parliament assembled in the autumn he opened up with all guns blazing. The army was slashed to a mere 7,000 men. A continual threnody of complaint was kept up against naval mismanagement. A Bill went through the Commons to wrest the militia from royal control. An Irish Land Commission was tacked to supply. When William sent down a personal appeal begging to be allowed to keep his Dutch Guards, the House, whipped on by Harley, remorselessly swept aside his request.[44] By the end of January 1699 even the government's financial time table was being determined by Harley.[45] In the following session his grip on supply was, if anything, tighter still. Vernon's nonchalant, matter-of-fact descriptions of the way money was being raised are staggering. On 20 January 1700 he wrote to Shrewsbury:

> We went today into the Committee of Supply. Mr. Harley, who governs in what relates to taxes, was for avoiding any disputes about the horse or foot, and proposed, as it was last year, £300,000 should be allowed for the guards and garrisons this next year; and reflections were made upon the exceeding that sum the last year, and, at the same time, it was declared that they should not concern themselves with the payment of any surplus beyond what they allotted. Their being put in mind that this surplus arises from maintaining a regiment in Guernsey and Jersey, and another in the West Indies, which was necessary in those places, and they had given no direction for disbanding them, signified nothing; but the question was carried, with a little opposition for £300,000.

And on the twenty fifth:

> We have been today in a Committee of Ways and Means, and have voted a Land Tax, not exceeding 2/- in the pound;

[43] Somers to William III, 28 Aug, 1698, P. Grimblot (ed.), *Letters of William III and Louis XIV and of their Ministers* (London, 1848), vol. II, p. 144.

[44] These moves may be followed in Cobbett, *op. cit.*, vol V., pp. 1191–9, and *Vernon Corr.*, vol. II, p. 229 *et seq.* William's touching appeal is printed in *Journals of the House of Commons*, XII, pp. 601–2.

[45] Vernon to Shrewsbury, 31 Jan. 1699, *Vernon Corr.*, vol. II, p 258.

though Mr. Harley computed that the particulars already agreed to amounted to £1,300,000; but the surplus of the Civil List, and what they pretend to save by a better management of the Excise, is, in part, to supply the rest; and wherein it falls short must be provided for next winter. They talk of doing something for deficiencies; but what this is does not yet appear, more than that Mr. Harley hinted as if the Irish forfeitures might be of some use that way. The officers, therefore, may be pretty much disappointed, who expect their whole arrears out of that fund.

On 30 May he concluded mournfully:

What your Grace observes of the behaviour of the Whigs, that even while they were discountenanced, the success of affairs in Parliament was in a great measure, owing to them, since it was in their power to obstruct them if they would; may of late, too, be said of the Tory Party: particularly of Mr. Harley, who for these two years past, has given what turn he pleased to the taxes, and could have made things worse than they are.

Montagu had been utterly eclipsed.[46]

Faced in this way with a House of Commons completely under Harley's thumb, the ministry began to disintegrate. In May 1699 Orford resigned. A few months later Montagu, his nerve gone, retreated into a harmless sinecure. By the spring of 1700 even William, with all his high sense of the prerogative, was beginning to see that he must bend before the wind. In April he dismissed Somers. In May and June he made a number of tentative overtures to Harley and several of the Court Tories. Finally, when, at the end of July, the death of Princess Anne's only surviving child, the infant Duke of Gloucester, made further parliamentary provision for the succession—and hence a strong ministry—an absolute necessity, he began negotiations in earnest.[47] By Christmas all was settled. Rochester and

[46] Vernon to Shrewsbury, 20 Jan., 25 Jan., and 30 May 1700, *Vernon Corr.*, vol. II, pp. 415 and 422, and vol. III, p. 67.
[47] The collapse of the Junto is skilfully described in Ellis, "The Whig Junto", chapter VI. For William's gradual shift of position see *Vernon Corr.*, vol III, *passim*; the Harley–Guy letters in *H.M.C. Portland MSS.*, III, p. 625; and above all Harley's "Large Account: Revolution and Succession", B.M. Portland Loan, 165, misc. 97, ff. 6–10.

Godolphin were taken into the Cabinet; Harley's friend and neighbour Robert Price became a Welsh Judge; and preparations were set in motion for a new Parliament. When, in February 1701, the new assembly met, Littleton, the former Speaker, pointedly absented himself from the Chamber, and Harley was elected to the chair in triumph with Court backing. Harley had done what every politician dreamed of doing, but what precious few achieved. He had stormed the Closet. Moreover, he had done this under a monarch who was the arch opponent of party rule, and who had a more than ordinary attachment to the King's prerogative of freely choosing and dismissing ministers. Not even Shaftesbury, the most revered of all Country heroes, had done more.[48]

There is one specially interesting feature about Harley's Country policy in the 1690's. His political approach was more positive than that of many Country M.P.s. His best energies were absorbed in constructive measures like the Trials for Treason Bill and the Triennial Act.[49] The cry for enemy blood was secondary. From 1694 onwards, too, both he and Foley gave the government valuable help over finance. Before this date ministerial requests for aid had nearly always met with stony faces from the back benches, and with the demand that a full scale enquiry into grievances should precede the granting of any money. But when, on 29 November 1694, the House went into committee to consider the government's request for £2,705,102 9s. 6d. for the army, Foley at once rose to his feet, sweet and reasonable, and without further ado offered

---

[48] Shaftesbury's own grandson, the Whiggish third Earl, paid generous tribute to Harley's prowess as Country Party leader. He was particularly impressed by the Herefordshire man's taming of the Tories. In 1703, looking back on Harley's performance in the latter part of William's reign, Shaftesbury wrote: "He [Harley] is truly what is called in the world a great man, and it is by him alone that that Party [the Tory Party] has raised itself to such a greatness as almost to destroy us. 'Tis he has taught them their popular game, and made them able in a way they never understood, and were so averse to, as never to have complied with, had they not found it at last the only way to distress the government". Shaftesbury to Furley, 30 Jan. 1703, T. Forster (ed.), *Original Letters of Locke, Algernon Sidney, and Anthony Lord Shaftesbury* (London, 1830), p. 192.

[49] For Harley's close links with these measures see Corbett, *op. cit.*, vol. V, pp. 714, 737–41, 760–1, 787–8 and 860–2; Robert Harley to Sir Edward Harley, 31 Dec. 1691, 2 Jan. and 5 Jan. 1692, B.M. Portland Loan, 79 (2); same to same 28 Jan. 1693, *H.M.C. Portland MSS.*, III, p. 512; Sir Edward Harley to Abigail Harley, 19 Dec., 1693, *ibid.*, pp. 548–9; Boyer, *op. cit.*, vol. II, p. 398; Oldmixon, *op. cit.*, p. 95.

£2,500,000, to which sum he pledged the support of his friends. The administration's naval estimates produced a similar reaction. Both gestures were snapped up with alacrity by the ministry.[50] From now on, whatever other steps it might take against the government, the Harley-Foley group, as its opposition to the attempted tacking of the Land Qualification Bill in January 1697 illustrates,[51] always loyally voted the supplies necessary for carrying on the war. This positive tendency was given the acid test in the summer of 1700 when Harley was at last embraced by William. Could he build as well as destroy? Could he serve a ministry or just bully it? In short, could he make the leap from Country to Court?

The evidence is curiously contradictory. In some respects Harley shaped up well to his new task. It was at his suggestion, for instance, that the Commons unanimously agreed to fulfil England's treaty obligations to the United Provinces. Guided by him too, the House passed the Act of Settlement, allotting the Crown to the House of Hanover on the death of Anne.[52] Again, turning his back resolutely on the past, he stoutly opposed an attempt by Bromley to revive the Public Accounts Commission.[53] But there was also a darker side to his activities. Sir Keith Feiling paints a picture of Harley in these months as a man genuinely trying to please William, struggling hard to rein in the wilder elements of his Party, and, in particular, doing his best to frustrate Country Tory attempts to impeach the former Whig ministers for their part in the Partition Treaties with Louis XIV.[54] Unfortunately the available evidence does not

[50] *Journals of the House of Commons*, XI, pp. 176–8 and 181; Bonnet's report, 4/14 Dec. 1694, Ranke, vol. VI, p. 252. Probably what eased the Harley-Foley group into a more accommodating frame of mind in November 1694 was an indication from the government that William was going to let through the Triennial Bill. The King had previously set his face against the measure. See Burnet, *op. cit.*, vol. IV, p. 232.

[51] Vernon to Shrewsbury, 26 Jan. 1697, *Vernon Corr.*, vol. I, p. 189.

[52] Bonnet's reports, 21 Feb./4 March 1701 and 7/18 March 1701, B.M. Additional MSS., 30,000 E, ff. 48 and 67–8; Harley was particularly proud of his contribution to the Act of Settlement. As Abel Boyer observed, he "valued himself so much upon his having promoted the Act of Succession, which was passed while he was Speaker, that he caused his picture to be drawn with the label of the said Act in his hand". A. Boyer, *The History of Queen Anne* (London, 1735), p. 125. The portrait, which is now in the possession of the Duke of Portland, is by Kneller.

[53] Hammond to Coke, 7 June 1701, *H.M.C. Cowper MSS.*, II, p. 428.

[54] Feiling, *op. cit.*, pp. 341–59.

square with this happy scene. Far from holding back the Tory wolves Harley set them on. He lent records, for example, to Charles Davenant, the Tory pamphleteer, for the latter's attack on the Partition Treaties.[55] Worse still, when the House went on to consider Somers's conduct in affixing the Great Seal to the Second Treaty, Harley throwing all restraint to the winds, angrily declared that "if the crime went unpunished the ruin of English liberties would follow from that moment".[56] Even the Act of Settlement[57] had a huge sting in its tail. Admittedly it solved the succession problem, but it also put on the statute book a sizeable piece of the Country programme. The Act stipulated that Sovereigns were henceforward to be in communion with the Anglican Church. It barred the monarch from involving England, without parliamentary consent, in war on behalf of non-British territories; it banished placeholders from the Commons; it removed the right of the King to dismiss judges; it stopped the issue of royal pardons to persons impeached by the Commons; and it forbade the sovereign to leave the country. Under its terms, also, aliens were excluded from the Privy Council and from civil and military office—an obvious slap at William's Dutch favourites. Ominously, the whole polyglot measure went under the description of "An Act for the Further Limitation of the Crown, and Better Securing the Rights and Liberties of the Subject".

In any event, all this is largely academic, for Harley was not given enough time to prove himself. Before the year was out William had plumped for another ministerial reshuffle. Parliament was accordingly dissolved, and when the new assembly met in December 1701, Harley was no longer Court candidate for the Speaker's chair, and he was elected by only four votes

[55] Davenant to Harley, 19 Sep. 1700, *H.M.C.Portland MSS.*, IV, p. 5. Cf. Vernon to Shrewsbury, 22 Aug. 1700, *Vernon Corr.*, vol. III, p. 132. Davenant's pamphlet, which eventually appeared in March 1701, was entitled *An Essay upon I the Balance of Power, II the Right of Making War, Peace and Alliances, III Universal Monarchy.*

[56] "Harley, contre sa prudence ordinaire, dit que si ce crime demeuroit impunis, qu'on pouvoit datter dès ce moment là la ruine de la liberté Anglicane". Bonnet's report, 1/12 April 1701, B.M. Additional MSS., 30,000 E, f. 121. Cf. Bonnet's report of 15/26 April, *ibid.*, f. 144, and Shaftesbury to Furley, 27 Feb. 1702, *Original Letters of Locke, Sidney and Shaftesbury*, pp. 171–5. The Whigs never forgave Harley for his belligerent attitude over the impeachments. See, for example, the third Earl of Sunderland's cutting allusion to it in the "no peace without Spain" debate over a decade later. Cobbett, *op. cit.*, vol. VI, p. 1037.

[57] 12 and 13 Will. III, C2.

after "a great contest" and "contrary to all expectations".[58] A few months later the King was dead, his frail body, which had withstood the turmoil and hazard of so many battlefields, broken by a fall from his horse in the park at Hampton Court. William's reign had demonstrated conclusively that Harley was a Country politician of quite exceptional stature. His deep conviction, and his willingness to spend long and toilsome hours at politics had carried him to the front. Once in charge he had proved his worth as leader both in adversity and at happier times. But it was left to the reign of the King's successor, Queen Anne, to show whether or not Harley could perform with equal merit as a Court politician.

[58] Anthony Hammond's Diary, Bodl. Rawlinson MSS., A 254, f. 67; E.S. de Beer (ed.), *The Diary of John Evelyn* (London, 1955), vol. V, p. 484. The voting was 216 : 212, *Journals of the House of Commons*, XIII, p. 645.

4 Court Politician

THE ACCESSION OF Queen Anne on 8 March 1702 gave a vigorous shake to the political kaleidoscope. For much of the previous reign Anne had been hopelessly at loggerheads with William, and her first speech to Parliament in 1702 showed that the old hatred still burned undiminished. In her clear, sweet voice she took a cruel cut at the dead King's memory by coolly informing the assembled Lords and Commons that her heart was "entirely English".[1] She followed this up by jettisoning her predecessor's closest servants, regardless of their ability. The Junto, for example, was omitted *en bloc* from the new Privy Council. Even the pension which Somers had procured for Joseph Addison, then a struggling young writer, was cancelled.[2] The ageing Sunderland, who had survived so many earlier political turn-abouts, could see no future for himself under the new regime. Instead, he concentrated his energies on launching the career of his madcap son, Lord Spencer.[3] Anne's prejudices, however, were not simply negative. As a devout Anglican she inclined towards Churchmen. In particular she extended her blessing to Marlborough, the husband of her companion Sarah Jennings, and to Marlborough's friend Godolphin. Marlborough secured the glittering post of Captain-General of the army, and Godolphin was placed at the head of the Treasury with its vast acreage of patronage.

One of the most interesting features of the new Court scene

[1] As Burnet observed, the expression "was looked on as a reflection on the late King". Burnet, *op. cit.*, vol. V, p. 3. Henry St. John, however, while he "owned it was a reflection" suggested that it was "not so much upon the late King as his ministers, who, he said, were the worst any Prince ever had". E. Lewis to T. Mansell, 27 Oct. 1702, N.L.W., Penrice and Margam MSS., L. 455. But St. John's explanation overlooks the fact that it was William who was the foreigner, not his ministers, and that, in any case, the ministers were the choice of the Monarch.

[2] J. Campbell, *Lives of the Chancellors and Keepers of the Great Seal of England* (London, 1846), vol. IV, pp. 174–6.

[3] Kenyon, *op. cit.*, pp. 325–7.

was, without doubt, the extraordinary degree of deference which was paid to Harley. Offices were showered on him and his entourage with an open hand. He himself was elected Speaker with Court backing. Associates like Price, Powlet and Bannister were either promoted or confirmed in their judicial posts.[4] Thomas Trevor was kept on as Lord Chief Justice, and Harley's old school-fellow Simon Harcourt received a knighthood plus the post of Solicitor-General. Within a year Paul Foley's son, Thomas, had been advanced to the office of Protonotary of Common Pleas,[5] and Harley's own brother, Edward, had been made Auditor of the Imprest—for life.[6] Moreover, honours and inducements of this sort were not the only marks of distinction accorded Harley. It is clear that from the beginning his opinion was being canvassed on every variety of issue by the new Court favourites. Already in 1702 we find him drafting the Queen's speeches jointly with Godolphin and a chosen few from the Cabinet. In the summer of that year we catch a glimpse of him busily managing elections on behalf of the ministry. In August he was helping to negotiate a loan for the Emperor. October saw the Treasurer begging his aid in ecclesiastical matters. In December he was doing his best to pilot Anne's proposed grant to Marlborough through a storm of High-Tory protest in the Commons.[7] And so on. Indeed, so high did Marlborough and Godolphin rate Harley that they felt it necessary to have special policy-making meetings with him. On the very first day of the reign the Treasurer had arranged one of these gatherings. Before the month was out the mode of summons had become stereotyped. "If it will consist with your convenience", wrote Godolphin on the twenty ninth, "my Lord Marlborough would be very glad to meet you this night about nine at my house". A year later the formula was in all essentials unchanged: "I design to call upon you at your own house before one if you have

---

[4] W. R. Williams, *The History of the Great Sessions in Wales, 1542–1830, together with the Lives of the Welsh Judges* (Brecknock, 1899), pp. 142–5.

[5] Foley to Harley, 29 Sep. 1702, B.M. Portland Loan, 136; Trevor to Harley, 2 Oct. 1702, *ibid.*, 159.

[6] Robert Harley to Abigail Harley, 2 March 1703, *ibid.*, 67.

[7] *H.M.C. Portland MSS.*, IV, pp. 34, 43–4, 48–9, 53–4; B.M. Additional MSS., 28,055, ff. 3–4; B.M. Portland Loan, 64, *passim*; Burnet, *op. cit.*, vol. V, p. 48; J. Johnson to R. Norris, 15 Dec. 1702, T. Heywood (ed.), *The Norris Papers* (Chetham Society, Manchester, 1846), pp. 106–7; Longleat, Portland Misc. MSS., *passim*.

no engagement to hinder me from it".[8] Frequently such meetings took place immediately before or straight after sittings of
the formal Cabinet.[9] One is forcibly reminded of the "inner
ring" or "directing group" which Sir Lewis Namier saw as the
engine of quite a number of eighteenth-century ministries.[10]

At first glance such preferential treatment may seem more
than a trifle puzzling. After all Harley was neither an orthodox
Churchman nor, at this stage, a friend of the Queen. In reality,
however, Marlborough and Godolphin had very sound reasons
for courting Harley. For one thing they were both members of
the Lords, and thus needed someone to keep an eye on things in
the Lower Chamber. As Lady Marlborough put it: "they
thought him [Harley] a very proper person to manage the
House of Commons", adding the significant rider "upon which
so much depends".[11] Even more important were the personalities of the Queen's two favourites. Neither really felt at home
at Westminster. Timid, of "awful serious deportment", hyper-
sensitive to criticism, Godolphin was scarcely ideally equipped
for the stresses and strains of political life.[12] Marlborough was
still less effective. In part, of course, this was a natural conse-

[8] Godolphin to Harley, 8 March 1702, H.M.C. Portland MSS., IV, p. 34; same
to same, 29 [March] 1702 and 10 March 1703, B.M. Portland Loan, 64(8) and (9).
[9] Ibid., 64, passim; Longleat, Portland Misc. MSS., passim.
[10] L. B. Namier, Crossroads of Power (London, 1962), pp. 93–110.
[11] W. King (ed.), Memoirs of Sarah, Duchess of Marlborough (London, 1930), p. 121.
[12] Memoirs of the Secret Service of John Macky (London, 1733), p. 24. Cf. Dartmouth's portrait in Burnet, op. cit., vol. II, p. 240. Godolphin's letters, printed in
Coxe, passim, depict the Treasurer as a formal, testy, rather unimaginative creature,
more at home on the racetrack than in the rough and tumble of political life.
Billingsgate criticism always hurt him deeply, especially when it came from the
pulpit. In 1705, for example, he was reduced to "great concern and very near
weeping" by High Church attacks on government policy (T. Sharp, The Life of
John Sharp, D.D., Lord Archbishop of York (London, 1825), vol. I, pp. 365–6, quoting
Archbishop Sharp's diary), while four years later the inflamatory language of
Henry Sacheverell's notorious 5 November sermon threw him into a state of
"passionate pique" (J. Swift, "Memoirs relating to that Change which happened
in the Queen's Ministry in the Year 1710", Temple Scott (ed.), The Prose Works of
Jonathan Swift (London, 1901), vol. V, pp. 373–4). The proper way to handle such
clerical squibs was, of course, neither to succumb to self-pity nor fly into a rage but,
as Harley appreciated, to counter them with more effective propaganda. This,
however, the essentially unpolitical mind of Godolphin could never grasp. Here
the verdict of Arthur Maynwaring, as recorded by Oldmixon, upon the disgrace
suffered by the Treasurer in 1710 is illuminating. "Mr. Maynwaring told me",
Oldmixon avers, "the Earl of Godolphin had the last contempt for pamphlets, and
always despised the press. He added, 'I have often blamed it in him, and now he
feels the effects of it, when his exalted reputation is levelled with infamy' ". (Oldmixon, op. cit., p. 456.)

quence of his position. As a soldier he was compelled to spend all summer on the continent fighting, and even when he was not abroad much of his time was absorbed in recruiting and re-equiping for the next campaigning season. But, in addition, it is clear that the Duke hated politics. His pomp and aristocratic chivalry, so admirable in the military and diplomatic fields, were wholly unsuited to the mud-slinging and intrigue of every-day politics. The instability and waywardness of parliamentary life unnerved him. Above all his sensitive spirit was unable to endure the venom and the hatred that so often issued from the press. Over and over again Marlborough's political corres-pondence touches a note of almost unfathomable weariness. In July 1703, surveying the party squabbles from the distance of the continent, he wrote to Godolphin:

> I do from my heart pity you and everybody that has to do with unreasonable people; for certainly it is much better to row in the galleys than to have to do with such as are very selfish and misled by everybody who speaks to them.

In 1707 the tone was still the same. In September of that year he confided to his wife:

> You may be sure I shall never mention Mrs. Masham either in letter or in discourse. I am so weary of all this sort of management, that I think it is the greatest folly in the world to think any struggling can do any good when both sides have a mind to be angry.[13]

It is highly significant that whenever the ministry was under pressure in the Lords it was rescued not by Marlborough and Godolphin but by the Junto. When, in the winter of 1704, for example, the ministers faced the prospect of censure over their Scottish policy, it was the Whig lords who saved the day by

[13] Marlborough to Godolphin, 22 July 1703 (N.S.), Coxe, vol. I, pp. 272–3; Marlborough to the Duchess, 19 Sep. 1707 (N.S.), *ibid.*, vol. II, p. 377. Marl-borough's political shortcomings are discussed in greater detail in A. McInnes, "The Appointment of Harley in 1704" *The Historical Journal*, vol. XI (1968), pp. 255–71. My views on Marlborough owe a good deal to conversation with Mr. J. A. Garrard.

3

smoothly setting in motion the machinery which led on to the Union.[14] Again, it was Somers and his aides who, in the 1705–6 session, first defeated Haversham's move to invite the Electress Sophia of Hanover to England, and then adroitly turned the tables on the High Tories by introducing a foolproof Regency Act.[15] In all this the Duke and the Treasurer were little more than helpless spectators. Politically both men often left much to be desired.

It was, more than anything, this political nakedness which induced Marlborough and Godolphin to chase Harley so hard in 1702. Had they only required a government mouthpiece in the Commons a subordinate figure would have done well enough. In William's reign Sir John Lowther had been firmly tied to Carmarthen's apron strings; Henry Guy was Sunderland's puppet. However, the need of Duke and the Treasurer was much more pressing. For them a performing doll in the Lower Chamber was insufficient. Politically uncertain, they were on more than one occasion at a loss to know what orders to give or what strings to pull for the right results. What they desperately wanted in the Lower House was a politician of the front

---

[14] The trouble arose when Godolphin advised the queen to sign the Act of Security, a measure which had gone through the Edinburgh Parliament in 1704. The Act stipulated that on the death of Anne Scotland would not feel bound to choose the same sovereign as England chose. The prospect was thereby opened up of the establishment of a Jacobite fifth column in Scotland, and this caused widespread alarm south of the border. Godolphin was accordingly severely criticized in the Lords for placing the country in a "dangerous" condition. For a time things looked black for the ministry, but then the Junto lords took a hand. Somers suggested that in order to bring home to the Scots the folly of separation from England "some laws might pass here for cutting off all their trade with England". This proposal eventually crystallized into the Aliens Act. At the same time as Somers was, in this way, attempting to bring the Scots "to an understanding of their true interests", Wharton moved for the establishment of a new Union commission —thus offering them a way out of their folly. The combination of stick and carrot worked perfectly. Within a year or so the Union Treaty was an accomplished fact. See Tullie House, Carlisle, Bishop Nicolson's MS. Diary, 29 Nov. 1704 *et seq.*; the Earl of Minto (ed.), *The Correspondence of George Ballie of Jerviswood* 1702–8 (Edinburgh, 1842), pp. 13–16.

[15] Tullie House, Carlisle, Bishop Nicolson's MS. Diary, 15 Nov. 1705 *et seq.*; Burnet, *op. cit.*, vol. V, pp. 225–35. Note also the important marginal comments of Dartmouth, Onslow and Hardwick in Burnet's account. Wharton's "charming" speech is pure delight. By moving the invitation the High Tories thought they had trapped the government. They believed that if Godolphin opposed the motion then he would offend the heir to the throne. On the other hand, if he voted for it he would incur the wrath of Anne who viewed the prospect of a Hanoverian Court in England with deep distaste. The Junto's solution pleased the Queen while at the same time—since it set the protestant succession on a surer footing—winning the applause of Hanover.

rank, a man who could act on his own initiative. Far from directing their House of Commons man they wished him to tender
them political advice, and to relieve them of the burdens of intrigue, public relations and electioneering. It was this crying
need of the ministry which formed Harley's chief *raison d'être* in
1702. Marlborough and Godolphin had observed and been impressed by Harley's performance in William's reign. They had
seen him sweep Montagu aside, and coolly take control of the
Lower Chamber. In the brief Country administration of 1701
they had worked side by side with him, and they had come to
like him so much that in December of that year they actively
supported his candidature for the Speaker's chair against that of
the Court nominee, Littleton.[16] The Duke and the Treasurer
knew that at heart they were not politicians. They had the good
sense to realise that Harley was. Hence, strictly speaking, it is inaccurate to describe Anne's first administration—as Sir Keith
Feiling does—as "the Marlborough-Godolphin ministry".[17] In
1702 England's fortunes were in the hands of three men, not
two. Marlborough was the soldier, Godolphin the slogging
administrator,[18] and Harley the politician of the trio.

As Country leader Harley's chief task had been to seize every
available opportunity to harry the government of the day. Now
that he had transferred his energies to the Court side his priorities
were, of course, completely changed. In his new role as Court

[16] Shaftesbury to Furley, 6 Jan. 1702, *Original Letters of Locke, Sidney and Shaftesbury*, p. 165; Harley, "Large Account: Revolution and Succession", B.M. Portland
Loan, 165, misc. 97, f. 18.
[17] Feiling, *op. cit.*, chapter 2.
[18] Godolphin's stolid dependability is beautifully caught in Charles II's phrase
"never in the way, nor out of the way" (Burnet, *op. cit.*, vol. II, p. 240, Dartmouth's
note). The Duchess of Marlborough was more long winded in her assessment of the
Treasurers' administrative virtues: "He was a man of few words, but of remarkable
thoughtfulness and sedateness of temper; of great application to business, and of
such despatch in it, as to give pleasure to those who attended him upon any affair;
of wonderful frugality in the public concerns, but of no great carefulness about his
own. He affected being useful without popularity; and the inconsiderable sum of
money, above his own personal estate, which he left at his death, showed that he had
been indeed the nation's treasurer, and not his own, and effectually confuted the
vile calumnies of his enemies and successors". (*Sarah Corr.*, vol. II, pp. 125–6). It was
this administrative capacity which saved Godolphin from becoming quite the
political cipher that Marlborough was. Even though the Treasurer was often
unadventurous, jittery, and coldly unbending, his beaver-like qualities did at least
make him a conscientious convener of meetings and drummer-up of votes. This aspect of Godolphin is explored in H. L. Snyder, "Godolphin and Harley: A Study
of Their Partnership in Politics", *Huntington Library Quarterly*, vol. XXX (1967), pp.
241–71.

manager his first concern was inevitably to ensure the smooth passage of vital war supplies. Here the major obstacle in his pathway soon proved to be the revitalized Tory Party. Anne's accession had not seen simply a shake-up at Court; it had also witnessed the return of the Whig/Tory cleavage to the forefront of the political stage. This re-emergence of half-buried enmities stemmed from a variety of causes. In part it was a corollary of the re-opening of the succession issue precipitated by the Duke of Gloucester's untimely death. Another stimulant was religion. The recall of Convocation in February 1701 had produced a bitter altercation between the High Church and Tory dominated Lower House, and the Low Church and Whiggish Upper Chamber. In addition there was mounting concern on the part of many Anglicans over the "abominable hypocrisy" of Occasional Conformity. This was a practice whereby Dissenters could evade the provisions of the Test and Corporation Acts by spasmodically partaking of communion according to the Anglican rite. The whole issue had been brought to a head in 1697 by the exhibitionist conduct of the Dissenting Lord Mayor of London, Sir Humphrey Edwin, who had proceeded to Mead's Meeting House in the Mayor's official coach with the sword and insignia of the City carried before him.[19] But the most important of all the factors contributing to the re-awakening of Whig/Tory strife was the accession of a High-Church Queen. Many Tories felt that Anne's coming marked the long awaited "sunshine day" when Whiggery would at length be overthrown and Tories rule "the promised land in peace".[20] Consequently, ignoring repeated ministerial appeals for domestic peace in the face of the enemy abroad, they bent their efforts in the first years of Anne's reign to pushing through violent

---

[19] The pejorative description of Occasional Conformity is William Bromley's. Bromley to Charlett, 22 Oct. 1702, Bodl. Ballard MSS., 38, f. 137. For Edwin's significance see Burnet, *op. cit.*, vol. V, p. 49, Dartmouth's note, and *Calendar of State Papers Domestic, 1697*, p. 467.

[20] *Memoirs of Sarah, Duchess of Marlborough*, p. 60, and W. Walsh, "The Golden Age Restored", *The Works of the Most Celebrated Minor Poets* (London, 1749), vol. 11, p. 127. Cf. Normanby to Nottingham, 10 March 1702, Leicestershire R.O., Finch MSS., G.S., bundle 22; Sir R. Tracy to Robert Harley, 15 March 1702, *H.M.C. Portland MSS.*, IV, p. 35; Lady Pye to Abigail Harley, 25 March 1702, *ibid.*, pp. 35–6; Sir J. Perceval to T. Knatchbull, 21 March 1702, *H.M.C. Egmont MSS.*, II, p. 208; *Ailesbury Memoirs*, vol. II, p. 525; and W. A. Aiken (ed.), *The Conduct of the Earl of Nottingham* (New Haven, 1941), p. 139.

partisan measures such as the Occasional Conformity Bill. "Do they forget", wrote Godolphin angrily as he contemplated the incendiary behaviour of the Tory diehards, "that not only the fate of England but of all Europe depends upon the appearance of our concord in the despatch of supplies?"[21] But his words fell on deaf ears. The hot heads of the Party were resolved upon exacting their due revenge, even if it meant holding up supply and seeing the allied cause trampled under foot.

Harley at once set about formulating plans to deal with the situation "by supplying proper antidotes".[22] His first resource was to adopt diversionary tactics. As soon as the 1702 election results were in he wrote to Godolphin suggesting that a decoy be set up for Tory marksmen:

> I doubt not but what is to be done as to supplies and the ways of raising them will be as well thought on as is possible before the actual meeting. Will there not be a party that will find imaginary faults unless they be led to what is real and what is expected to be animadverted upon—I mean some accounts? I fear else they will run at riot and do mischief.

In her speech from the Throne at the opening of Parliament in October, Anne obliged by directing members' thoughts to the iniquities of the past. Having first requested the necessary monies for carrying on the struggle against Louis, she continued:

> And, that my subjects may the more cheerfully bear the necessary taxes, I desire you to inspect the accounts of all public receipts and payments; and, if there have been any abuse or mismanagements, I hope you will detect them; that the offenders may be punished, and others be deterred by such examples from the like practices.

Bromley and company took the bait to perfection. The Accounts Commission was revived, and promptly buried itself in a protracted investigation into the financial misdoings of William's

[21] Godolphin to Harley, 10 Dec. 1702, *H.M.C. Portland MSS.*, IV, p. 53.
[22] Harley to Godolphin, 9 Aug. 1702, B.M. Additional MSS., 28,055, f. 3.

Paymaster General, Lord Ranelagh.[23] Meanwhile Harley pressed quietly on with the money bills.

But diversion, though useful, was a tool of limited value. Even the wide-eyed innocents on the Tory back benches could not be fobbed off for ever with chimeras from the past. Already in January 1703 Seymour, Musgrave, and Granville, angered by the Lords' mangling of the Occasional Bill, were attempting to delay the passage of the Malt Tax. In the following year there was talk of tacking the Bill to supply.[24] Harley saw that if the money votes were not to be subjected to the possibility of dangerous delays something more elaborate than smoke screens and stool pigeons would soon be necessary. Accordingly he set to work to buy off a section of the Tory leadership. In September 1703 there is evidence that he was reaching out towards some sort of accommodation with William Bromley.[25] But in the end the project foundered. However, in the following spring success came in the shape of Henry St. John and his following. St. John, a sparkling debator, had begun his career as a high-flying Tory. In part his commitment to the Tory side seems to have been emotional. He saw the Tory Party as the repository of landed values and gentlemanly ideals, and as such he warmed to it instinctively.[26] But his Toryism had also a more basic rationale. Lively and aspiring, he quickly realised that a sure way to focus attention on himself was to pose as the brilliant captain of the earthy, inarticulate Tory squirearchy.[27] In any event, whatever the reasons for the young man's party zeal they

[23] Harley to Godolphin, 2 Aug. 1702, A. W. Thibaudeau (ed.), *Catalogue of the Autograph Letters... Formed by Alfred Morrison* (London, 1883–92), vol. V, p. 77; *Journals of the House of Commons*, XIV, pp. 4 and 27 *et seq.* W. Cobbett, *op. cit.* pp. 97–143. Halifax was also attacked by the Commission.

[24] Tullie House, Carlisle, Bishop Nicolson's MS. Diary, 15 Jan. 1703; T. Johnson to R. Norris, 16 Jan, 1703, *The Norris Papers*, pp. 123–4; O. Klopp, *Der Fall des Hauses Stuart* (Wien, 1875–88), vol. X, p. 224, citing Hoffman's report of 19/30 Jan. 1703; Anon to Trumbull, 23 Dec. 1703, *H.M.C. Downshire MSS.*, I, p. 818; C. Davenant to H. Davenant, 4 Jan. 1704, B.M. Lansdowne MSS., 773, f. 12.

[25] Bromley to Harley, 25 Sep. 1703, *H.M.C. Portland MSS.*, IV, p. 67.

[26] On this aspect of St. John see J. Hart, *Viscount Bolingbroke, Tory Humanist* (London, 1965).

[27] In the latter part of Anne's reign St. John was again to join the Tories. Of his reconversion he later wrote: "The principal spring of our actions was to have the government of the state in our hands". "A Letter to Sir William Windham", *The Works of the late Right Honorable Henry St. John, Lord Viscount Bolingbroke* (London, 1754), vol. I, p. 8. The confession indicates that St. John's Toryism was not entirely a philosophical affair.

were soon to be undermined by a third facet of his personality. St. John had an extraordinary capacity for hero worship. The first political figure to whom he fell captive in this way was the retired and ageing William Trumbull.[28] But soon Trumbull began to be replaced in his affections by Harley. The Speaker, sensing the change, was quick to profit by it. On 4 April 1704 St. John was, at Harley's bidding, duly enrolled into the service of the ministry as Secretary-at-War.[29] Shortly afterwards his boon companion Thomas Coke was made Teller of the Exchequer, while Sir Godfrey Copley, another St. John follower, got an Army Comptrollership.[30] From now on "faithful Harry" was a government man. A gaping hole had thereby been torn in the fabric of the Tory Party, and the Court's position neatly consolidated.

Even this bold coup, however, proved insufficient to dispose completely of the Tory menace. Before long Bromley and Seymour were busy mounting another attack. Acutely conscious that the initiative had been wrested from them, they determined on a last desperate bid to reassert control in the Commons. In the hope of enticing back into the fold at least some of the lost Tory sheep, they resolved, when Parliament met in the autumn, to tack the Occasional Bill to the Land Tax. Harley, who had not at first been inclined to take the rumours of an impending Tory assault very seriously,[31] was suddenly brought face to face with reality by an urgent note he received from Solicitor-General Harcourt on 18 November:

[28] St. John to Trumbull, 23 May 1698 and subsequent correspondence, *H.M.C. Downshire MSS.*, vol. I, p. 277 *et seq.*

[29] Most contemporary accounts point to Harley as the prime mover in St. John's advancement (e.g. Boyer, *History of Queen Anne*, p. 125). Moreover, it was to Harley that St. John attached himself and it was upon him that he poured out his gratitude: "You have been so kind in millions of instances to me that I really look on myself as accountable to you for all my actions". (St. John to Harley, 26 Oct. 1705, *H.M.C. Bath MSS.*, I, p. 79).

[30] *Calendar of Treasury Books*, vol. XIX, p. 227; Prior to Coke, "Thursday morning", *H.M.C. Cowper MSS.*, III, p. 54; Luttrell, vol. V., p. 417. For a list of the St. John connection in Sir William Trumbull's hand see *H.M.C. Downshire MSS.*, I, p. 817.

[31] See Harley's optimistic assessment of Court strength in the paper headed "October 30 1704 list", B.M. Portland Loan 35. The day after he compiled this list Harley wrote to George Stepney telling him that although there was much "noise of distant winds" he had reason to hope that "no such storms can rise as will endanger the public". Harley to Stepney, 31 Oct. 1704, B.M. Additional MSS., 7,059, f. 39.

> Universal madness reigns. The more enquiry I make con-
> cerning the Occasional Bill, the more I am confirmed in my
> opinion that if much more care than has been be not taken, that
> Bill will be consolidated. I find the utmost endeavours have
> been used on one side, and little or none on the other. If this
> be of any moment you'll think of it.[32]

Harley's reaction was electric. He alerted Godolphin, and at
once hastened to draw up a list of the more amenable of those
M.P.s reputedly for the tack. In the next week or so these men
—92 in all—were approached either by Harley or by one of his
deputies and their votes assiduously canvassed. Meanwhile
Godolphin hustled the placeholders into action. Meeting
followed meeting in rapid succession, with every minister pooling ideas and information. When on 28 November the critical
debate eventually came on, government tactics were impeccably
rehearsed. So as not to frighten off any of Harley's new-won
Tory converts, the Court spokesmen, to a man, refrained from
attacking the Occasional Bill itself. Instead they concentrated
their fire exclusively on the iniquity of tacking. Bromley and
Seymour, sensing that the moment of truth was upon them, gave
as good as they got, and the speeches raged on for hour after
hour. When members at length filed into the division lobbies the
candles had long been burning. The drama of those last
moments was vividly caught by William Nicolson, the moderate
Bishop of Carlisle, in his diary:

> The Commons sat this evening till eight o'clock from one,
> warmly debating whether the Occasional Bill should be
> committed to the same committee with the Land Tax. Which
> question being at last put, was carried in the negative: Yeas
> 134, Noes 251. This defeat sat very uneasy upon many of our
> high flyers, who were venturing the Parliament and the
> nation's falling into any sort of confusion, rather than not carry
> their point. When the coaches began to move I sent out my
> servant to enquire how matters went. And he presently
> returned with a lamentable story that 'the Church has lost it'.

[32] Harcourt to Harley, 18 Nov. 1704, B.M. Portland Loan, 138.

This he said he had from several clergymen, as well as others. With submission, I am of a contrary opinion.[33]

Thus Bromley's counter-stroke had been brilliantly repulsed. Only 28 of the 90 odd members listed in Harley's canvass voted with the opposition. The tack lay in ruins, and with it the Tory threat to supply. In the ensuing elections Tory numbers were slashed, 59 of the 134 tackers alone losing their seats. Henceforward, thanks to Harley's "prudent management", the money votes were to create no more major headaches for the ministry.[34]

Although finance was easily Harley's main worry as Court manager, it was by no means his sole concern. Other facets of the government programme called for equally meticulous handling. On these issues, too, Harley performed in creditable fashion. His contribution to the Scottish Union, for instance, was a significant one. He was, of course, in charge of the parliamentary side of things. As a curtain-raiser he had, in the 1705–6 session, guided the repeal of the Aliens Act through the Commons despite strong opposition, and later on he was to watch with similar care over the passage of the completed Union Treaty itself.[35] In addition, however, he lent a hand on many other fronts. He was an active member of the Union Commission.[36] He had agents planted all over Edinburgh to keep the ministry posted on developments there. He pumped

[33] Tullie House, Carlisle, Bishop Nicolson's MS. Diary, 28 Nov. 1704. Cf. Harley's description, Harley to Marlborough, 28 Nov. 1704, Blenheim MSS., F II–16. Harley's list is scribbled on the back of Harcourt's warning letter of 18 November. It has been printed and analysed by P. M. Ansell in *Bulletin of the Institute of Historical Research*, vol. XXXIV (1961), pp. 92–7. Evidence on the flurry of government meetings at this time is contained in 5 undated letters from Godolphin to Harley preserved at Longleat. See Godolphin to Harley, "Tuesday, 10 at night", "Monday at 2", "Sunday past two", "Wednesday at 8", and "Saturday at noon", Longleat, Portland Misc. MSS., ff. 126, 134, 138, 140 and 196. For ministerial tactics on 28 November see Cobbett, *op. cit.*, vol. VI, pp. 361–2 and Burnet, *op. cit.*, vol. V, pp. 177–8, and for the wisdom of this conduct E. Brereton to R. Myddleton, 3 March 1704, N. L. W., Chirk Castle MSS., E. 4204.

[34] Marlborough to Harley, 16 Dec. 1704, Coxe, vol. II, p. 69. The division lists are printed in *Somers Tracts*, XII, pp. 471–6, and Oldmixon, *op. cit.*, pp. 346–7. R. R. Walcott, "Division-Lists of the House of Commons 1689–1715", *Bulletin of the Institute of Historical Research*, vol. XIV (1936–7), pp. 28–9, discusses the relative merits of these lists.

[35] A. Aufrere (ed.), *The Lockhart Papers: containing Memoirs and Commentaries upon the Affairs of Scotland from 1702 to 1715* (London, 1817), vol. I, p. 139.

[36] *Acts of the Parliaments of Scotland*, XI, Appendix, pp. 146–90, *passim*; D. Defoe, *The History of the Union of Great Britain* (London, 1784), pp. 105–6 and 121. Harley attended 40 of the 46 meetings of the Commission.

3*

encouragement and propaganda into men like Leven and Carstares. Last, but not least, for well over a year he effectively marooned the Jacobite leader Hamilton by skilfully dangling government bait before him.[37] But even more interesting than Harley's efforts on behalf of the Union was his conduct over the Regency affair in 1706. At the close of William's reign Harley had shown by his vigorous advocacy of the Act of Settlement that at that stage he was still firmly wedded to the classic Country ideal of banishing placeholders from the Commons. When, however, in the spring of 1706 the back-bench element in the House attempted to consolidate the 1701 victory by incorporating further anti-placeholder provisions in the Regency Bill, Harley rallied decisively to the Court side. In the event the Country forces proved so powerful that he only managed to achieve a compromise on the issue. But this was, relatively speaking, unimportant. What really counted was the stand he had taken. By coming out heart and soul on the government side he demonstrated once and for all that he had shed the atttitude which in 1701 threatened to spell his doom as a Court politician. Delighted, Godolphin hurried to congratulate his reformed colleague on having "fought it so stoutly" against his old cronies.[38]

Examples of Harley's managerial conduct in these years could easily be multiplied. Especially impressive were his efforts to tame the High Church clergy, first by wooing their leader George Hooper, and subsequently by pressing for financial assistance for the lower paid clerics.[39] Enough has been said,

[37] Harley's correspondence with Leven and Carstares in *H.M.C. Portland MSS.*, IV and VIII; R. Story, *William Carstares* (London, 1874), pp. 287–9; Brenanaud's letters in B.M. Portland Loan, 127; Earl of Minto (ed.), *Correspondence of George Ballie of Jerviswood, 1702–8* (Edinburgh, 1842), pp. 35–7 and 102. See also p. 79 *et seq.*, below.

[38] Harley's conduct in the anti-placeholder agitation of 1706 is recorded in detail in an anonymous parliamentary diary to be found in Cambridge University Library, Additional MSS., 7093. See also Godolphin to Harley "friday noon", B.M. Portland Loan, 64(16), and Harley's draft speech dated 23 Jan. 1706, B.M. Portland Loan, 9(26). For the background to the whole affair see G. S. Holmes, "The Attack on 'The Influence of the Crown' 1702–16", *Bulletin of the Institute of Historical Research*, vol. XXXIX (1966), pp. 47–48.

[39] G. V. Bennett, "Robert Harley, the Godolphin Ministry, and the Bishoprics Crisis of 1707", *English Historical Review*, vol. LXXXII (1967), pp. 729–30. Harley's concern for the poorer clergy led to the introduction into the Commons in 1704 of Queen Anne's Bounty restoring to them the royal taxes of first fruits and tenths.

however, to illustrate the point. Both on the crucial problem of finance, and also in other areas, Harley transferred his political talents from Country to Court smoothly and easily. But in fact this is only half the story. Harley did not simply adjust to a new situation. He grew in stature in his Court role. In particular, he succeeded in building up a superb system of political intelligence that became the envy even of foreign observers.

One of the consequences of the friction between the Tory Party and the ruling triumvirate was that many of the Tories who held ministerial posts either found themselves summarily dismissed because of their growing obstructiveness, or else felt bound to resign. In the spring of 1704 the government was particularly discommoded when, in a fit of pique, Lord Nottingham the Tory Secretary of State, suddenly threw in the sponge. The triumvirs, who had not anticipated the move, had no successor lined up, and for a whole month after Nottingham's untimely departure Godolphin was compelled to cast about desperately in search of a suitable replacement. Even under normal conditions it was not always easy to lay hands at short notice on serviceable ministerial timber. But in 1704 things were very far from normal. Indeed the range of choice open to the ministers was almost unbelievably restricted. They could scarcely appoint a prominent Tory since Nottingham's withdrawal was regarded by the Tory hierarchy as symbolising ritualistic severance with the ministry. On the other hand, in view of Anne's current political prejudices, a front-bench Whig was equally out of the question. What the triumvirs needed was a man of stature who was also politically colourless. And men of this calibre were nowhere to be found. In the end Harley was obliged, much against his better judgement, to accept the seals himself in order to plug the gap.[40]

Hitherto discussions of Harley's record at the Secretariat have tended to be strongly coloured by the revelations of the traitor clerk William Greg.[41] Stress has been laid on the bad organisation

---

[40] For a detailed analysis see A. McInnes, "The Appointment of Harley in 1704", *The Historical Journal*, vol. XI (1968), pp. 255–71.

[41] Greg, a clerk in Harley's office, acted as chief censor of the correspondence of French prisoners of war in England. This work brought him into contact with Chamillart, the French Minister of War. In November 1707 Chamillart managed to persuade Greg, who was deep in debt, to sell secret military information to the

of Harley's office, on the mere pittance paid to his clerks, on the system which forced them to work long and irregular hours, and above all on the almost criminal lack of the most elementary security precautions. Basing his verdict on these disclosures Professor Mark Thomson has selected Harley as the epitome of secretarial incompetence. With equal assurance Sir Winston Churchill has dismissed the unfortunate triumvir as an arrant rogue guilty of "culpable negligence in public business".[42]

There seems no reason to doubt the substantial accuracy of Greg's testimony. Had he wished to damage Harley by misrepresenting facts the Scot could have done much more than simply paint a black picture of his employer's administration. He could with ease have accused Harley of being implicated in treason. As it was Greg went to almost incredible lengths to protest Harley's innocence. On more than one occasion he was offered his life if he would implicate his master, but he refused to do so. His dying act on the scaffold was to issue a statement denying that his former employer had in any way been privy to his own treasonable activities. Clearly Greg's disclosures were not inspired by malice. It does, nevertheless, seem strange that Harley, who had, with the utmost industry, in William's reign, mastered the details of parliamentary procedure, should suddenly have become so slack and negligent when appointed Secretary. It seems even stranger that after his fall in 1708 he should with equal suddenness have recovered his former industry in compassing the destruction of the Marlborough-Whig administration.

The explanation of these apparent incongruities of conduct is in fact a simple one. The truth is that although Greg's evidence cannot itself be challenged, the construction placed upon it by later scholarship is in large measure misleading. Thus while it is incontestable that security precautions in Harley's office were hopelessly inadequate, it is wrong to ascribe such conditions to

---

French government. The clerk's treason, however, was discovered, and at the subsequent investigation of his conduct it became painfully obvious that the lax set up in Harley's office virtually invited disloyalty of the Greg kind. Greg's evidence may be found in T. B. Howell (ed.), *A Complete Collection of State Trials* (London, 1816), vol. XIV, pp. 1380–7.

[42] M. A. Thomson, *The Secretaries of State, 1681–1782* (Oxford, 1932), p. 19; W. S. Churchill, *Marlborough, His Life and Times* (London, 1947), book II, p. 315.

Harley's particular slackness. Nottingham's office was no better organised. "I have been in the Secretary's office of a post night", wrote Defoe, "when had I been a French spy I could have put in my pocket my Lord Nottingham's letters directed to Sir George Rooke and to the Duke of Marlborough, laid carelessly on the table for the doorkeeper to carry to the post office".[43] Similarly, although Harley paid his clerks poorly he cannot be condemned for so doing. He was simply following customary practice—a practice which continued long after his fall in 1708.[44] In brief, the bad organisation of Harley's office was not at bottom the outcome of his own negligence; it was rather a product of the times, a concrete instance of the low ebb of administrative efficiency characteristic of Augustan England. Harley did not create the system which led to the tragic death of his gifted clerk; he inherited it.

But the stress so often laid on the laxity of Harley's administration is not only unfair. In one respect at least it is grossly inaccurate. An integral part of the duties of the Secretaries of State was the task of furnishing the government of the day with news. The bulk of such information was fairly run-of-the-mill in character, and came from a chain of regular correspondents scattered throughout Europe. These observers were, for the most part, government officials, varying in status from ambassadors and envoys to postmasters and customs officials. Their task as intelligencers was to provide the government with a regular account of the day to day happenings in various parts of the globe.[45] On top of this more formal structure, however, Harley took it upon himself to embroider an elaborate network of domestic spies and agents. As a result of the fact gathering activities of this more flexible instrument he became the most informed politician of his day.

By far the most prominent of all Harley's spies was the irrepressible Daniel Defoe. Daniel had first made Harley's acquaintance in 1703. The occasion of their meeting was a pleasant one, for it was bound up with Harley's successful efforts to engineer the pamphleteer's release from Newgate whither he had been

---

[43] *Defoe Letters*, pp. 38–9.
[44] Burnet, *op. cit.*, vol. V, p. 346, Hardwicke's note.
[45] P. Fraser, *The Intelligence of the Secretaries of State and their Monopoly of Licensed News 1660–88* (Cambridge, 1956).

swept by the storm of protest raised by his biting satire *The Shortest Way with Dissenters*.[46] From that time onwards until the final collapse of the triumvirate Dan Foe, the Cripplegate butcher's son, was to figure as Secretary Harley's leading agent.

Daniel obtained his first commission as a roving political spy in the summer of 1704 when he was entrusted with a mission in the eastern counties of England. His job had a dual character: he was to forward Harley a first hand account of the political complexion of the counties through which he travelled, and at the same time do what he could to spread "principles of temper, moderation and peace" among all the people with whom he came into contact.[47] The journey proved so successful that in the following year Defoe was packed off to western England on a similar mission. On this occasion one of his main tasks seems to have been to probe Seymour's "Western Empire",[48] but his travels took him through much of the midlands and the north as well. It was election time in all these counties and Daniel had much to say about the heats dividing the country at this time. He was firmly convinced that "the greatest hindrance to the forming the people into moderation and union among themselves, next to the clergy, are the justices". "Wherever there happen to be moderate justices", he added, "the people live easy and the parsons have less influence, but the conduct of justices in most parts is intolerably scandalous".[49] Harley took the warning to heart; in the autumn of 1705 Lord Keeper Wright who had been prevailed upon by Sir Edward Seymour to sanction a "general displacing of moderate men" from the bench was removed from office.

In 1705 the elections had been the central political concern. By 1706 men's attention had shifted. Scotland and the Union

---

[46] It is sometimes stated that Defoe's release was not effected until August 1704. (E.g. W. Lee, *Daniel Defoe: His Life and Recently Discovered Writings* (London, 1869), vol. I, p. 91, and W. Minto, *Daniel Defoe* (1879), p. 49.) This is wrong. On 26 September 1703 Harley was given authority to release Defoe (Godolphin to Harley, 26 Sep. 1703, *H.M.C. Portland MSS.*, IV, p. 68), and by 9 November the Dissenter was out of gaol (Defoe to Harley, 9 Nov. 1703, *Defoe Letters*, p. 10).

[47] *Defoe Letters*, pp. 57–62. The quotation is from p. 60. Daniel was accompanied on his tour by another Dissenter, Christopher Hurt.

[48] "Seymsky's Western Empire", Defoe records on one occasion, "may with much ease be overthrown". Defoe to Harley, 14 Aug. 1705, *ibid.*, p. 100.

[49] Abstract of Defoe's western journey in *ibid.*, p. 113.

were fast becoming the touchstone of politics. Accordingly
Defoe's next assignment carried him into the northern kingdom.[50] His task was still the same—in part to record opinion,
in part to forward the government programme. But the scene
of his operations was vaster and the character of his work
immensely more varied. His previous journeys had been a mere
apprenticeship. It was in Scotland that he won his spurs as a
secret agent. Daniel remained Harley's chief agent in Edinburgh
throughout the union crisis. The long and almost daily reports
which he sent to his master represent only a fraction of the effort
he put into the Union project. In addition he aided the Union
managers at every turn, supplying them with debating material
and checking their attempts to carve up the Treaty.[51] Under a
variety of disguises he wheedled his way into every kind of
company and there preached the necessity of Union.[52] He
attended meetings of the Kirk daily and was "entirely confided
in" by the Scottish divines.[53] All this time a stream of Union
propaganda poured from his pen in the form of pamphlet, tract
and poem.[54] He even found time to act as Scottish correspondent of de Fonvive's *Post Man*.[55] His energy was indeed truly
remarkable, and his contribution to the success of the Union
project in Scotland was by no means inconsiderable.

In contacting Harley from Newgate Defoe had used as inter-
mediary the distinguished Scottish economist William Paterson.[56] The choice was oddly appropriate for Paterson's name
was soon to be added to the list of the Secretary's agents in
Edinburgh. Since the golden days of Darien and the Bank of

[50] He arrived in Edinburgh early in October. This was not his first visit to
Scotland. He had made a tour of the country in William III's reign. See J. R.
Moore, *Daniel Defoe, Citizen of the Modern World* (Chicago, 1958), chapter XV,
passim.

[51] *Defoe Letters*, pp. 154–6, 160–2, 176–8.

[52] Defoe to Harley, 26 Nov. 1706, *ibid.*, pp. 158–9. On occasion he even beguiled
a Jacobite audience with his blandishments. Early in January 1707, for example, he
had by "an unexpected success . . . obtained a converse with some gentlemen belonging to the Duke of Gordon who are very frank". *Ibid.*, pp. 189–90.

[53] Defoe to Harley, 26 Nov. 1706, *ibid.*, p. 159.

[54] Note especially his celebrated six *Essays at Removing National Prejudices*, and the
soothing poem *Caledonia*, the avowed purpose of which was to convince the dubious
Scots that merger with England involved no base affront to their ancient dignity.

[55] Moore, *op. cit.*, pp. 157–162.

[56] On Paterson see generally J. H. Burton, *The History of Scotland* (Edinburgh,
1905), vol. VIII, pp. 14–30, and W. A. Steel, "William Paterson", *English Historical
Review*, vol. XI (1896), pp. 260–81.

England Paterson had fallen on hard times, and he spent the first four years of Anne's reign bemoaning his ill fortune, forwarding snippets of economic information and advice to Harley and Godolphin, searching always for some kind of permanent employment in the government. Eventually his hopes were fulfilled. In 1706 he was employed by the government to help calculate "the equivalent", and then sent up to Scotland to speed the Union there. His official status in the northern kingdom was that of economic adviser to the Union managers, but unofficially he acted as one of Harley's secret agents.[57]

Defoe was more than once to criticise Paterson for confining his attention too exclusively to economic matters and thereby failing to make contact with the people of the Scottish capital.[58] No doubt Daniel was a little jealous of his confrere, but all the same his strictures do have some foundation. Paterson was certainly less energetic than his English colleague. Even so, the Scot's reports to Harley were both interesting and useful. They painted a graphic picture of the disturbed state of Edinburgh, and also provided the Secretary with an almost verbatim account of proceedings in the Scottish Parliament.[59] Moreover Paterson did on occasion make some attempt to convince a fairly wide audience of the economic advantages which Union would bring to Scotland.[60]

Defoe and Paterson were not the only agents whom Harley had at work in Edinburgh in 1706. Another man who was reporting regularly from the Scottish capital at this time was David Fearn,[61] a Cameronian of high social rank, and a close friend of the Earl of Stair.[62] Fearn was in some ways the most

---

[57] Paterson's letters to Harley, *H.M.C. Portland MSS.*, IV, p. 18 *et seq., passim,* and *ibid.*, VIII, *passim*; J. M. Gray (ed.), *Memoirs of Sir John Clerk of Penicuik* (London, 1895), p. 61.

[58] See Defoe's letters to Harley, 22 Nov., 26 Nov., and 21 Dec. 1706, *Defoe Letters*, pp. 157–8, 160 and 178–9.

[59] For Paterson's reports see *H.M.C. Portland MSS.*, IV, *passim*.

[60] Note his pamphlet *An Enquiry into the Reasonableness and Consequences of an Union with Scotland*, and also the two manuscript treatises on the Union in B.M. Additional MSS., 10,403.

[61] In contemporary documents Fearn's name is variously spelt, Fearn, ffearn, Fearns and Fearne, but he usually signed himself Fearn.

[62] William Houston writes to Fearn of "our fraternity, of which you have formerly been provost". (*H.M.C. Portland MSS.*, VIII, p. 331). That Houston was a Cameronian is proved by his memorial, *ibid.*, pp. 371–4. On Fearn's social rank and his relations with Stair see *ibid.*, IV, pp. 401–2.

valuable of all Harley's Scottish agents. Not only did he maintain contact with the Cameronian west through the person of
Dr. William Houston, but he also had an intimate knowledge of
the issues and personalities underlying Scottish politics, and was
at the same time "in credit with the Kirk".[63] This background
enabled Fearn to supply Harley with a series of memorials on
various aspects of the Scottish scene.[64] It also gave a certain dis-
tinctiveness to Fearn's analysis of the situation in Edinburgh,
and it is noticeable that his weekly reports to Harley were much
less pessimistic in tone than were the letters of Defoe.[65]

The importance of Fearn's reports increased in the summer of
1707 when Defoe left Edinburgh to make a tour of Scotland.[66]
Then for a brief space the Cameronian became Harley's chief
agent in the Scottish capital, and it was only at this late hour
that Godolphin was made aware of Fearn's existence.[67] Harley
had in fact deliberately kept his association with Fearn a tight
secret. In particular he had been at great pains to prevent
Defoe from getting wind of the Scot's presence in Edinburgh.[68]
Clearly the Secretary was using Fearn as a check on
Defoe.

In a sense David Fearn had more of the professional spy about
him than either Defoe or Paterson. Both these last had performed a double role in Scotland. They had gathered information for Harley, but they had also done much to smooth the
passage of the Union Treaty. Fearn was much more the pure
informer. He himself did very little in the way of forwarding the

[63] See generally Fearn's correspondence in B.M. Portland Loan, 135, *H.M.C.
Portland MSS.*, IV, and *ibid.*, VIII. The quotation is from Harley's letter to
Godolphin, 19 June 1707, *ibid.*, IV, p. 421.

[64] Only one of these memorials survives—a list of the noblemen and landed
gentry of Scotland with notes on their political and religious proclivities. (*Ibid.*,
VIII, pp. 202–8). For evidence that there were other memorials see Fearn's letters
to Harley of 1705, B.M. Portland Loan, 135(1). All these memorials were drawn up
before Fearn was sent to Edinburgh as a secret agent.

[65] *H.M.C. Portland MSS.*, IV, *passim*; B.M. Portland Loan, 135(1).

[66] Defoe to Harley, 25 March 1707, and subsequent correspondence. *Defoe
Letters*, p. 212 *et seq.*

[67] Harley to Godolphin, 19 June 1707, *H.M.C. Portland MSS.*, IV, p. 421.

[68] Note especially John Bell's letter to Harley of 19 Nov. 1706, *ibid.*, p. 353: "Mr
D[e] F[oe] knows nothing in the least from me of D. F[earn]'s concerns in that
country [Scotland], and the like Mr. D. F[earn] knows as little of Mr. D[e] F[oe]'s,
and this your honour may depend upon, and nobody could have kept matters more
private than I have done".

Bell, the post-master at Newcastle-on-Tyne, was the medium through whom
Harley sent orders and money to both Defoe and Fearn while they were in Scotland.

Union.[69] This was even truer in the case of another of Harley's Scottish agents, the ill-fated William Greg. Greg had been sent to Edinburgh early in June 1705, and he remained there until October of the same year. The reports he sent to Harley were lengthy and frequent, but the Scot seems to have confined himself to the single task of ascertaining "the pulse of this boiling nation". He appears to have made no effort to regulate that pulse. This, perhaps, was why Greg was recalled to London in the winter of 1705 to be replaced in Edinburgh by the more volatile Defoe.[70]

A spy who far outshone Greg in importance was Captain John Ogilvie, yet another Scot. Ogilvie, a former officer in James II's army, had gone into exile with the King, and had ever since remained in contact with the main stream of Jacobite intrigue. From time to time in the period 1705 to 1707 the Scot was employed by the unsuspecting French as a secret service agent, and throughout much of the same period Ogilvie's wife, a "very close minded" woman, was resident at St. Germains taking careful note of happenings there. On his return from the continent in July 1707 Ogilvie was despatched to Scotland where he visited a number of leading Jacobite houses, and was welcomed as a friend and confidant.

Ogilvie's intimate association with Jacobitism made him a spy of immense value. The reports which he forwarded to Harley were always interesting and often of exceptional importance. It was, for instance, from Ogilvie that the Secretary obtained a copy of the cipher of the French foreign minister Torcy. It was the Scot too who alerted Harley about the activities of the French agent Nathaniel Hooke. Later Ogilvie was to supply the

---

[69] This did not mean that Fearn was in any way lukewarm in his support of the Union. In fact, he was fervently pro-Union and anti-Jacobite. "I desire", he wrote on one occasion, "to live no longer than I see the throne filled with a successor of the true Protestant line". (Fearn to Harley, 24 March 1705, B.M. Portland Loan, 135(1)). Moreover, Fearn did occasionally materially aid the Union cause. "There is talk of issuing forth a proclamation to discharge the bringing in of foreign coin to clog the Equivalent", he informed Harley, and added, "*verbum sapientis* I had a hand in that matter". *H.M.C. Portland MSS.*, VIII, p. 276.

[70] For biographic material on Greg see *State Trials*, vol. XIV, pp. 1380–7. As early as February 1705 Greg was in Harley's pay (*H.M.C. Portland MSS.*, IV, p. 159), and by May of that year the details of Greg's mission to the northern capital had been settled. (*Ibid*., pp. 181–4). For Greg's reports from Edinburgh see *ibid*., pp. 194–248, *passim*. The frequency of his letters may be gauged from those dated 28 Aug., 30 Aug., 1 Sep., 6 Sep. 8 Sep. 1705.

government with details of the French plan to invade Scotland in the spring of 1708 months before the project actually materialised. The value Harley attached to these reports is indicated by the fact that he was prepared, for three years, to pay the erstwhile army captain sufficient to enable him to mix on an equal footing with the upper strata of Jacobite society. Well might the Secretary do so, for John Ogilvie was no common informer. He was, in fact, nothing less than Harley's ears and eyes among the Jacobites.[71]

The five men examined above have been dwelt on at some length to give an idea of Harley's spy network in action. The network, however, was more intricate than the careers of these men might seem to suggest. For one thing it included many more agents. Some of these—John Toland[72] for instance—like Defoe combined the functions of both spy and writer. Others such as John Clare,[73] the printer whom Harley employed to track down wanted pamphleteers, played a more limited role. Moreover, we must also bear in mind the fact that Harley's major agents had deputies and assistants of whom very little is known. Defoe, for example, speaks of having established "a settled correspondence in every town and corner" of the Seymour country.[74] In Scotland, too, the wily Dissenter had his helpers, and in the winter of 1706 he sent one of these men, John Pierce, on a pacifying mission to the Cameronian country.[75] Furthermore, clustered about the edges of Harley's spy network was another group of informants—a motley collection of men

[71] On Ogilvie's relations with Harley see *ibid.*, p. 160 *et. seq.*, *passim*, and *ibid.*, VIII, p. 319. Ogilvie was first employed by Harley in the spring of 1705. Ogilvie to Harley, 11 Feb. 1705, B.M. Portland Loan, 152. The Secretary's first recorded payment to Ogilvie is 5 May 1705, *ibid.*, 163.

[72] John Toland, the Deist (1670–1722). In Harley's pay 1705. (*H.M.C. Portland MSS.*, IV, p. 409). Penned the government reply to Drake's *Memorial of the Church of England.* 1707 spying in Germany for Harley. (*H.M.C. Portland MSS.*, IX, pp. 289–90). See also *D.N.B.*, vol. LVI, pp. 438–42; E. Calamy, *Historical Account of My Own Life* (London, 1829), vol. II, pp. 37–8; *Wentworth Papers*, p. 132; *H.M.C. Portland MSS.*, IV, pp. 408–10, 486, 491; *ibid.*, VIII, p. 279.

[73] Little is known of Clare beyond the fact that when brought into Harley's employ in 1705 he was in a destitute condition. B.M. Portland Loan, 130(4).

[74] Defoe to Harley, 14 Aug. 1705, *Defoe Letters*, p. 100.

[75] *Ibid.*, p. 163 *et. seq.*, *passim*. Considerable uncertainty exists concerning Pierce's true identity. Andrew Lang thought that Pierce was a pseudonym for John Ker of Kersland (A. Lang, *History of Scotland* (Edinburgh, 1907), vol IV, pp. 124–31). Paul Dottin, on the other hand, has identified Pierce with a man of that name implicated in the publication of *Legion's Humble Address*. (P. Dottin, *Daniel Defoe et ses Romans* (Paris, 1924), pp. 139 and 165).

who were, strictly speaking, neither professional spies nor their deputies. Into this rather ragged category fell friends like the Earl of Leven[76] and William Carstares,[77] officials of the stamp of Edmund Dummer,[78] and an odd assemblage of other people such as John Tutchin[79] and John Forster[80] who, imbued with patriotic zeal, forwarded information "without purchase or pay". The web, indeed, when viewed in its fullness, was a very tangled one. Its threads spread imperceptibly across the whole countryside. When Auditor Harley compared his brother's knowledge of the domestic scene with that of Queen Elizabeth's celebrated spy chief Francis Walsingham, his judgement was not being hopelessly distorted by brotherly affection. He was expressing little more than the plain truth.[81]

Harley's intelligence system, then, clearly shows that his period as Court politician was a time of growth as well as adaptation. Moreover, his powers were maturing in other ways as well. As the dual character of the work of so many of his agents indicates he was anxious to mould opinion and develop to the full government use of the press. Indeed, Defoe's highly popular newspaper the *Review*, a publication from the start sponsored by Harley, was, in the first half dozen years of the reign, unrivalled as an organ of political propaganda. In addition Harley was carefully extending the range of his political contacts. He penetrated especially deeply into the

[76] David Melville, third Earl of Leven (1660–1728). Commander-in-Chief of the Scottish forces; Governor of Edinburgh castle. Corresponded with Harley. His view on Scottish affairs was useful; it represented the opinion of one who, although wholly in favour of the Revolution and all it entailed, was yet outside the ministry. See *H.M.C. Portland MSS.*, IV, pp. 99–100, 103–4; *ibid.*, VIII, pp. 130–1.

[77] William Carstares (1649–1715) the famous Scottish divine. Principal of Edinburgh University. An intimate friend and frequent correspondent of Harley. *Ibid.*, VIII, *passim*; Story, *op. cit.*, pp. 287–9.

[78] Edmund Dummer, surveyor of the navy. Wrote often to Harley on naval matters. Encouraged by the Secretary he set up a scheme for a monthly intelligence between London and the West Indies. P.R.O. State Papers Domestic, 4, *passim*; *ibid.*, 7, no. 84; B.M. Portland Loan, 9, 64, 125(2), 134(3) and (4), 167; *Calendar of State Papers Domestic, Anne*, vol. I, pp. 213–4; *H.M.C. Portland MSS.*, VIII, *passim*.

[79] John Tutchin (1661–1707). Editor of the *Observator*. He had occasionally sent oddments of information to Nottingham. He was to do the same for the Earl's successor. *Ibid.*, IV, pp. 86, 91, 294–5.

[80] John Forster, an obscure figure. Resident in the north of England. Sent Harley occasional information on Jacobite activities. *Ibid.*, pp. 296, 424, 449.

[81] Edward Harley's "Memoirs", *ibid.*, V, p. 647. Cf. Schulenburg to Leibnitz, 31 March 1714, J. M. Kemble (ed.), *State Papers and Correspondence Illustrative of the Social and Political State of Europe* (London, 1857), p. 491.

religious theatre. Among his associates in the opening years of
the reign he numbered the distinguished Dissenting minister
Edmund Calamy, William Penn the Quaker, Dr. George
Hooper, friend of the Non-Juring Ken, William Carstares the
influential Scottish Presbyterian, the Low-Churchman John
Potter, Dr. George Smalridge the High-Church divine, the two
Archbishops—Sharp of York and Tenison of Canterbury, and,
incredibly, Francis Atterbury the darling of the high flyers.[82]
Here was the whole spectrum of ecclesiastical opinion. No
other politician in Queen Anne's day could lay claim to such
mastery. Yet, as measures like the Occasional Conformity Bill
and the Schism Act demonstrate, religion had once again come
to occupy the forefront of the political stage. Hence Harley's
clerical contacts were a priceless asset. Godolphin, for one, was
not slow to realise this. Within a year of the Queen's accession
he had handed over the ministry's ecclesiastical concerns to
Harley's safe keeping. "I shall not move in anything of this
kind," he informed the Speaker in November 1702, regarding
clerical preferment, "except as you will guide me".[83]

Glancing back across the evidence one is tempted to conclude
that Harley the Courtier was as much a triumph as his Country
predecessor. In the Commons he performed with all the old
panache. Each year his talents climbed toward maturity. But
there was one great difference. Harley's Country career culminated in a blaze of glory. Through sheer ability he forced the
ministry to bow before him. His spell at Court, however, ended
in disaster and disgrace. In February 1708 he was brusquely
thrust from office. Moreover, his departure was not the result of
defeat at the polls. He was rejected by his own patrons Marlborough and Godolphin. On the evening of 29 January
Godolphin despatched Attorney-General Harcourt to Harley
with a message severing their long association. Next day the
Secretary hurried to see Marlborough who furnished him with
details of his offence. Fortified with these, Harley at once wrote

[82] B.M. Portland Loan, 125 (3), 129(6), 147(3), 153(6), 153(4), 156(7), 163(8)
and 306; Bodl. Ballard MSS., 6, f. 99; W. Graham (ed.) *The Letters of Joseph Addison*
(Oxford, 1941), pp. 92 and 96; *H.M.C. Bath MSS.*, I, p. 57; *Carstares State Papers*,
pp. 718–22, 727–9 and 774–6; *Defoe Letters*, pp. 193, 255 and 397; *H.M.C. Portland
MSS.*, IV *passim*, V, p. 648 and VIII, p. 297; H. C. Beeching, *Francis Atterbury*
(London, 1909), pp. 143–4.
[83] Godolphin to Harley, 4 Nov. 1702, *H.M.C. Portland MSS.*, IV, p. 50.

to Godolphin protesting his innocence and begging a chance to explain himself. The Treasurer's reply was searing:

> I have received your letter, and am very sorry for what has happened to lose the good opinion I had so much inclination to have of you, but I cannot help seeing and hearing, nor believing my senses. I am very far from deserving it from you. God forgive you![84]

From now on all doors began rapidly closing. By 6 February it was all over. On that day Marlborough wrote to the Queen informing her that neither he nor the Treasurer could serve any longer in the same ministry with "Mr. Secretary Harley". Stung by the ultimatum Anne made a spirited effort to keep her Secretary. Even threats of resignation from Somerset, Pembroke Cowper, Devonshire and "Harley's friend" Newcastle, failed to shake her resolution. Only on 9 February, when the Commons ominously "let the Bill of Supply lie on the table, though it was ordered for that day", and the Junto lords even more ominously set in train the first steps of what seemed to be a projected impeachment of Harley, did she give way. On 10th the Secretary had his final audience with his royal mistress, and the following day he departed into the political wilderness. His friends Mansell, Harcourt and St. John, in a surprising show of group solidarity, elected to accompany him out of office.[85] Thus, before passing final judgement on Harley's career as triumvir it is essential to take a close look at his fall from grace. Was he ousted simply because of a personal quarrel with Godolphin? Had he perhaps overreached himself in some way? Or was the trouble more serious? Had he, in short, failed, in the end, to come up to expectation as Court politician? These are the problems which are explored in our next chapter.

---

[84] Godolphin to Harley, 30 Jan. 1708, *H.M.C. Bath MSS.*, I, p. 190. See also Marlborough to Harley, "Thursday night" [29 Jan. 1708], B.M. Portland Loan, 12(5), and Harley to Godolphin, 30 Jan. 1708, *H.M.C. Bath MSS.*, I, pp. 189–90.
[85] Marlborough to Anne, [6 Feb. 1708], Churchill, *op, cit.*, book II, pp. 312–3; Swift to King, 12 Feb. 1708, *Swift Corr.* vol. I, pp. 74–6; Cropley to Shaftesbury, 7 Feb. 1708, P.R.O. 30/24/21/146; Burnet, *op. cit.*, vol. V, p. 344, Dartmouth's note, and p. 345; Tullie House, Carlisle, Bishop Nicolson's MS. Diary, 9 Feb. 1708.; Harley's memorandum for his final audience on 10 Feb. 1708, B.M. Portland Loan, 9(52).

5 Failure of a Court Politician

HARLEY'S DRAMATIC FALL from grace in the spring of 1708 is by no means the easiest political phenomenon to explain away. After all, the triumvirate administration had, by any yardstick, proved itself an extraordinarily effective political combination. It had successfully staved off the divisive threat from the Tory right; it had watched over the Union with Scotland; above all it had, with machine-like regularity, produced the money votes that enabled Marlborough to crush the flower of Louis XIV's armies at Blenheim and Ramillies. Indeed, many even of the best informed of contemporaries were sent reeling by the news. Lord Halifax, for instance, confessed himself "at a loss how to understand" the happy turn of events. The "great changes" at Court, he confided to Portland, were "as new, as surprising and as unexpected to me, and some other of your friends here, as they were to your Lordship at Bulstrode." Somers was equally in the dark, while three years later another observer was still so puzzled by the "many intricate pipes" of the Secretary's disgrace that he felt obliged to "lodge it amongst the mysteries of state".[1]

At first sight it might easily seem that the real source of the trouble was Harley's undistinguished administrative record at the Secretariat.[2] The fact that Greg's defection—the incident which exposed his administrative shortcomings—came to light only a short time before his dismissal, gives a certain plausibility to this theory. So, too, does the intense play made of the whole affair by Whig politicians at the time. Not only was every means of suasion, fair and foul, brought to bear on Greg to get him to

[1] Halifax to Portland, 19 Feb. 1708, N.U.L., Portland MSS., PWA, 945; Somers to Portland, 14 Feb. 1708, *ibid.*, PWA, 1188; P.H., *An Impartial View of the Two Late Parliaments* (London, 1711), p. 117.
Charles Montagu had been raised to the peerage as Baron Halifax, co. York, on 13 Dec. 1700.
[2] On Harley's administration see A. McInnes, "Robert Harley, Secretary of State" (M.A. Thesis, University of Wales, 1961), pp. 48–76 and 181–91.

smear his employer, but as late as the spring of 1709 the Junto lords were still dredging the affair in Parliament.[3] There is, however, no evidence to suggest that either Marlborough or Godolphin was at all vexed by Harley's failure to tighten up security precautions in his office. Both men realised that as Secretary and party manager he was shouldering an inordinate burden, and the Treasurer at least seems to have been more than satisfied with the effort Harley was putting in at the Secretariat.[4] In any case the complete nature of the rift in the triumvirate in 1708, and the bitterness felt on both sides, make it obvious that the Churchill coterie regarded Harley's fault as something more serious than administrative incapacity. Had the Secretary's deficiency as an administrator been the real point at issue, then this might perhaps have been ground enough for removing him from the Secretariat to some more congenial employment. It would not, however, have been sufficient to smash a ministry and end, without hope of renewal, a deep rooted, long standing friendship. Sentiment apart, this would still remain true, for Harley, the Commons' manager, was far too valuable to be so lightly cast aside.

But administration is not the only blind, attractive alley. Equally engaging possibilities are opened up by the fall of Nottingham, Harley's predecessor. The Tory Earl forfeited the confidence of Anne and her political advisers because he persisted in advocating policies regarded by them as prejudicial to the interests of the government. If we put Harley's career under the microscope we find that he too seems, at times, to have been guilty of the same sort of indiscretion. In 1707, for example, his conduct over the affair of the "Drawback Bill" shook the government to the very foundations. The Bill, which was introduced at the behest of irate English merchants, was designed to stifle an attempt being made by certain speculators in Scotland

---

[3] *Journals of the House of Commons*, XVI, pp. 71 and 105–6; Edward Harley to Abigail Harley, 18 Feb. 1709, *H.M.C. Portland MSS.*, IV, pp. 520–1. Greg, who had been condemned to death, was respited from week to week and beset by Whig agents offering him his life if he would betray Harley. But the prison chaplain, Paul Lorrain, successfully exhorted the unhappy captive to stand firm. G. M. Trevelyan, *England Under Queen Anne* (London, 1930–4), vol. II, p. 332. Greg was eventually executed on 28 April 1708.

[4] Godolphin to Harley, May 1706, *H.M.C. Bath MSS.*, I, p. 81; B.M. Portland Loan, 64 *passim*; Longleat, Portland Misc. MSS., *passim*.

to manipulate to their own advantage a number of the economic clauses of the Union Treaty. This manipulation was made possible by the time lag which occurred between the signing of the Union in February 1707 and its coming into force in May of the same year. During that period large quantities of foreign merchandise were imported into Scotland at the existing rate of Scottish customs duties, a rate which was considerably below the level of duties operative in England. The intention was to re-ship these goods to England after 1 May when a uniform high tariff was to be introduced in both kingdoms and the old duties on trade between the two countries abolished. No doubt Harley gave his tacit support to the Drawback Bill—for he made no attempt to kill the measure—in the hope of winning over the mercantile interest at the next election. His attempt to dish the Whigs in this way, however, misfired badly. All over Scotland the cry went up that the Union had been broken, and in England a battle royal developed between the Lords and Commons. For a time the situation was very serious. At one stage Defoe feared the "unaccountable fermentation" might lead to the "unravelling of all we have been doing". The introduction of a retroactive clause by Harley, aimed at penalising fraudulent importers while protecting the interests of native Scots, came far too late to produce any beneficial results. In fact in certain parts of Scotland the nature of Harley's clause was misreported, and as a result the situation became even more strained. At length the Queen herself was compelled to intervene. On 8 April, in an effort to cool boiling tempers, she prorogued Parliament for a week. But even this drastic measure failed, and a few days later Anne brought the session to an abrupt end in order to prevent the dispute getting completely out of hand.[5]

The Drawback affair must undoubtedly be ranked as an extremely interesting political controversy, and in view of Nottingham's experiences it is tempting to conclude that it was this sort of thing which brought about Harley's downfall. Again, however, as in the case of Harley's administrative

[5] Burnet, *op. cit.*, vol. V, pp. 290–1; T. Johnson to R. Norris, 5 April 1707, *The Norris Papers*, p. 159; Defoe's letters to Harley of 22 Feb., 22 April, 24 April and 16 May 1707, *Defoe Letters*, pp. 203–5, 215, 216 and 219–22; Godolphin to Harley, 19 March and 17 April 1707, *H.M.C. Bath MSS.*, I, pp. 166–7 and 169. For drafts of the retroactive clause in Harley's hand see B.M. Portland Loan, 31(1).

limitations, appearances are misleading. Too much can be read into the Drawback ferment. In fact the controversy bears only a superficial resemblance to the earlier conflicts in which Nottingham was involved. In advocating such measures as the tack Nottingham was deliberately attempting to press home measures which were distasteful to the government. In supporting the Drawback Bill Harley was doing no such thing. Nottingham had ventured to disagree with the ministry's stated objectives. Harley simply committed a tactical blunder. That it was no more than this is proved by the nonchalance with which Godolphin treated the whole affair.[6] The Treasurer knew only too well how easy it was to make such errors of judgement. Accordingly he was ready enough to forget Harley's occasional slips.

Once the innocuous nature of Harley's conduct in such incidents as the Drawback dispute is appreciated, then it becomes clear that, throughout his term of office as Secretary, his policy remained in harmony with that of his colleagues. It is true that he seems to have been far more deeply disappointed than they at the failure to secure peace in 1706 following the successes of the Ramillies campaign. Nevertheless there is no solid evidence to suggest that because of this he began dragging his feet on the war issue. Even over the vexed question of the struggle in Spain there is no sign of a division before the Secretary's ejection from the ministry. In 1705 Harley had stated his opinion clearly that "the restoring of the monarchy of Spain to the House of Austria" was "the only way to secure peace". At a later date he was to rise from his sick bed to defend ministerial expenditure in the peninsula, and only a few weeks before his fall he gave his support to Somers's momentous resolution that no peace could be safe or honourable while the Spanish crown remained in Bourbon hands.[7] Moreover, Harley's attitude was far from being one of mere passive acceptance. As his extensive efforts on behalf of the Union with Scotland amply demonstrate he was at pains to do all he could to forward the government's programme. All this, of course, serves yet again to emphasise

---

[6] See Godolphin's letters to Harley of 19 March, 11 April, 15 April and 17 April 1707, *H.M.C. Bath MSS.*, I, pp. 166–9.

[7] Harley to Abigail Masham, 16 Oct. 1706, Longleat, Portland MSS., X, f. 55; Harley to Marlborough, 4 Dec. 1705, Coxe, vol. II, p. 245; Harley to Stepney, December 1706, B.M. Additional MSS., 7,059; Feiling, *op. cit.*, p. 398.

Harley's value to the administration. It shows that Marlborough and Godolphin would never have consented to drop the Secretary in 1708 had they not thought this absolutely essential for the survival of the ministry.

A third red herring is provided by the work of the von Noorden school. In the eighteen eighties the German historian Carl von Noorden first put forward what was subsequently to prove a most influential thesis. He argued that the real source of trouble in 1708 arose out of the Commons' investigation into the Almanza fiasco. In April 1707 the cause of the Grand Alliance in Spain had suffered a sharp set back as a result of the heavy defeat of the allied forces at the Battle of Almanza. When, in the ensuing session of Parliament, an enquiry into the disaster was mounted, it was discovered, from papers laid before the Lower Chamber by St. John, the Secretary-at-War, that of the 29,000 men voted by Parliament for service in Iberia in 1707, less than 9,000 were actually in the peninsula at the time of the allied reversal. On 29 January 1708 this shattering revelation produced an explosive debate in which the ministry was subjected to most damaging criticism at the hands of opposition members. Von Noorden and his disciples, men like Leadam and Trevelyan, suggested that St. John had, with Harley's connivance, deliberately "blurted out" the contents of "the scandalous muster roll" in order to sink the government, or at least that Godolphin and the Duke interpreted the Secretary-at-War's behaviour in those terms. In 1951, in a skilful article, Godfrey Davies drastically modified the original theory by completely exonerating both Harley and St. John from any suggestion of political crookedness. Nevertheless, Davies still insisted that the Almanza debate was of crucial importance in explaining the Secretary's fall. Harley's poor showing on the 29th., he asserted, may not have been regarded as double dealing by Marlborough and Godolphin. But what it did do was just as vital, for it finally convinced the two men that their right hand man had lost control of the Lower House, and had thus outlived his usefulness.[8]

[8] C. von Noorden, *Europaische Geschichte im achtzehnten Jahrhundert* (Dusseldorf, 1870–82), vol. III, pp. 219–20; I. S. Leadam, *The History of England from the Accession of Anne to the Death of George II* (London, 1912), p. 130; Trevelyan, *op. cit.*, vol. II, p. 327; Churchill, *op. cit.*, book II, pp. 299–316; G. Davies, "The Fall of Harley in 1708", *English Historical Review*, vol. LXVI (1951), pp. 246–54.

On the surface there is undoubtedly a good deal to recommend Dr. Davies's revision of the von Noorden thesis. For one thing there is the apparent coincidence of dates: Harley received his marching orders from Godolphin on the evening of 29th—the very day of the debate. In addition there can be no question that Harley's grip on the Commons had been very shaky throughout the 1707–8 session. Not only was government policy in Spain called in question. The ministry also took a heavy battering on the Scottish Privy Council affair, and over naval mismanagement.[9] Even so Dr. Davies's analysis will not in the end stand up to detailed scrutiny. Recently a series of letters, penned by the major actors in the 1708 drama, has come to light which proves conclusively that, even in its diluted form, the Almanza explanation is totally misleading. The letters clearly show that Harley had already fallen foul of his imperious colleagues several days before the Almanza debate came on in the Lower Chamber. Moreover, quite apart from this chronological point, the language used by the Duke and the Treasurer at the time of the crisis simply does not square with a technical failing of the sort specified by Dr. Davies. Phrases like Marlborough's "false and treacherous proceedings of Mr. Secretary Harley" and Godolphin's "God forgive you" imply something more ominous than a mere winding down of political energies on the Secretary's part.[10]

With the major false trails identified and labelled we are now in a position to grasp exactly what it was which convinced the two kinsmen of the necessity of breaking with their much valued colleague. The root cause of the fissure in the triumvirate was indeed political in character. But it had little directly to do with Harley's loss of grip in the Commons, and still less was it

⁹ R. R. Walcott, *English Politics in the Early Eighteenth Century* (Oxford, 1956), chapter VII provides a detailed account of ministerial vicissitudes in the 1707–8 session.

¹⁰ Harley to Marlborough, 28 Jan., 1 Feb., 6 Feb., and 18 Feb. 1708, B.M. Portland Loan, 12(5) and (6), and 130(3); Marlborough to Harley, 29 Jan. (2 letters), and 7 Feb. 1708, *ibid.*, 12(5). The first published analysis of this new material may be found in G. S. Holmes and W. A. Speck, "The Fall of Harley in 1708 Reconsidered", *English Historical Review*, vol. LXXX (1965), pp. 673–98. For an earlier unpublished use of it see A. McInnes, "Robert Harley, Secretary of State", pp. 131–9 and 192–202. Cf. Harley to Godolphin, 30 Jan. 1708, *H.M.C. Bath MSS.*, I, pp. 189–90; Godolphin to Harley, 30 Jan. 1708, *ibid.*, p. 190; and Marlborough to Anne, [6 Feb. 1708], Churchill, *op. cit.*, book II, pp. 312–13.

connected with his attitude to policy. The split was not the result of a disagreement over the ministry's objectives; it was the outcome of the failure of the triumvirs to see eye to eye on the means of attaining those objectives. The problem was a problem of strategy not of policy, and it was expressed in the differing attitudes adopted by the Harley and Churchill groups to the warlike evolutions of the Whig Junto and its well drilled regiments.

Nottingham's fall in 1704, we have seen, was not an isolated incident: it was part of the larger crisis which saw the rejection of the High-Tory alliance by the triumvirate. The alienation of the high-flyers which was virtually completed with Nottingham's resignation meant that the ministry then rested on rather shaky foundations, and it quickly became apparent that sooner or later the government would have to recruit additional support from somewhere. Naturally enough it was Harley, the political manager of the ministry, who assumed responsibility for securing the necessary support,

The Secretary wasted no time. Moving with complete coolness and assurance, he at once focused his attentions on John Holles, Duke of Newcastle, an intimate of the Junto and a Whig nobleman of great wealth and electoral influence.[11] As early as April 1703 Harley had been studiously exchanging courtesies with the Whig Duke,[12] and now that the fabric of the ministry was collapsing about the ears of the triumvirate, Speaker Harley began to court his Grace's favour with more earnestness.[13] It seems that Harley's first idea was that Newcastle should succeed Jersey as Lord Chamberlain, but the Queen put an end to his hopes on this score by appointing the Earl of Kent to the vacant office. The disconsolate Harley did, however, succeed in obtaining a promise from the Treasurer that when "a fit opportunity" presented itself the Duke would receive his true deserts. More important, perhaps, the Queen herself expressed much delight at the news that Newcastle was seriously contemplating throwing in his lot with the government.[14]

---

[11] Walcott, *English Politics*, pp. 47–50, and O. R. F. Davies, "The Wealth and Influence of John Holles, Duke of Newcastle 1694–1711", *Renaissance and Modern Studies*, vol. IX (1965), pp. 22–46.
[12] Monckton to Harley, 3 April 1703, *H.M.C. Portland MSS.*, IV, p. 59.
[13] B.M. Portland Loan, 147(1); *H.M.C. Portland MSS.*, II, p. 184 *et seq.*, *passim*.
[14] Harley to Newcastle, 23 April, and 9 May 1704, *ibid.*, pp. 184–5.

Thus encouraged Harley quickly marked out another post for his new-won friend. His eyes turned to the Privy Seal, an office then in the hands of the high-flying and obstruent Duke of Buckingham. Here again, however, there were difficulties. Buckingham, a close friend of the Queen, was well entrenched in office.[15] Moreover, Marlborough, fearing that the Whig Duke might prove "too much of a party man", was putting a brake on events.[16] Even Newcastle was adding to the difficulties. Annoyed at the delay in effecting his promotion, the Whig magnate began to show signs of becoming restive, and Harley found it expedient to humour him by advancing his candidates to the bench of magistrates in Nottinghamshire, and by obtaining from Anne the promise of a peerage for his brother-in-law and chief political supporter Thomas Pelham.[17] But as things transpired the Speaker need have worried little. Newcastle hastened to give assurances that he would be "everything the Queen would have of him", and these, together with the fact that his Grace's estate was "so very great", finally overcame Marlborough's qualms. On the other side Buckingham, continuing heedlessly along his wayward path, at last exhausted the Queen's store of good will. By the end of March 1705 all was over. Newcastle became Lord Privy Seal, and shortly afterwards his cousin and political follower Lord Rockingham was offered the Lord Lieutenancy of Kent, while he himself succeeded Buckingham as Lord Lieutenant of Yorkshire.[18]

Newcastle's appointment was the first positive step taken by the triumvirate towards some sort of understanding with the Whig groups in Parliament. It was, moreover, a step which had been taken almost wholly at Harley's bidding. He it was who first brought forward Newcastle as a candidate for government favour, and right up to the day of Buckingham's fall he continued to handle all negotiations between the ministry and the

---

[15] Sir J. Percival to T. Knatchbull, 21 March 1702, *H.M.C. Egmont MSS.*, II, p. 208.
[16] Marlborough to Godolphin, 3 Nov. 1704 (N.S.), Coxe, vol. II, p. 48.
[17] Harley to Newcastle, 29 July 1704 and 16 March 1705, *H.M.C. Portland MSS.*, II, pp. 186 and 189. Pelham got his peerage in December 1706.
[18] Marlborough to Godolphin, 3 Nov. 1704 (N.S.), Coxe, vol. II, p. 48; Godolphin to Harley, 1 April 1705, *H.M.C. Bath MSS.*, I, p. 67; Godolphin to Newcastle, 26 March 1705, *H.M.C. Portland MSS.*, II, p. 189; Hedges to Newcastle, 28 March 1705, *ibid.*, Harley to Newcastle, 31 March 1705, *ibid.*

Whig Duke.[19] Throughout Harley led the way. Godolphin, Marlborough and Anne all trailed behind in his footsteps, at times a little uneasily.

Soon, however, the political diagram began to change. Once Newcastle's intrusion into the ministry had been effected Harley's interest in Whiggery seems to have waned. On the other hand, Marlborough and Godolphin began to display more enthusiasm for the Whig connection. It was these last two it seems who were responsible for the crop of Whig appointments which accompanied the elections of 1705.[20] Harley at least took little part in these promotions. Indeed a number of the changes seem to have occasioned him not a little disquiet. The advance-ment of Cowper is a case in point. On the very day Cowper took office as Lord Keeper Godolphin wrote to Newcastle begging him to intercede with Harley who was proving unco-opera-tive.[21] Again the Secretary at first came out strongly against the choice of John Smith as Court candidate for the Speaker's chair, and for a time it seemed that a political crisis was brewing.[22] Eventually, however, the trouble was resolved, and Harley agreed to support Smith's candidature. Even so, the incident was an ill omen for the future peace of the ministry. It showed that while Harley, who had initiated the swing towards the Whigs, was now drawing back, Marlborough and Godolphin were bent on pressing forward with a new vigour. On the question of political strategy the triumvirs had begun to drift apart.

In 1706 the drift was accelerated and the division in the ministry over the Whig association began to assume really serious proportions. In the summer of that year the Junto de-manded the replacement of Secretary Hedges by the Whig Earl

[19] Even Godolphin, who was apparently quickly convinced by Harley that Newcastle would be a useful addition to the ministry, did none of the negotiating. The Treasurer's letter to Harley of 1 April 1705 (*H.M.C. Bath MSS.*, I, p. 67) proves that at that time he was still unacquainted with the Whig Duke.

[20] Argyll was appointed commissioner for Scotland. The Earl of Sunderland was sent as envoy to Vienna. John Smith became Speaker. Robert Walpole won a seat on the Prince's Council. William Cowper succeeded Nathan Wright as Lord Keeper of the Great Seal.

[21] Godolphin to Newcastle, 11 Oct. 1705, *H.M.C. Portland MSS.*, II, p. 191. In this letter the Treasurer calls Harley by the code name "M. Guidot".

[22] W. A. Speck, "The Choice of a Speaker in 1705", *Bulletin of the Institute of Historical Research*, vol. XXXVII (1964), pp. 20–46. Harley's preference for the chair was his old school-fellow Simon Harcourt.

of Sunderland, and as autumn approached the Whig lords made it clear that if their desires were not speedily effected then they would carry their followers into opposition when the next session of Parliament opened. Neither Marlborough nor Godolphin had any particular liking for the insolent and hot tempered Sunderland,[23] but they could not help noting facts. In the 1705-6 session the ministry had been forced to rely heavily on Whig support, especially in the Regency affair. Again, the Junto, and particularly Somers,[24] had played a prominent part in the Union negotiations. Convinced that without the continuance of such support everything "must end in confusion", the two kinsmen decided that they must bury personal predilections for the sake of the public good. They must give the Junto lords their pound of flesh. Before, the move towards the Whigs had seemed desirable; now it was a dire necessity.

The Queen, however, had other ideas. With typical Stuart stubbornness Anne determined to resist any invasion of her prerogative. She found a welcome ally in Harley, by now more hostile than indifferent to proposed Whig advancements. Throughout the autumn and early winter of 1706 the Secretary plied his colleagues with arguments against a surrender to the Junto. The Whigs, he was convinced, were a minority. "Nothing but unnecessary compliance", he insisted, "can give these people strength". The Duke and the Treasurer had no need to capitulate. If they would only play a bold hand and take

[23] Even so rabid a Whig as Sarah, Duchess of Marlborough, thought very little of the Earl. In later years she was to write of her erstwhile son-in-law: "it is certain he had not much in him". *Sarah Corr.*, vol. II, p. 194.

[24] Full justice has never been paid to Somers for his part in the Union. He initiated the Aliens Act (*Correspondence of George Ballie*, p. 16; A. S. Turberville, *The House of Lords in the Eighteenth Century* (Oxford, 1927), p. 79), was a leading member of the 1706 Commission, was trusted by the Scots (*Carstares State Papers*, p. 774), co-operated closely with Godolphin (P. H. Brown (ed.), *Letters Relating to Scotland in the Reign of Queen Anne by James Ogilvy, Earl of Seafield, and Others* (Edinburgh, 1915), p. 63; *Correspondence of George Ballie*, p. 169), advised Queensberry and other Scottish nobles (P. Yorke (ed.), *Miscellaneous State Papers from 1501 to 1726 from the Collection of the Earl of Hardwicke* (London, 1778), vol. II, p. 200; Campbell, *Chancellors*, vol. IV, pp. 192-4), and defended the Treaty in the Lords (Cobbett, *op. cit.*, vol. VI, p. 568). Addison's high estimate of Somers's importance (J. Addison, *The Freeholder* (Glasgow, 1752), p. 184) is confirmed by the Duchess of Marlborough (*Memoirs*, p. 260), by Burnet (Burnet, *op. cit.*, vol. V, p. 274), and by Hardwicke (notes to *ibid.*, pp. 276 and 287). The latter's judgement is particularly significant because it is based on manuscript evidence which has since been destroyed by fire.

the issue to the country, they would soon discover which side was the stronger.[25]

But the two kinsmen remained unconvinced. They knew that the Whigs were ruthless, that they would not scruple "to tear everything to pieces". Accordingly Marlborough and Godolphin would have no truck with Harley's airy schemes. Harsh political reality dictated a surrender to the Whigs. So, for some months, a state of deadlock ensued, the two sides diametrically opposed, both refusing to budge an inch. It was the story of Speaker Smith all over again, only this time the stakes were higher, the conflict vaster and more bitter. As the meeting of Parliament drew nearer Whig voices grew more strident, Godolphin more despondent. At last, in desperation, the beleaguered Treasurer began to talk of resignation. This tipped the scales. On 3rd December, the very day that Parliament was due to meet, Anne gave up the struggle, and Sunderland was appointed Secretary.[26]

For the triumvirate Sunderland's triumph was the beginning of the end. Any hopes which Marlborough and Godolphin might hitherto have entertained that Harley's attitude to Speaker Smith was a temporary aberration were well and truly shattered. There could no longer be any question that the unpleasantness over Smith's candidature was an expression of a fundamental difference of outlook on Harley's part. Accordingly, from now on the triumvirate moved rapidly down hill, lurching from one dispute to the next. More and more as time wore on the Churchill group came to see Harley's hand behind every obstructive move of the Queen. This was especially the case after the summer of 1707 when Sarah, Duchess of Marlborough, made the terrible discovery that Harley had secured a means of access to the royal palace through the person of his

---

[25] Harley to Godolphin, 15 Oct. 1706, *H.M.C. Bath MSS.*, I, pp. 109–11; Harley to Marlborough, 12 Nov. 1706, Coxe, vol. III, p. 126; Harley to Godolphin, 16 Nov. 1706, *ibid.*, pp. 123–5; Harley to Poulett, 21 Sep. 1706, B.M. Portland Loan, 153(7).

[26] Correspondence in chapters LI and LII of Coxe; *Memoirs of Sarah, Duchess of Marlborough*, pp. 113–16; Godolphin to Harley, 10 Oct. 1706, *H.M.C. Bath MSS.*, I, p. 107; same to same, November 1706, *H.M.C. Portland MSS.*, IV, p. 363. Sunderland's appointment was followed by a number of other concessions to the Whigs. James Montagu, Halifax's brother, became Solicitor General. Wharton got an earldom. The names of Rochester, Nottingham, Jersey and Buckingham were struck off the Privy Council.

distant cousin, the "ungrateful chambermaid" Abigail Hill.[27] Indeed, when, that same year, the news broke that Anne had appointed two Tory divines to the sees of Exeter and Chester over the heads of her ministers matters almost came to a final showdown. To the Duke and the Treasurer as well as to the Junto lords—who were at that moment pressing the names of Whig clergy on Godolphin—it seemed that the appointments were entirely the doing of Harley and his new ally Abigail, and the two kinsmen did not scruple to accuse the Secretary openly of shady behaviour. Only a vigorous denial by Harley, backed up by an equally categorical assurance from the Queen saved the day. Nevertheless it had been an ugly incident, and it left Godolphin and Marlborough more sullen and prickly than ever. Certainly there was no guarantee that if a crisis of similar magnitude blew up in the future the Secretary's colleagues would, in their present frame of mind, again feel disposed to swallow his professions of innocence.[28]

This is, in fact, precisely what happened in the spring of 1708. Harley, who had, throughout the previous autumn and winter, continued to press his anti-Whig line, once more fell beneath a

[27] Duchess of Marlborough to Burnet, 29 June 1710, Bodl. Additional MSS., 191, fl; *Memoirs of Sarah, Duchess of Marlborough*, p. 125 *et seq*. Actually Harley had won Anne's confidence long before he established relations with Abigail. From very early in the reign he had access to the back-stairs (Godolphin to Harley, 7 July 1702, *H.M.C. Portland MSS.*, IV, p. 43) and already in June 1705 the Queen was signing her letters to Harley "your very affectionate friend". (*H.M.C. Bath MSS.*, I, p. 30). Thus Abigail was merely an additional channel of approach to the Queen.

[28] Harley's denial may be found in *Miscellaneous State Papers from the Collection of the Earl of Hardwicke*, vol. II, pp. 483-4, and Anne's in *H.M.C. Marlborough MSS.*, p. 41. For the rest see the correspondence in Coxe, chapters LVIII, LXII and LXIII. The importance of the bishoprics question has, perhaps, been under-estimated in recent studies of Harley's fall. (See, for example, the slighting reference to it in G. S. Holmes and W. A. Speck, "The Fall of Harley in 1708 Reconsidered", *English Historical Review*, vol. CCCXVII (1965), pp. 673-4). In fact the whole affair bears a striking similarity to the crisis which actually brought Harley down in February 1708. As in 1708, so in 1707, the two kinsmen seem, for a time at least, to have been convinced that the Secretary was working on an alternative "scheme" of government (Marlborough to the Duchess, 11 July 1707 (N.S.), Coxe, vol. III, pp. 273-4). In 1708 Godolphin broke with Harley through the medium of Attorney-General Harcourt. Over the bishoprics crisis Marlborough counselled similar action (same to same, 4 July 1707 (N.S.), *ibid.*, p. 267). When the Duke and the Treasurer finally succeeded in ousting Harley they did it by withdrawing from Court. In 1707 they seriously contemplated playing the same card (Anne to Marlborough, 25 Aug. 1707, *H.M.C. Marlborough MSS.*, p. 41). Finally, on both occasions Harley claimed to be the innocent victim of "sly insinuations, and ground-less jealousies" (Harley to Marlborough, 16 Sep. 1707, *Miscellaneous State Papers from the Collection of the Earl of Hardwicke*, vol. II, p. 483. Cf. Harley to Marlborough, 6 Feb. 1708, B.M. Portland Loan, 12(6)).

cloud of suspicion, and this time the Marlborough coterie just refused point-blank to have any further truck with the Secretary's explanations. What the exact nature of Harley's offence really was on this occasion does not appear from the correspondence of the Duke and the Treasurer. Their letters simply accuse the Secretary in general terms of indulging in despicable underhand "transactions" aimed, it seems, particularly at Godolphin. For the details we have to look elsewhere, and here the evidence of Joseph Addison, friend of Somers and Under-Secretary to Sunderland is of the first importance. On 13 February, two days after Harley's fall, Addison wrote to Manchester:

> It is said Mr. Harley and his friends had laid schemes to undermine most of our great officers of state and plant their own party in the room of them. If we may believe common fame he himself was to have been a peer and Lord Treasurer, though others say Lord Rochester was designed for that post. Mr. Harcourt was to have been Lord Chancellor, Mr. St. John Secretary of State, the Duke of Buckingham Lord Privy Seal and so on.

Shortly afterwards the Whig protégé was able to add further particulars:

> It seems my Lord Rochester and Mr. Bromley were taken no care of in the intended promotions, and 'tis supposed were not in the secret. The Treasury they say was to have been in commission and Mr. Harley at the head of it in order to have it broken in a short time and himself to have been Lord High Treasurer of Great Britain.... They did not question it seems but my Lord Marlborough would have acted with them and therefore thought their scheme good till His Grace refused to sit any longer in council with the late Secretary. I am credibly informed that the same resolution has been taken by the Lord Treasurer, High Steward, Privy Seal, President of the Council, Lord Chancellor and the other Secretary of State. How this so much talked of scheme proved abortive and came to light before its time is still a mystery.[29]

[29] Addison to Manchester, 13 Feb. and 27 Feb. 1708, *Letters of Joseph Addison*, pp. 91 and 95.

Unfortunately the authenticity of Addison's picture is not as firmly established as one would like. Much of what he wrote is by his own admission based on nothing more than "common fame". Even so he was not repeating mere idle gossip. Addison, the Junto's darling, was a man standing at the centre of affairs, his finger on the pulse of government, a man well able to sift fact from fiction. If he reported what he heard, at least he was "credibly informed". Further, he was not the only political commentator to sense which way the wind was blowing. Swift's keen nose ferreted out much the same story. Most important of all, apologists of both the Harley phalanx and the Marlborough group, people who spoke the thoughts and feelings of the chief antagonists, were later to incorporate the same thesis in their writings.

Thus, what in the end brought Harley down in February 1708 was the belief which Marlborough and the Treasurer came to entertain that the Secretary, whose "prying genius and ambitious spirit could not be contented to act an under-part", was secretly plotting "to form a scheme of government in which the first proposition was to remove my Lord Godolphin".[30] How justified such suspicions were it is hard to gauge. High Tories like Sir Thomas Hanmer, Sir Henry Bunbury and Peter Shakerley certainly seem to have believed that they had the Secretary in their pocket. On one occasion, too, Harley was distinctly observed by a number of M.P.s shiftily engaged in bargaining with another Tory, William Clayton, behind the Speaker's chair. In addition, there exists among the Harley papers a scribbled note in the Secretary's own hand which is evidently an outline agenda for two meetings to be held on 13 and 14 January 1708. The contents of the paper leave one in no doubt that the principal object of these gatherings was to discuss the details of a possible *rapprochement* with the Tory Party.[31]

All the same the case against Harley is by no means over-

---

[30] Boyer, *History of Queen Anne*, p. 321; "Lord Coningsby's Account of . . . Parties during the Reign of Queen Anne", *Archaeologia*, vol. XXXVIII (1860), p. 7.

[31] Brereton to Oxford, 10 Nov. 1713, B.M. Portland Loan, 127(7); T. Johnson to R. Norris, 17 Jan, 1708, *The Norris Papers*, pp. 161–2; "preliminaries Jan. 13 1707/8 and Jan. 14", B.M. Portland Loan, 9 (51). Harley's agenda has been printed and analysed in Holmes and Speck, *loc. cit.*, p. 683 *et. seq.*

whelming. We know from other sources, for instance, that the meetings of 13 and 14 January were official government affairs, and that to the second of them at least Godolphin himself was summoned.[32] Moreover, High Tories were notorious optimists. As early as the summer of 1706 the Hanmer group was convinced that ministerial adjustments were about to occur which would bring "a fine change of weather" to "our longing wishes and prayers".[33] It is also worth noting that neither Harley's correspondence with Abigail, nor his memoranda for his private meetings with the Queen give any hint of a plot to overthrow the administration. On more than one occasion, too, the Secretary roundly denied the charge of treason levelled at him. Moreover, he did not simply protest his innocence to his outraged colleagues. He was equally unbending in his private and family correspondence where there was no real need to dissemble. On 15 February 1706, for example, he wrote solemnly to his brother Edward:

> I thank God that I have a true sense of my sins against Heaven, but as to anything else I can profess that in the affairs of the office and station I was in I have walked in truth and with a perfect heart. But for peace I have had great bitterness. I have not only the quiet of my own mind in having done my duty as to man, but also the satisfaction and calmness of spirit under what is brought upon me. I desire only to know my duty in this juncture, and beg ability to perform it. I can assure you that I have not the least grudge or resentment in my mind against the authors of it; though I do know they have contrived against my life, but I do daily pray to God to do them good for all that they have done or designed against me.

Two years later, when he again came into his own, Harley was still resolutely declaring that he had been the innocent victim of wicked rumours sedulously fomented by his political enemies who falsely "gave out that he had been working underhand to

---

[32] Harley to Devonshire, 13 Jan. 1708, B.M. Portland Loan, 264, pp. 202–3; Harley to Godolphin, 14 Jan. 1708, *ibid.*, 64(1).
[33] Cholmondeley to Hanmer, 31 Aug. 1706, N.L.W., Bettisfield MSS., 85.

throw out the very ministers themselves" in order to jeopardise his relations with his two beleagured colleagues.[34] It is well known that where Harley was concerned the Marlborough group was frequently prone to get things out of perspective. The evidence clearly demonstrates, for instance, that the Duchess's belief that in the months following his dismissal Harley was repeatedly admitted to Anne's presence by Abigail "privately by the back garden" was totally misplaced. In fact, not once during the whole of the summer did the ex-Secretary have even the briefest of audiences with his Sovereign.[35] It is consequently not beyond the realms of possibility that the suspicions of the Duke and Treasurer the previous spring may also have been alarmist.

Happily, however, it is not vital for us to decide one way or the other upon Harley's culpability in 1708. The thing which it is imperative to establish is not so much the Secretary's guilt or innocence, but rather what made it possible for such a climate of distrust to arise at all. Why, in other words, did Harley oppose the drift towards the Whigs with such dogged determination after 1705? Here the vital clue is his courtship of Newcastle. It is important to grasp that in making his bid for the Newcastle group Harley was not, as it might seem at first glance, throwing out overtures to the Whigs in general. The wooing of Newcastle was just one aspect of a very carefully laid scheme. Its complement was the Secretary's simultaneous capture of the St. John Tories. In each case the ministry, prompted by Harley, was attempting to gain the allegiance of groups on the periphery of the party. The plan was to win over the more moderate or less partisan elements both Whig and Tory, and in this way to draw the sting of both parties. St. John's sympathy with Tory belligerancy, we have seen, was on the wane in 1704; Newcastle was frequently critical of the extremism of the Junto.[36] Harley hoped that by capturing men of this type he would be able to smash

[34] Robert Harley to Edward Harley, 15 Feb. 1708, B.M. Portland Loan, 70(9); S. Clement, "Faults on Both Sides", *Somers Tracts*, vol. XII, p. 693. Harley's correspondence with Abigail may be found in *H.M.C. Portland MSS.*, IV, *passim*, and his notes for meetings with Anne in B.M. Portland Loan, 10.

[35] *Memoirs of Sarah, Duchess of Marlborough*, p. 158; Harley to Abigail Masham, 16 Oct. 1708, Longleat, Portland MSS., X, f. 55.

[36] E. L. Ellis, "The Whig Party 1702-8" (M. A. Thesis, University of Wales, 1949), pp. 106-25.

both Whigs and Tories,[37] and set up a scheme of non-party government drawing its strength from dissidents, moderates and independents. "I have", he asserted time and again, "no partiality to one side more than another". In his view there was no difference between "a mad Whig and a mad Tory". Both were equally obnoxious.[38]

To this ideal of a ministry free of party domination Harley adhered through thick and thin right up until the time of his fall.[39] His opposition to the appointment of Sunderland, for instance, did not stem from a hatred of the Whigs as such. He simply believed that surrender to the Junto on this issue would lead inevitably on to the monopoly of office by a single party. As he explained in a draft letter, presumably intended for Godolphin's eye:

[The] Queen began her reign upon the foot of no parties. She has thrived in it, and had success. Will you set up another? Which shall it be? The least or the greatest? The Queen would not give herself up to the Tories when they were unreasonable, though much the majority. Shall she do that for the Whigs who can never be so?

The foundation of the Church is in the Queen; the foundation of Liberty is in her! Let her therefore be arbitress between them. Should the Whigs be complied with in everything they ask can you carry on business? Certainly no.

Relieve therefore those who are gone too far. Can you stop the Whigs that they will not possess themselves (as a faction)

[37] Defoe, at this time in Harley's pay, agreed with his master. "Divide them", he urged in regard to the Whigs, "caress the fools of them most . . . Buy them with here and there a place". (Defoe to Harley, 2 Nov. 1704, *Defoe Letters*, pp. 65–70). The Dissenter's antipathy to Toryism, of course, needs no comment.

[38] Harley to [Godolphin] draft, n.d., B.M. Portland Loan, 10(19); same to same, 15 Oct. 1706, *H.M.C. Bath MSS.*, I. pp. 109–11; same to same 16 Nov. 1706, Coxe, vol. III, pp. 123–5.

[39] This did not mean that Harley wished to ban party men entirely from the ministry, nor even that he wished, at all times, to maintain an exact balance between the two contending parties. But what Harley did insist on was that any party man who happened to be taken into the government should be freely chosen by the Queen and remain strictly subordinate to her, "for if a man can be turned out or put in for being of a party, that party is the government and none else". (Memorandum in Harley's hand, dated 25 Aug. 1706, N.U.L., Harley MSS., PW2, HY, Secretary of State's box, folder (1)). On this point see the interesting discussion in Geoffrey Holmes, *British Politics in the Age of Anne* (London, 1967), pp. 366–81.

of your authority? If you stand not here? Can you hold the government a moment in this measure of the Whigs without success? Will not the least ill success slow that up?

Do the Whigs deserve to enjoy all the Queen's success? And nobody else?

A year later he was still preaching the same message:

I see very well the knavery of one side and the folly of the other, and I am disheartened by neither, because I hope there are enough notwithstanding all the usage they meet with, who will join to open the eyes of honest gentlemen sufficient in numbers to rescue us from the folly of one side and the violence of the other.[40]

Throughout Harley's aim was to compose differences and to cool tempers. His desire was a truly national government reflecting all shades of political opinion. Hatred of the Whigs was symbolic of something else—hatred of party rule.

At bottom, then, it was the Secretary's unwavering opposition to government controlled by party which lay at the root of his conflict with Marlborough and Godolphin. What made this particularly annoying from the Duke and the Treasurer's point of view was that they themselves had no real liking for party rule, and they certainly did not intend to sell out to the Junto lock, stock and barrel if they could possibly avoid it. As Somers once observed a "cautious and prudent management between parties" was Godolphin's "ordinary road". As late as the spring of 1708, in fact, rumour had it that the two kinsmen were trying "to make a party of Whigs and Tories", while even after the fall of the Harley group it is noticeable that it was not the Junto lords who reaped the immediate benefit, but the milder, more accommodating Lord Treasurer's Whigs.[41] Nevertheless, despite their antipathy to party, Marlborough and Godolphin firmly believed that it was absolutely essential from time to time

---

[40] Harley to [Godolphin], 25 Sep. 1706, B.M. Portland Loan 9(38); Harley to Stratford, 26 June 1707, *ibid.*, 171.

[41] Pringle to Marchmont, 20 July 1708, G. H. Rose (ed.), *A Selection from the Papers of the Earls of Marchmont illustrative of Events from 1685 to 1750* (London, 1831), vol. III, p. 332; Cropley to Shaftesbury, 30 Dec. 1707, P.R.O. 30/24/20/141; Walcott, *English Politics*, p. 149.

to surrender to Junto pressure. Without such periodic concessions, the two kinsmen felt, Whig support of the ministry's war policy would be thrown in jeopardy, and if this happened the whole allied cause might easily founder. "But madam", Marlborough retorted when the Queen declared against Sunderland's advancement in 1706, "the truth is that the heads of one party [the Tories] have declared against you and your government, as far as it is possible, without going into open rebellion. Now, should your Majesty disoblige the others [the Whigs] how is it possible to obtain near five millions for carrying on the war with vigour, without which all is undone". When, in the following year, Anne again began to flaunt her hatred of the Junto, Godolphin's voice was equally sombre:

The liberties of all Europe, the safety of your Majesty's person and of the Kingdom, the future promotion of the Protestant religion, and the glory of your reign, depend upon the success of the next session of Parliament, and indeed upon every session of Parliament while this war lasts, to which, except it please God to give a favourable conclusion, your Majesty can never hope to enjoy any settled quiet during your whole reign. This being truly the case what colour of reason can incline your Majesty to discourage and dissatisfy those [the Whigs] whose principles and interest led them on with so much warmth and zeal to carry you through the difficulties of this war?...."[42]

The Duke and the Treasurer were convinced that Harley, in refusing to rally to arguments like this, was unnecessarily, perhaps even wilfully, rocking the boat.

Why did the Secretary decline so stubbornly to compromise his non-party ideal in the face of the facts as his colleagues had done? Part of the reason was that his analysis of the political situation differed radically from theirs. He believed that it was possible to resist the Junto and at the same time keep the ministry's head above water. Somers and company, he maintained, were merely paper tigers, "pretended leaders", men

---

[42] Marlborough to Anne, 24 Oct. 1706, Coxe, vol. III, p. 118; Godolphin to Anne, 11 Sep. 1707, *H.M.C. Marlborough MSS.*, p. 41.

"who make much noise and have no real strength". If the government took no notice of them their bullying attempts "to bend everybody to one measure" would eventually disgust the rank and file of their party who would thereupon desert and rally to the ministry. In this way the "foundation" would be "laid" of "blowing up" the Whig Party. Moreover, quite apart from Junto weakness, there were the Tories to consider. Harley insisted that the Duke and the Treasurer were grievously mistaken in writing off the entire Tory Party as beyond redemption. "I think the distinction of the tackers was what they justly deserved", he wrote to Godolphin in 1706, "but my lord, this is now carrying farther. Not only the 134 [tackers] are to be persecuted, but all the rest; not only those who opposed them [the Whigs], but those without whose assistance these gentlemen could not have been an equality, much less a majority". Those Tories who had opposed the tack, Harley argued, had always loyally supported the administration's war policy and would continue to do so provided they were not senselessly persecuted.[43]

Whether or not Harley's reading of the situation was a correct one it is difficult to say. A recent study has stressed the hardening of the two party division after 1705,[44] and, if correct, this would seem to bear out the assessment of Marlborough and Godolphin rather than that of the Secretary. On the other hand it is indisputable that by 1708 a number of former Junto supporters, the Lord Treasurer's Whigs, had become disillusioned with "the wild embroilments" of the Party leaders.[45] Moreover, Harley, seems to have been quite correct in assuming that the Tories who had rallied to the government over the tack were loyal supporters of the ministry's war policy. When, for example, one of these men, Edward Brereton, heard it rumoured that he had "turned a Whig" he retorted:

---

[43] Harley to Godolphin, 15 Oct. 1706, *H.M.C. Bath MSS.*, I, pp. 109–11; Harley to Marlborough, 12 Nov. 1706, Coxe, vol. III, pp. 126–8; Harley to Godolphin, 16 Nov. 1706, *ibid.*, pp. 123–5; Harley's manuscript tract "Plain English to All who are Honest or would be so if they knew how", B.M. Portland Loan, 10(1).

[44] W. A. Speck, "The House of Commons, 1702–14: A Study in Political Organization" (D. Phil. Thesis, Oxford University, 1965), part I.

[45] For the Lord Treasurer's Whigs see Walcott, *English Politics*, p. 149. The quotation is from "Lord Coningsby's Account", *Archaeologia*, vol. XXXVIII (1860), p. 8.

I cannot guess at the reason of it, unless it be, that I did not stay in the House to vote for the tacking of the Bill against Occasional Conformity to the Land Tax Bill. I reasoned that the Lords had formerly published their resolution not to pass any Bill that had another tacked to it, and that the former misunderstandings between both Houses were rather increased than diminished, and that it would be a dangerous experiment to try the success of that proposed tack, lest the miscarriage of the Land Tax Bill might bring difficulties upon the nation, and delay the necessary supplies both for the fleet and armies.

He added:

But I must not forget to acquaint you that I was heartily zealous for the Bill itself against Occasional Conformity; and when the motion was made for leave to bring it into the House it was vigorously opposed; and I divided for it; and afterwards I appeared for the Bill in all the steps which it made in the House (except in the tacking part); and now you have the history of my fanaticism; and I had rather be called a pick pocket than a Whig.[46]

Harley could not have put his case more forcefully himself.

Correct or incorrect, however, the Secretary stuck to his guns. In any case his divergent assessment of the tactical situation in Parliament was neither the only nor the most important reason for his failure to adjust his non-party ideal. Behind his inflexibility lay a second and far more significant factor. Indeed, Harley's optimistic analysis of the parliamentary situation after 1705 may well have been, to some extent at least, wishful thinking, a mere rationalisation of his second, deeper motive. Certainly the Secretary would never have argued his case with such persistent vigour, or driven things anywhere near breaking point had his difference with Marlborough and Godolphin been merely the result of disagreement over the weighing of political possibilities. The truth is that Harley's commitment to the non-

[46] E. Brereton to R. Myddleton, 3 March 1704, N.L.W., Chirk Castle MSS., E.4204.

party notion was entirely different in quality and depth from the more workaday attitude of his two colleagues.

The approach of the Duke and the Treasurer to the problem of party was thoroughly practical. They disliked party rule because the demands of party politicians were irksome and tended to disrupt administration and the smooth passage of government business. But if the political situation dictated some sort of limited surrender to the party chiefs then they were willing enough to modify their position. Harley's attitude, on the other hand, was worlds apart from this kind of pragmatism. He viewed party not with the eyes of the bureaucrat, but with those of the passionate constitutional idealist. His writing was saturated with emotive overtones. "Vile and profligate"; "persuading all honest, well-meaning men"; "the public good"; "the scum of their own party"; "the rights of electors"; "wicked arts"—such outbursts are the exclamations of the moralist rather than the cold calculation of the political tactician.[47] Indeed, at times Harley's language assumed an almost prophetic note:

> I said days should speak and multitudes of years should teach wisdom; but great men are not always wise, neither do the aged understand judgement. Therefore I said hearken to me, I also will shew mine opinion, I will not accept any man's person, neither will I give flattering titles unto man, but my words shall be of the uprighteousness of my heart, and my lips shall utter knowledge clearly.[48]

Harley hated party rule because it represented the domination of the minority over the majority, the extremist few over the moderate many; because it kindled hatreds and set people at odds instead of uniting them in common brotherhood; because so many of the party chiefs were not really interested in the pursuit of principle but only in "the public spoils"; above all, because party control threatened to disrupt the balance of the "ancient constitution", and, in particular, to wrest from the Crown its immemorial right of appointing and dismissing mini-

---

[47] For examples of these phrases see Harley to Marlborough, 12 Nov. 1706, Coxe, vol. III, p. 127; "Plain English", B.M. Portland Loan, 10(1); and "Faults on Both Sides", *Somers Tracts*, vol, XII, p. 678 *et seq.*
[48] "Plain English", B.M. Portland Loan, 10(1).

sters. The Crown was the centre piece of Harley's whole political system. His ideal was an administration, freely chosen by the Queen to meet the needs of the moment, governing with the support and approbation of the independent, back-bench gentry, the "unlisted men". "The foundation is", he wrote to Godolphin in 1705, "persons or parties are to come in to the Queen, and not the Queen to them". "If the gentlemen of England are made sensible that the Queen is the head, and not a party", he continued, "everything will be easy, and the Queen will be courted and not a party; but if otherwise—". "The embodying of the gentlemen (country gentlemen I mean) against the Queen's service", he insisted "is what is to be avoided".[49]

Thus, the ultimate source of the great rift within the ministry was a ghost from the past. Despite all his undoubted achievements in the first half dozen years of Anne's reign, Harley had, in the last resort, failed to make the grade as a Court Politician. He was still obsessed, as he had been in former days, with clean government, with the health of the constitution, and with the rule of the gentry. His reflexes were still those of the opposition man. Admittedly, on details there was some mellowing. With William's malignant influence removed he was willing enough to revise his back-bench attitude on things like place and royal grants. But deeper down there was no change. At heart he remained a Country Politician. This is what caused him to quarrel so violently with his colleagues, this is what occasioned the recurrent ministerial crises after 1705, and this is what, in the end, brought the triumvirate to its ignominious close.

Of course, one might argue that all this is only what was to be expected. The Secretary's failure to make a clean break with his Country past immediately was quite natural. Children do not

---

[49] The Harley-Godolphin correspondence in *H.M.C. Bath MSS.*, I, *passim*, especially Harley's letter of 4 Sep. 1705, pp. 74–5; Harley's letters to Marlborough in the 1704–8 period, Coxe, vols. II and III, *passim*; Harley to Marlborough, 29 June 1705, Blenheim MSS., A.1–25; Memorandum in Harley's hand, 25 Aug. 1706, N.U.L., Harley MSS., PW2, HY, Secretary of State's box, folder (1); Harley to Poulett, 21 Sep. 1706, B.M. Portland Loan, 153(7); "Plain English", *ibid.*, 10(1). In addition boxes 9 and 10 of the Portland Loan contain numerous jottings and memoranda in Harley's hand which throw light on his attitude to party rule. E.g. a memorandum dated 3 April 1708 in box 10 bundle 22 reads: "The power of the Crown ought to protect against the violence of men and parties, now the power of the Crown is given to a party to destroy others". On all this cf. A. McInnes, "The Political Ideas of Robert Harley", *History*, vol. L (1965), pp. 309–22.

become adults overnight. Harley's sojourn at the Secretariat was his political adolescence. Fortunately we have a chance to test this hypothesis. An examination of the final phase of Harley's career will show whether such an explanation is tenable.

6 Prime Minister

IN THE SPRING and summer of 1708 Harley's political fortunes
reached their nadir. At Westminster he was almost totally
isolated. In 1704 he had broken with the High Tories. The
Whigs hated him implacably. Even the moderate Churchill
group had now parted company with him. Nor were his enemies
content to let him be once he was down. Long after his fall he
remained "the mark at which every dart of faction is levelled".[1]
The Junto lords in particular displayed such unseemly eagerness to implicate the fallen minister in Greg's treason that even
some of their best friends turned away disgusted. Marlborough's
chaplain, Francis Hare, for example, while willing enough to
censure Harley for his carelessness, confessed that he was "sorry
in point of common justice to see the matter so furiously
pursued".[2] Then, on top of all this, came the general election of
1708 when the Harley group took another heavy mauling. An
especially hard blow was the defeat of Henry St. John, the ex-
Secretary's chief lieutenant. "Faithful Harry" had had the mis-
fortune to quarrel with his father at the family seat of Wootton
Bassett, and although he took steps to canvass support in at least
half a dozen other constituencies he was unable to find an
alternative anchorage. "Those whom it is my inclination and
principle to serve have left me out", St. John lamented bitterly,
"and I conclude that they do not want me".[3] The scene indeed
looked bleak. Yet, within the space of two years, the prospect

---

[1] St. John to Harley, 6 Nov. 1708, Longleat, Portland MSS., VI, f. 227.
[2] Hare to Duchess of Marlborough, 1 Dec. 1710, *Sarah Corr.*, vol. II, p. 54.
[3] St. John to James Grahme, 18 July 1708, *H.M.C. Bagot MSS.*, p. 341. See also
Lockhart Papers, vol. I, p. 295; St. John to Harley, 1 May 1708, Longleat, Portland
MSS., VI, f. 222; Granville to Harley, 20 May 1708, *H.M.C. Portland MSS.*, IV,
p. 489; Atterbury to Harley, 14 Aug. 1708, *ibid.*, p. 500; Edward Harley to Abigail
Harley, 15 Dec. 1708, *ibid.*, p. 515; St. John to Harcourt, 20 Dec. 1708, *ibid.*;
Harcourt to Harley, 20 Dec. 1708, *ibid.* The seats canvassed by St. John were
Cricklade, Devizes, Lostwithiel, Milborne Port, Weobley and Westbury.

had been utterly transformed. With a splendid virtuoso display of political talent, Harley had succeeded in pulling his connection up out of the dust, and establishing a ministry, the record of which may bear comparison with that of any of the other governments in the 1689 to 1714 period.

The first act in the drama was the destruction of the Marlborough-Whig administration. Both as Country politician and as Secretary Harley had demonstrated how expertly he could operate inside the Commons. He was now to show that he possessed equal facility outside its walls. His most pressing need was clearly to re-establish the links with the Tory opposition so rudely shattered in 1704. Accordingly, straight after his fall from office in February 1708, he made a number of tentative moves in this direction. On several occasions, for instance, he spoke vigorously in the Lower House against the Bishops' Visitation Bill. He also rallied to an unsuccessful Tory motion which attempted to blame the administration at home for the shortage of English troops at Almanza.[4] But his efforts at reconciliation met with little response from the Tory benches. The high flyers, smarting still at the memory of previous rebuffs, exulted in their old adversary's disgrace. Hence, when summer came, Harley found it prudent to retreat to Brampton Bryan and wait upon events. "I am master of no news or intelligence", he wrote philosophically in July from his rural lair, "and take no more pleasure in the schemes and projects which are every day new, than in hearing the dreams of a sick man".[5]

The erstwhile Secretary, however, did not have to lick his wounds for long. In the 1708 elections, conducted in the wake of an attempted Jacobite invasion of the kingdom, the Tories suffered a severe setback. Harley, quick to appreciate the chastening effect of such a defeat, at once threw out new feelers in the direction of the Tories. On 20th August he penned a letter of the first importance to Bromley, the Tory chief in the Commons. In it he set out his opinion that the Whigs were at present enjoying the fruits of office because they had "taken advantage of the mistakes of others", and he followed this up

[4] Tullie House, Carlisle, Bishop Nicolson's MS. Diary, 24 Feb. and 9 March 1708; Addison to Manchester, 24 Feb. 1708, *Letters of Joseph Addison*, p. 94.
[5] Harley to Newcastle, 17 July 1708, *H.M.C. Portland MSS.*, II, p. 205.

by hinting that an alliance between himself and his old associate might go a long way towards restoring the political balance. Bromley's reply was cautious. He clearly did not like the Herefordshire man's cutting reference to past mistakes.

> I will not enter into a nice discussion of that point, [he wrote] but you will forgive me telling you what immediately occurred to my thoughts upon reading it, an expression that I have met with of a blasphemous fellow in his prayer on one of their fasts in the late times. 'O God, many are the hands that are lift up against us, but there is one God, it is Thou thyself O Father, who hath done us more mischief than they all'.

He also wanted Harley to be more "free and open" in his dealings, and "more particular" in his proposals. Nevertheless, the general tone of the letter was encouraging. "I am determined", he informed Harley, "notwithstanding anything past, to join with you, not as you observe they do on the other side, though they hate one another, but in affection as well as zeal to preserve the whole, and for the service of the public".[6]

Once the ice had been broken in this way the two men began to draw rapidly together. Three weeks after his initial letter Bromley wrote again to Harley reassuring him of his friendship. "I will", he continued, "on all occasions use my utmost endeavours to disappoint all arts that may be used to prevent our coming to a good understanding". Then, in mid-October, came Harley's crucial decision to support the Tory leader's candidature for the Speaker's chair. By the beginning of November St. John was able to congratulate his mentor on the palpable success of his courtship.[7] Old enmities, of course, could not be laid aside in a trice. For some little time one can discern undercurrents of recrimination. On 11 November, for instance, we find Bromley complaining to Nottingham that "Mr. H[arley], notwithstanding his professions, is not yet come to town". A month later he evinced similar unease:

---

[6] Harley to Bromley, 20 Aug. 1708, B.M. Portland Loan, 128(3); Bromley to Harley, 18 Sep. 1708, *H.M.C. Portland MSS.*, IV, pp. 504–5.
[7] Bromley to Harley, 12 Oct. 1708, B.M. Portland Loan, 128 (3); Harley to Harcourt, 16 Oct. 1708, *H.M.C. Bath MSS.*, I, p. 193; St. John to Harley, 6 Nov. 1708, Longleat, Portland MSS., VI, f. 228.

Mr. H[arley] writes to his old friends with all possible
professions of sincerity, and of his going entirely into the same
interest with them. He proposes schemes, that, if they are
pursued, may perhaps save a penny, but what is that when
all is at stake? He certainly can lay others and give his assistance in them that are more material and serviceable, and if
he will not soon do so, I think he may be justly suspected for
the future.[8]

Nevertheless, from the spring of 1709 onwards, Bromley's letters
become steadily more cordial, and with Bromley secured the
rest was easy. Through him Harley was quickly on terms once
more with his old enemy Rochester, and soon he had the bulk of
the Church Party at his command.[9]

Although a *rapprochement* with the Tories was unquestionably Harley's first priority in 1708, it in no sense marked the
limit of his political ambition. The former minister's keen eye
was swift to observe that all was not well in the government
camp. In fact, ever since Harley's fall in February, the Junto
and the Marlborough-Godolphin group had been behaving
more like two hostile packs of wild animals than like colleagues.
The Whig lords' appetite for power seemed insatiable. In the
course of 1708 they bludgeoned Somers and Wharton into office.
At the same time they pressed Orford's claims to the Admiralty.
Early in 1709 it was even rumoured that they were grooming
Halifax for Godolphin's position at the Treasury.[10] Battered
and bruised by these incessant demands, Godolphin found that
his interest in politics, never very great, was rapidly ebbing
away. "I suffer so much", he complained to Marlborough in
January 1709, "that I must give myself the vent of saying the
life of a slave in the galleys is paradise in comparison of mine".[11]
Whenever the Treasurer did manage to screw up enough
courage to do something he only made matters worse. His

---

[8] Bromley to Nottingham, 11 Nov. 1708, Leicestershire R.O., Finch MSS., G.S.,
bundle 23; same to same, 7 Dec. 1708, *ibid.*
[9] See generally Bromley's letters to Harley in B.M. Portland Loan, 128 and 310.
For Bromley's importance in smoothing relations with Rochester - Marlborough to
Godolphin, 23 Aug. 1708, Coxe, vol. IV, p. 202.
[10] W. Thomas to Edward "Lord" Harley, 3 Feb. 1709, *H.M.C. Portland MSS.*,
IV, p. 519.
[11] Godolphin to Marlborough, 10 Jan. 1709, Coxe, vol. IV, p. 356.

attempt, for example, to seduce a section of the Whig following
during the struggle for the nomination of the new Speaker in
the autumn of 1708 only stirred up a hornets' nest about his
ears.[12] Again, when, early in 1709, he passed over the Junto
candidate, Montrose, and instead appointed Queensberry as
Secretary for Scotland, he was well and truly "roasted" at
Westminster.[13] The tension between the Junto and the
Churchill group, however, though significant, was only part of
the ministry's trouble. The dry rot had entered into the Whig
Party itself. Before the end of 1708 George Lockhart of Carn-
wath had noted deep unrest among the rank and file:

> But as all the Whigs, especially in the House of Commons,
> were not included [in the government] . . . such as were
> neglected continued to exclaim against the Court and express
> a great resentment against their old friends, whom they
> termed deserters of the cause and Court Whigs, assuming the
> name of staunch Whigs to themselves.

Lockhart's assessment of the dissidents' motives was, no doubt,
blighted and ungenerous, but that his belief in the reality of a
back-bench revolt was not entirely a figment of his Jacobite
imagination is clearly indicated by Lord Hervey's later reflections on the "courtly manner" of "our bastard Whigs".[14]
Moreover, the Country wing was by no means the only section
of the Party that was showing signs of discontent. As the months
wore on a group of "Lord Treasurer's Whigs" was coming more
and more to resent the unscrupulous pressure being brought

[12] Godolphin, in alliance with a section of the Whig Party led by Lord Coningsby
Spencer Compton and John Smith, and without consulting the Junto tried to
secure the nomination of Sir Richard Onslow to the chair. Angered by this attempt
to manoeuvre behind their backs, the Junto lords advanced the name of Sir Peter
King. For a time the contest generated great bitterness, and it was only after the
Treasurer had "declared he would stand and fall by the party he had espoused
[i.e. the Junto]" that the five lords agreed to drop their support of King. Sunderland
to Newcastle, 19 Oct., 26 Oct., and 4 Nov. 1708, Trevelyan, *op. cit.*, vol. II, pp.
414-6; Maynwaring to Duchess of Marlborough, "Wednesday morning", *Sarah
Corr.*, vol. I, p. 138; same to same, "Tuesday, one o'clock", *ibid.*, p. 143; Bromley
to Nottingham, 11 Nov. 1708, Leicestershire R.O., Finch MSS., G.S., bundle 23;
E. Lewis to Harley, 5 Oct. 1708, *H.M.C. Portland MSS.*, IV, p. 506.

[13] Peter Wentworth to Lord Raby, 21 Jan. 1709, *Wentworth Papers*, p. 72; same
to same, 1 March 1709, *ibid.*, p. 77.

[14] *Lockhart Papers*, vol. I, p. 296; *Letter-Books of John Hervey, First Earl of Bristol*,
vol. I, pp. 265 and 271.

upon Godolphin by the Junto.[15] In addition, "the five tyrannizing lords", in the exuberance of their triumph, were beginning to neglect a number of useful, if prickly, Whig magnates—
men like Argyll, Somerset and Peterborough. Cowper, sensing
the atmosphere of crisis, wrote in alarm to Newcastle of his fears
of "a division among honest men". "If nothing be done to alter
things from what they are at present", he observed gloomily,
"I am afraid we may see part of them fighting with, if not under,
the Tories, and the other part further engaged as courtiers than
we would wish them to be".[16] Well might Cowper be worried,
for time was to show that not even the Junto itself was immune
from the disease. When, in 1709, Halifax was passed over and
the youthful Lord Townshend appointed instead as principal
envoy to the peace negotiations at Gertruydenberg, the great
financier's relations with Somers, his chief, visibly cooled.[17]

   With such a rich field of opportunity opening out before him
Harley moved smoothly into action. His first success was among
the most singular of all. Charles Talbot, Duke of Shrewsbury,
was a Whig statesman of immense repute.[18] He had been
prominent at the time of the Revolution, had served with
applause as William's Secretary of State, and was again to play
a decisive role in events during the crisis of 1714. Charming,
intelligent, palpably sincere, Shrewsbury had a magnetic
personality. To many of the rank and file Whigs he was an
object of adoration. Even his political opponents treated him
with an esteem rare in Queen Anne's England. Notwithstanding his many qualities, however, Shrewsbury had contrived to
fall foul of the Junto. Towards the close of William's reign the
Duke had surrendered his seals as Secretary of State and hurried
abroad, ostensibly to repair his shattered health. But to the five
Whig lords, facing the prospect of impeachment, it seemed as

---

[15] Peter Wentworth to Lord Raby, 11 Jan. 1709, *Wentworth Papers*, p. 69; same
to same, 25 Jan. 1709, *ibid.*, p. 73.
   [16] Cowper to Newcastle, 4 Oct. 1708, *H.M.C. Portland MSS.*, II, p. 205. The
phrase "the five tyrannizing lords" is Queen Anne's. Anne to Marlborough, 27
Aug. 1708, Coxe, vol. IV, p. 204.
   [17] Maynwaring's assertion that Halifax was "highly dissatisfied with Somers"
(*Sarah Corr.*, vol. I, p. 264) is borne out by the Whig lord's own remarks in two undated letters to Somers in B.M. Additional MSS., 34, 521, ff. 39–40.
   [18] The standard life of Shrewsbury is T. C. Nicholson and A. S. Turberville,
Charles Talbot, Duke of Shrewsbury (Cambridge, 1930). See also D. H. Somerville,
The King of Hearts (London, 1962).

though Shrewsbury was deserting the Whig cause in its hour of peril, and when, even after his return to England in 1705, his Grace still refused to lend a helping hand, Junto chagrin knew no bounds. Bitterly disappointed, the five lords wrote off their old associate as beyond redemption, a spent political force.[19]

The Junto's loss was Harley's gain. As early as 1701 Harley had been in touch with Shrewsbury via their mutual acquaintance James Vernon, and in the course of the next few years he went out of his way to perform a number of small services on behalf of the illustrious exile. At the Duke's request, for example, Harley used his "authority in the House" to shield Vernon from certain charges he feared might be brought against him as a result of one of the Commons enquiries. Again, in the summer of 1703, Harley forwarded to Rome a manuscript from the Cotton Library which Shrewsbury wished to borrow.[20] Favours of this kind worked like yeast upon the great nobleman's mind, and predisposed him more and more to look with favour on Harley and his schemes. The change was not lost on the Herefordshire man, and accordingly when, in the early summer of 1708, his plans were beginning to ripen, Harley decided that the moment had come to move in and clinch matters. In May the Duke announced that he was "ready to meet" Harley's close friend, Sir Simon Harcourt, and in July further consultations were arranged at Shrewsbury's country house, Heythrop in Oxfordshire.[21] Before the year was out his Grace's conversion had been accomplished, and in the months which followed he was to render invaluable assistance to Harley both as a link with other discontented Whigs and as a lever upon the Queen.

Another Harley captive at this period was his one-time Cabinet colleague Newcastle. During and after the ministerial

[19] For Shrewsbury's refusal to come meekly to heel in 1705, and its stunning impact, see Shrewsbury to Halifax, 24 Aug. 1705, and Halifax's perplexed reply, *Private and Original Correspondence of Shrewsbury*, pp. 653–4. The extent of Junto disappointment is perhaps indicated by the malicious delight evinced by the Whig lords upon hearing the news of Shrewsbury's unfortunate marriage to an ageing Italian widow. See in particular the comments of Halifax and Orford, B.M. Additional MSS., 34, 521, ff. 50 and 63–4.

[20] Vernon to Shrewsbury, 9 June 1701, *Vernon Corr.*, III, p. 148; same to same 24 Sep. 1703, *ibid.*, pp. 236–7; Shrewsbury to Harley, 28 June 1704 (N.S.), *H.M.C. Bath MSS.*, I, pp. 57–8; same to same 11 Aug. 1703 (N.S.), *ibid.*, pp. 54–5.

[21] Shrewsbury to Harley, 6 May 1708, *H.M.C. Bath MSS.*, I, p. 191; Harley to Shrewsbury, 27 July 1708, *H.M.C. Buccleuch and Queensberry MSS.*, II, p. 720; Shrewsbury to Harley, 29 July 1708, *H.M.C. Bath MSS.*, I, p. 191.

crisis of February 1708 Newcastle had rallied decisively to the
Junto side. In April, for instance, he had, along with Devonshire,
sought an interview with the Queen and endeavoured to impress
upon her the justice of Somers' claim to a seat in the Cabinet. A
month or so later he again sided with the Party leaders when
they challenged Queensberry's right to an hereditary seat in
the House of Lords in virtue of his recent creation as Duke of
Dover.[22] At this point, no doubt, many a political pundit
would have given up Newcastle as irretrievably lost. Harley,
however, was far from despairing. He knew that the Whig
Duke was at heart a moderate, and that in the past he had
come to resent deeply the Junto's indecorous bullying of Anne.
Hence, in the summer of 1708, Harley again began to corres-
pond with the Lord Privy Seal, and to feed him with notions of
"the state and condition of the country" and "the miseries
which will inevitably follow unless a speedy care be admini-
stered".[23] He did not hurry things too much. He remained content simply to open up a channel of communication, and then
to sit back and let the Junto lords work their own ruin. In the
fulness of time his patient handling of the situation received its
due reward. When, in 1710, the moment of decision at length
came, Newcastle did not again succumb to the Junto's blandishments.

Shrewsbury and Newcastle were both men of weight in the
Whig Party. But Harley was not content to net only the big fish.
No malcontent, however insignificant or seemingly unpromis-
ing, was neglected. Before the end of 1709 the ex-Secretary was
on terms with Rivers[24] and Peterborough,[25] and in the course of

[22] Godolphin to Marlborough, 22 April 1708, Coxe, vol. IV, p. 71; Sunderland
to Newcastle, 27 May 1708, Trevelyan, *op. cit.*, vol. II, p. 412.

[23] Monckton to Harley, 18 Aug, 1708, B.M. Portland Loan, 151; Harley to
Newcastle, 22 Oct. 1708, N.U.L., Holles MSS., PW2, 95.

[24] As early as July 1708 Rivers was having meetings "after dark" with Harley.
(Rivers to Harley, 15 July 1708, B.M. Portland Loan 156(3)). In September 1709
Harley informed Mansell that Rivers had solemnly promised "to join for the
public good". ([Harley] to [Mansell], 30 Sep. 1709, N.L.W., Penrice and Margam
MSS., L. 648). Rivers, a Junto ally since 1688, when, in company with Wharton he
had joined William at Exeter, had quarrelled with the five lords over the conduct
of the war in Spain.

[25] Already in January 1709 we find Shaftesbury ruefully lamenting the fact that
Peterborough was now "in the party" of Harley. (Shaftesbury to Furley, 15 Jan.
1709, *Original Letters of Locke, Sidney and Shaftesbury*, pp. 246–7). On Peterborough's
split with the Junto see E. L. Ellis, "The Whig Party, 1702–1708" (M.A. Thesis,
University of Wales, 1949), pp. 239–45.

the next year or so Haversham, Raby and Somerset were all edged over into the Harley orbit.[26] Even Halifax who, as a member of the Junto, might reasonably have been expected to have been proof against Harley's designs, had, by 1710, been wooed into a position of semi-neutrality.[27] Nor did Harley confine his attentions to England. As early as October we find him informing Harcourt of the Junto's breach with "the great men of Scotland". "Methinks", he continued, "some care should be taken to show them their condition, not only that of their country, but of their own persons". Within a short while Queensberry had been won over, and he was soon followed by Argyll, Orrery and Islay. By 1710 Hamilton, Mar, Wemyss and Northesk were also safe in Harley's pocket.[28]

Perhaps the most instructive of all Harley's triumphs in these crowded months was his capture of Jonathan Swift. Ever since his fortunes had begun to rise the ex-minister seems to have been on the look out for "some good pen" to put his programme to the country, and when, in the autumn of 1710, the disgruntled Swift loomed over the horizon he decided there and then that he need search no further. The choice could hardly have been bettered, for in the years to come the Irish cleric was to prove over and over again that he was by far the most gifted political controversialist of the age. Assailed by pamphlets like *The Conduct of the Allies*, and scorched by the merciless invective of Swift's *Examiners*, point after point of the Whig case shrivelled and turned to cinder. However, it is not just Harley's quick appreciation of Swift's potential which is impressive. Even more illuminating is the way he stalked his quarry. One of the things

[26] Haversham to Harley, 5 Sep. and 15 Sep. 1709, *H.M.C. Portland MSS.*, IV, pp. 524–5 and 526. Marlborough had noted Raby's intimacy with Harley as early as August 1708 (Marlborough to the Duchess, 2 Aug. 1708, Coxe, vol. IV, p. 185), but not until he succeeded Townshend at the Hague late in 1710 was Raby positively identified with the Tories. On Somerset see his letters to Harley in B.M. Portland Loan 156(6); also Shrewsbury to Harley, "Thursday morning", *H.M.C. Bath MSS.*, I, p. 198, and Somerset to Harley, 24 May 1710, *H.M.C. Portland MSS.*, IV, p. 542.

[27] By the end of 1709 Halifax was expressing "great friendship" for both Harley and Shrewsbury. (Shrewsbury to Harley, "Thursday morning", *H.M.C. Bath MSS.*, I, p. 198. Cf. Swift's opinion of the situation a year later: "I know he [Halifax] makes court to the new men, although he affects to talk like a Whig" (J. Swift, *Journal to Stella*, ed. H. Williams (Oxford, 1946), vol. I, p. 106). See also Halifax's letters to Harley in B.M. Portland Loan, 151.

[28] Harley to Harcourt, 16 October 1708, *H.M.C. Bath MSS.*, I, p. 192; *Lockhart Papers*, vol. I, pp. 314–15 and 319.

for which Swift had never forgiven the Junto lords was the way
they had repeatedly brushed aside his efforts to enlist their
support in his fight to get Queen Anne's Bounty extended to the
Church in Ireland. Harley made no such error. As soon as he
got wind of the Irish man's desire he hastened to arrange a time
when they might meet to thrash out the matter together. Swift,
with the experience of Whig promises still fresh in his mind,
repaired to the politician's house at the appointed hour, half
expecting to be fobbed off with some plausible excuse from
Harley's rogue of a porter. The reception he actually met with
must have surpassed his wildest hopes. Swift himself has left us
a first hand description of the master tactician at work:

> Mr. Harley came out to me, brought me in, and presented
> me to his son-in-law, Lord Doblane (or some such name) and
> his own son, and, among others, Will Penn the Quaker. We
> sat two hours drinking as good wine as you do; and two hours
> more he and I alone; where he heard me tell my business;
> entered into it with all kindness; asked for my powers and read
> them; and read likewise a memorial I had drawn up, and put
> it in his pocket to show the Queen; told me the measures he
> would take; and, in short, said every thing I could wish: told
> me he must bring Mr. St. John and me acquainted; and spoke
> so many things of personal kindness and esteem for me, that
> I am inclined half to believe what some friends have told me,
> that he would do everything to bring me over. He has desired
> . . . . me to dine with him on Tuesday, and after four hours
> being with him, set me down at St. James's coffee house in a
> hackney coach. All this is odd and comical, if you consider
> him and me. He knew my christian name very well.

Flattered to the top of his bent, Swift was already more than
half won over, and when, "in less than three weeks", the humble
suppliant learnt that his errand of mercy on behalf of the Irish
clergy had been "settled . . . at five meetings with the Queen"
his conversion was complete.[29]

[29] Swift, *Journal to Stella*, vol. I, pp. 36, 41 and 45-6; J. Swift, "Memoirs relating
to that Change which happened in the Queen's Ministry in the Year 1710",
Temple Scott (ed.), *The Prose Works of Jonathan Swift* (London, 1901), vol. V, pp.
379-83.

By the beginning of 1710, then, Harley had, by dint of much careful negotiation, built up a formidable combination against the ministry. At its core was the Tory following of Bromley, but it included also a sizeable number of discontented Whigs. At the same time, opinion in the country at large, increasingly alarmed by the Junto policy of war to the death, had swung decisively behind the Herefordshire man.[30] All that now stood between him and victory was the person of the Queen herself.

Undoubtedly Anne sympathised with what Harley was about, but, as the correspondence of Abigail Masham makes amply clear, she refused time and again to throw in her lot with the conspirators.[31] The truth was that Anne had lost face badly by rallying to Harley in February 1708, and, although as anxious as any to be rid of the Junto, she had no wish to subject herself a second time to similar indignity. What the Queen demanded before she would begin to move against the ministry was some massive indication of the opposition's power. Fortunately for Harley, in the spring of 1710 the opportunity for such a show of strength was conveniently provided by the ministry itself. In a moment of terrible political misjudgement the administration decided to impeach the Tory divine Henry Sacheverell for preaching a high-flying sermon before the Queen in St. Paul's Cathedral on 5 November 1709, the twenty first anniversary of William's landing at Torbay.

The decision to proceed against Sacheverell was the worst political blunder the Junto ever made. Overnight the firebrand preacher became a national hero, drawing about him all the disparate strands of discontent that had been slowly building up against the ministry over the previous two years. As the trial proceeded government support in the Lords began to drop away alarmingly. Outside the walls of the court room, too, it was the same story. A poem "found on the Queen's toilet" linked the doctor's cause with that of the martyred Laud. His lodgings were inundated with messages of support and good will, he was prayed for by name in several of the City churches, and his person was graced by visits from the Dukes of Beaufort,

[30] For the shift in public opinion see Trevelyan, *op. cit.*, vol. III, *cap.* II.
[31] E.g. see Abigail's letters to Harley of 27 July 1708, 6 Nov. 1708, and 4 Sep. 1709, *H.M.C. Portland MSS.*, IV, pp. 499, 510–11 and 525.

Leeds and Buckingham, and the Queen's uncle, the Earl of Rochester. Court ladies repaired to Westminster Hall at seven in the morning to make sure of a seat at the trial. The Queen, who attended the proceedings daily, was cheered upon her way by pro-Sacheverell crowds pressing round her coach. For several nights at the beginning of March it seemed as though the City might fall entirely into the hands of the mob. At least half a dozen meeting houses were pulled down, and their contents put to the torch. The mansions of many leading Whigs were threatened, and men like Cowper and Wharton were "insulted" by the insurgents. "Before my own door", declared Bishop Burnet, "one with a spade cleft the skull of another who would not shout as they did". At one stage the rioters were on the point of hanging Dolben, but in the nick of time he managed to convince them that he was someone else. In the end the cry went up to storm the Bank of England, the greatest of all Whig citadels, and the government, at its wits end, was forced to call out the Queen's Horse Guards to quell the tumult.[32]

Even then, however, the saga was not over. When, on 21 March, the doctor, having been duly found guilty, was allotted only the mildest of punishments, the country went wild with joy. At Oxford the effigy of Dr. Hoadley, the Low Church champion, was ceremonially burnt. When news of the light sentence reached Sherborne "the bells were set ringing, Dr. Sacheverell's health was publicly drunk in the town hall, and . . . some bottles of wine were sent into the church for another select company of both sexes, who drank the doctor's health at the top of the tower, with lights in their hands to give public notice". Everywhere bonfires were lit; loyal Tory addresses poured into the Queen from all parts of the country; and up and down the land High Church parsons thundered from the pulpits "like sons of Jehu". One divine—Hesketh—had to be forbidden to preach in the royal chapel after delivering before the Queen "a very high flying sermon far exceeding that of Dr. Sacheverell". The

---

[32] C. E. Doble and others (eds.), *Remarks and Collections of Thomas Hearne* (Oxford, 1885–1918), vol. II, pp. 350–2; John Bridges to Sir William Trumbull, 20 Dec. 1709, Berks. R.O., Trumbull MSS., LIII; Lady Wentworth to Lord Raby, 6 March 1710, *Wentworth Papers*, p. 113; Oldmixon, *op. cit.*, pp. 434–5; Burnet, *op. cit.*, vol. V, pp. 430–1; Abigail Harley to Edward Harley, 2 March 1710, *H.M.C. Portland MSS.*, IV, pp. 532–3.

doctor himself was provided with a rich cure in Shropshire by one of his admirers, and his journey northwards to his new living partook of the character of a royal progress. In Oxford the Vice Chancellor and the heads of colleges entertained him magnificently. At Banbury he was greeted by the corporation dressed in their scarlet and black gowns, and presented with a hamper of the best wine in the town. He got another hamper at Warwick. Near Wrexham close on two thousand Welsh gentry came out to convey him to the house of Mr. George Shakerley where he spent the night. To welcome the doctor the two steeples at Bridgnorth were draped with £50 worth of flags and colours, while he entered Ludlow with drums beating, trumpets sounding and banners flying. The only place that seems to have put up any show of resistance was Worcester. Here Bishop Lloyd gave express orders to his clergy to avoid contact with the doctor, and to make assurance doubly sure the clappers were removed from the bells of a number of churches in the diocese. Even this stern measure, however, proved only partially successful. Some of the choicer spirits of the town broke into St. Nicholas's church and rang the bells with hammers, while women garlanded the city's statue of Charles I with flowers.[33]

Queen Anne heartily disliked Sacheverell's exhibitionism and his brand of mob oratory. She told Burnet that she thought his sermon was a bad one, and that "he deserved well to be punished for it".[34] But if the messenger was a distasteful one, the news he bore was nonetheless welcome for that. The Sacheverell ferment showed, as nothing else could have done, that the conspirators had the tide behind them. In this respect the whole affair was, as the Earl of Ailesbury cynically remarked, "nuts for Mr. Harley".[35] The Queen now definitely began to move against the ministry. She was still capable of fits of wilfulness, as the letters of Abigail illustrate,[36] and at times she moved with

[33] Burnet, *op. cit.*, vol. V, pp. 436–7; *Remarks and Collections of Thomas Hearne*, vol. II, p. 369; A. T. Scudi, *The Sacheverell Affair* (New York, 1939), p. 124; W. Kennett, *The Wisdom of Looking Backward* (London, 1715), pp. 31–4; Anon, *The Age of Wonders* (London, 1710); Luttrell vol. VI, p. 602; Boyer, *History of Queen Anne*, pp. 478–9; Oldmixon, *op. cit.*, pp. 448–9; Foley to Harley, 17 July 1710, *H.M.C. Portland MSS.*, IV, p. 550.
[34] Burnet, *op. cit.*, vol. V, p. 432.
[35] *Memoirs of Ailesbury*, vol. II, p. 621.
[36] E.g. Abigail Masham to Harley, 17 April 1710, *H.M.C. Portland MSS.*, IV, p. 540.

glacier slowness. Nevertheless, with Sacheverell the Rubicon had been crossed.[37] In January 1710 Anne, without Marlborough's consent, appointed Harley's new-won convert Rivers Lord Lieutenant of the Tower, the most important military arsenal in England. On 13 April Shrewsbury replaced the Marquess of Kent as Lord Chamberlain. In June Sunderland went, in August Godolphin. By October the revolution was complete. Parliament had been dissolved and a new Tory-dominated assembly elected. Harley remained content with a seat on the Treasury Board, plus the comparatively minor post of Chancellor of the Exchequer. But few doubted that he was now the man who would "preside behind the curtain".[38] It was to Harley, not to Shrewsbury or any other magnate, that the aspiring Henry St. John wrote for a job in the new administration.[39]

Harley's accession to power rang down the curtain in triumph on the opening act of the play. The remainder of the performance was to prove equally colourful. The new prime minister's most pressing concern in 1710 was unquestionably the problem of finance. During the last twelve months of Godolphin's administration the huge demands of war had taken a terrible toll on the country's economy. Army debentures, which had stood at 91 in the slump of 1706–7, dwindled to 80 by the beginning of 1710. Bank stock also sank steadily. Taxes no longer reached their stipulated amounts, trade was overburdened, and many branches of the revenue were anticipated. In the royal household salaries were eighteen months in arrears. Edward Harley has left us a graphic picture of his brother's inheritance:

[37] Swift, who, as an intimate of both Harley and St. John, was in an excellent position to know the facts, later wrote regarding the change of ministry in 1710: "It was the issue of Doctor Sacheverell's trial that encouraged her [Queen Anne] to proceed so far". J. Swift, "An Enquiry into the Behaviour of the Queen's Last Ministry", *Prose Works of Swift*, vol. V, p. 438. Cf. Harley's statement in October 1710 that "the Queen has had an opportunity of seeing where the strength and inclination of the people are". Harley's plan of administration, 30 Oct. 1710, *Miscellaneous State Papers from the Collection of the Earl of Hardwicke*, vol. II, p. 486.
[38] J. Swift, "Memoirs relating to that Change in the Queen's Ministry", *Prose Works of Swift*, vol. V, p. 378. Cf. Burnet, *op. cit.*, vol. VI, p. 9; Brydges to Drummond, 24 Aug. 1710, C. Buck and G. Davies (eds.), "Letters on Godolphin's Dismissal in 1710", *Huntington Library Quarterly*, vol. III (1939–40), p. 236; Addison to Joshua Dawson, 1 Sep. 1710, *Letters of Joseph Addison*, p. 236. For a narrative of the changes see Trevelyan, *op. cit.*, vol. III, *cap.* IV.
[39] St. John to Harley, 8 March 1710, *H.M.C. Portland MSS.*, IV, p. 536.

When he came into the Treasury he found the Exchequer almost empty, nothing left for the subsistence of the army, but some tallies upon the third general mortgage of the customs; the Queen's civil list near £700,000 in debt; the funds all exhausted, and a debt of £9,500,000 without any provision of Parliament; which had brought all the credit of the government to a vast discount. In this condition the nation had then in pay 255,689 men.

"All these particulars", declared Edward, "appear by papers left in the Treasury by the Earl of Godolphin, of which I now have the authentic copies".[40]

What made Harley's task especially taxing was the fact that these financial troubles, which were basically the result of the strains imposed by the long continental war, had become interwoven with politics. The intermingling of the two had turned what was in any case a difficult situation into one of extreme gravity. Ever since the founding of the Bank of England under Whig auspices in the sixteen nineties Tory back-benchers had looked with suspicion upon the activities of the City. Wartime conditions greatly exacerbated this hostility, for while the Tory squire found himself racked by the heavy Land Tax, the City financier grew fat on the interest on money lent to the Treasury to help meet the growing war needs of the government. By 1710 the tension between the "landed interest" and the "moneyed interest" had reached such a pitch that many important men in the City genuinely believed that the establishment of a new Tory-dominated ministry would spell disaster for the financial world.[41] Hence, when in June Anne dismissed Secretary of State Sunderland, four Directors of the Bank—Heathcote, Scawen, Eyles and Gould—deeply alarmed, solicited an interview with the Queen in which they sought, with many "tragical

[40] Memorial to Queen Anne dated 31 Aug. 1710, B. M. Lansdowne MSS., 829, ff. 123–34; W. R. Scott, *The Constitution and Finance of English, Scottish and Irish Joint Stock Companies to 1720* (Cambridge, 1910–12), vol. I, p. 386, vol. III, pp. 228–9; Edward Harley's "Memoirs", *H.M.C. Portland MSS.*, V. p. 650. Cf. the premier's own account dated 6 June 1714, *ibid.*, p. 464. For Bank stock prices see J. E. T. Rogers, *History of Agriculture and Prices in England* (Oxford, 1866–1902), vol. VII, pt. 2, pp. 711–7.

[41] For an admirable account of the clash between the "landed" and the "moneyed" interests see Holmes, *British Politics in the Age of Anne, cap.* V.

expressions", to persuade her of "the danger of altering her ministers and dissolving the Parliament". Anne managed to calm their frayed nerves a little by assuring them that Sunderland's removal did not herald the beginning of the avalanche, and they returned to their counting houses in a somewhat happier frame of mind. However, a month or so later, when strong rumours again began to circulate of an impending change at Court, the Bank was once more thrown into a flutter, and on this occasion Heathcote and his confreres did not confine themselves to verbal warnings. When, at the close of July, Godolphin requested a loan of £100,000 together with certain smaller sums, the Bank refused to accommodate him. At the same time Sir Henry Furnese, the contractor in charge of the remittance of commercial bills of exchange in the Low Countries, Portugal and Spain ordered his agents in Amsterdam to refuse to accept any further bills until his outstanding account with the Treasury had been settled. Furnese's "malice", coming on top of the Bank's decision, meant that in Flanders "the very army was left without subsistence, and everything else in the same case".[42]

The financial problem, then, which confronted Harley when he took over the reins from Godolphin in August 1710 was one of appalling proportions. Not only was the economy beginning to feel the strain of war as never before, but, in addition, the City's fear of rising Tory fortunes seemed on the point of disrupting the whole of the government's credit machinery. Many felt that Harley could not possibly survive the crisis. Swift, for example, was sunk in gloom. "I am afraid the new ministry is at a terrible loss about money", he confided to Stella towards the end of October. "The Whigs talk so it would give one the spleen; and I am afraid of meeting Mr. Harley out of humour. They think he will never carry through this undertaking. God knows what will come of it. I should be terribly vexed to see things come round again : it will ruin the church and clergy for ever".

---

[42] Harley to Arthur Moore, 19 June 1710 (draft), *H.M.C. Portland MSS.*, IV, p. 545; James Brydges to George Brydges, 17 June 1710, Buck and Davies, *loc. cit.*, p. 230; Treasury minutes of 28 July and 3 Aug. 1710, *Calendar of Treasury Books*, vol. XXIV, p. 33; Brydges to Sencert, 17 Aug. 1710, Buck and Davies, *loc. cit.*, p. 232; Bank of England minute of 17 Aug. 1710, *ibid.*, p. 234; Benjamin Sweet to Marlborough, 15 Aug. 1710 (N.S.), Blenheim MSS., BII–9; Drummond to Harley, 9 Dec. 1710 (N.S.), *H.M.C. Portland MSS.*, IV, p. 637; Harley to Newcastle, 13 Aug. 1710, *ibid.*, II, p. 216.

On the day of Godolphin's dismissal Bank stock fell by five points to 108¼. On 30 October it dropped below 100 for the first time since 1707, and by 1 November it stood at 97. By this time even Halifax, who, in August, had generously offered to place his not inconsiderable financial skills at Harley's disposal, had given up hope. On 26 October he wrote a valedictory note to Newcastle informing the Duke that, in his opinion, credit had now "fallen past retrieve".[43]

But if others were despondent Harley was not. As soon as Godolphin was out of office the new Chancellor of the Exchequer hastened to summon the gentlemen of the Bank to attend upon him. Godolphin's unsuccessful request for a £100,000 loan was boldy renewed, and, after some hesitation, the Directors agreed to supply half this sum, though for two months only, not for four as requested, and on condition that repayment should be in gold. With this £50,000 safely in his pocket, Harley turned to explore other possibilities. There is evidence to suggest that even before Godolphin's fall the Herefordshire man, anticipating resistance from the Bank, had put himself in touch with several important private financiers. Labouring "night and day" he now redoubled his efforts in this direction. As a result "several rich merchants and bankers" agreed "to supply the urgent necessities of the government". A particularly valuable convert was Sir Theodore Janssen, one of the founders and first Directors of the Bank, who, by reason of his Dutch extraction, exercised great influence in Amsterdam. Equally important was the decision of Messrs. Lambert, Hoare and Gibbon to throw in their lot with Harley. Late in August these three agreed to supply the new ministry with the princely sum of £350,000. It was thanks largely to this particular loan that Harley was able, on 26 August, to report in triumph to Newcastle that, "notwithstanding all the arts and malice which have been used, we have found ways to remit yesterday subsistence for the whole army in Flanders till Christmas". What especially pleased the Chancellor was the fact that the whole transaction had been carried through "at a much easier rate" than would have been possible had he adopted

[43] J. Swift, *Journal to Stella*, vol. I, p. 76; Rogers, *loc. cit.*; Halifax to Newcastle. 26 Oct. 1710, *H.M.C. Portland MSS.*, II, p. 223.

Godolphin's customary method of working through the now delinquent Furnese.[44]

While these various negotiations were in train, Harley took pains to ensure that the government's voice was properly heard in all important quarters. Earl Rivers, for example, was despatched to Hanover in August to reassure the Electoral family, while in Amsterdam the Chancellor's agent, John Drummond, did all in his power, throughout the period of crisis, to sooth the apprehensions of the commercial fraternity in the Dutch capital. Naturally, the biggest part of this public relations effort was concentrated on the vital domestic scene. One of the more effective Harleyite pamphlets to appear at this time was *Faults on Both Sides*, a persuasive tract which argued the case against party bickering and division. A still more important publication was Defoe's *Essay on Loans* which set out to do much the same thing from a more strictly economic standpoint. Daniel maintained that in financial matters political opinions were of no account. What mattered was a person's honesty and his business acumen, and in this respect the new administration was every jot as credit worthy as its Whig predecessor. Meanwhile the *Review* continued to appear, preaching, as of old, the virtues of Harley and his entourage.[45]

Eventually this expert propaganda, together with the Chancellor's obvious success in meeting his immediate monetary needs, began to tell. It is true that the Bank continued, from time to time, to behave in a most infuriating manner. When, for instance, early in September, the principal officers of the Ordnance requested a loan of £20,000, the gentlemen of the Bank blandly replied that for the immediate requirements of the Ordnance "£10,000 at present would serve". Again, late in the following month, John Drummond was enraged when news reached him of a "villainous resolution" of the Directors to

[44] Treasury minutes of 15 Aug., 17 Aug., 22 Aug., and 25 Aug. 1710, *Calendar of Treasury Books*, vol. XXIV, pp. 35–6, 38, 39–40, 42 ; Harley's minutes of 15, 17 and 22 Aug. 1710, B.M. Portland Loan, 10(2) ; Francesco de Caseras' tender, *ibid.*, 290 ; Brydges to Harley, 21 Aug. 1710, *ibid.*, 291 ; Boyer, *History of Queen Anne*, p. 477 ; Harley to Newcastle, 26 Aug. 1710, *H.M.C. Portland MSS.*, II, pp. 217–8.

[45] James Cresset, not Rivers, had been the original choice for the Hanoverian mission, but Cresset died towards the end of July. (Somerset to Harley, 26 July 1710 *H.M.C. Portland MSS.*, IV, p. 552). For Drummond's importance see his letters to Harley, *ibid.*, p. 559 *et seq.*, *passim*. *Faults on Both Sides* has been reprinted in *Somers Tracts*, vol. XII, pp. 678–707.

discount no foreign bills. Indeed, so high was the feeling between the Bank and the administration that when, in the spring of 1711, the annual elections for Governor, Sub-Governor and Directors came around, the Harley ministry intervened and made a determined, though in the event unsuccessful, effort to oust Heathcote and his fellow Whigs and replace them with a more accommodating Board. Nevertheless, despite the Bank's often tiresome behaviour in these months, it is clear that, by the close of 1710, the government's position was on the upgrade. Here Swift is a useful barometer. Before the end of December the Irish cleric, who had, as we have seen, been among the most despondent of Harley's friends, was jauntily reporting to Stella that Bank stock had now climbed once more to 105.[46]

In this rising atmosphere of confidence Harley was, in the new year, able at last to lead the way out of the financial wood. Early in January he reached an important agreement with the Bank whereby the Directors undertook to cash all Exchequer bills of a certain issue at face value. The following month he launched a new government lottery, having first got the seal of approval for his plans from Halifax. In the new buoyant climate the lottery proved a spectacular success, and money poured in freely. As a result, for perhaps the first time since the summer of 1710, the ministry had enough ready money to meet its needs. Finally, with the ministry's immediate financial worries ironed out, the Chancellor crowned nine months unremitting effort at the Treasury by tackling the problem of government debt. In May, before a spellbound House of Commons, he announced his South Sea Company scheme. The chief purpose of the project was to fund the disturbingly large floating debt by making the state's creditors the first shareholders in the new Company. But, in addition, it had a subsidiary advantage in that it enabled Harley to reward his own loyal supporters in the City by securing their appointment to the Company's first Board of Directors. Tory back-benchers went wild with delight. Bonfires were lit in various parts of the capital, and church bells set ringing. The nation, declared a piqued Burnet, was "infatuated beyond the

[46] Treasury minute of 6 Sep. 1710, *Calendar of Treasury Books*, vol. XXIV, p. 48; Drummond to Harley, 7 Nov. 1710 (N.S.), *H.M.C. Portland MSS.*, IV, p. 617; Swift, *Journal to Stella*, vol. I, p. 135. For the Bank election see the Dutch despatches in B.M. Additional MSS., 17,677 EEE ff. 151, 166, and 172.

power of conviction".[47] The rejoicing was wholly apt, for the South Sea scheme symbolises Harley's emergence from the great credit crisis. From this time onwards the gentlemen of the Bank abandoned their sullen, carping attitude, and for the rest of the reign co-operated loyally with the ministry. Harley's cup of joy was rendered complete when on 24 May he was raised to the peerage as Earl of Oxford and Earl Mortimer, and five days later made Lord Treasurer. The immediate occasion of this out-pouring of royal favour was the Guiscard affair.[48] But, at a deeper level, it reflected the Queen's profound satisfaction with Harley's record in his first nine months as premier, no small part of which was his financial triumph.

The restoration of credit was unquestionably the new ministry's first priority in 1710. But it was by no means the government's largest task. A problem of far greater complexity was the necessity of bringing to an end the great European war. In the two years since the fall of the Harley group in 1708 war weari-ness had grown apace. It was not just the Exchequer which was creaking under the strain. The country at large was suffering. "Taxes", wrote Humphrey Prideaux from Norwich in Septem-ber 1708, "begin to come very heavy; and the reason is that rent comes heavier from the tenants; and, when the landlord receives nothing, how can he pay anything?" "The failure of the countryman's trade", Prideaux continued, "is the cause of this. We are now upon a very ticklish point abroad. If this cam-paign doth not succeed so well as to force the French to a peace next winter, I am afraid we shall not be able to find funds for another year". Aggravated by the harsh winter of 1708–9, when the Thames froze over so hard that booths and tents were set up upon it and an ice fair held, the price of food soared upwards.[49]

---

[47] Scott, op. cit., vol. I, p. 387; Halifax to Harley, 11 Feb. 1711, H.M.C. Portland MSS., IV, p. 658; Edward Harley's "Memoirs", ibid., V, p. 652; Lady Dupplin to Abigail Harley. 3 May 1711, ibid., IV, p. 683; Burnet, op. cit., vol. VI, p. 54. For the subsidiary motive behind the South Sea scheme see J. G. Sperling, "The Division of 25 May 1711 on an Amendment to the South Sea Bill: A Note on the Reality of Parties in the Age of Anne", Historical Journal, vol. IV (1961), pp. 191–202.
[48] For Guiscard see below, p. 151.
[49] Prideaux to Ellis, 13 Sep. 1708, E. M. Thompson (ed.), Letters of Humphrey Prideaux to John Ellis (London, 1875), p. 199; A. Boyer, History of the Reign of Queen Anne digested into Annals (London, 1703–13), vol. VIII, p. 361. So severe was the cold that when early in January, Peter Wentworth sat down to write to his brother he found that the ink was frozen in the pot. (Wentworth to Lord Raby, 4 Jan. 1709, Wentworth Papers, p. 68).

The thin harvest of the following summer did nothing to relieve the situation, nor did the influx of twelve thousand Protestant refugees from the ravaged Palatinate. The price of wheat, which had stood at 26 shillings a quarter in 1707, rose to 37s. 11d. the following year. By 1709 it had reached the alarming figure of 71s. 11d., and it maintained this dizzy level for the next twelve months.[50] Meanwhile, the difficulty of obtaining enough recruits to replenish the ranks of the army and navy, had led to an increasingly arbitrary use of the press gang. "Everything is run out of breath", observed Harley in the winter of 1708, "the mines are worked out",[51] and although the 1710 election was fought much more upon the Sacheverell issue than on the question of the prolongation of the war, few doubted that the new ministry would press earnestly for peace at the earliest available opportunity.

There seems little doubt that Harley himself was personally heavily committed to the idea of peace in 1710. His campaign against standing armies in the 1690s, and his obvious disappointment at the failure to terminate hostilities after the victory at Ramillies in 1706, both indicate his extreme sensitivity to the "extravagant burdens" of war. Moreover, as the tone of his correspondence shows, his sojourn at Brampton Bryan in the summer of 1708 had made him acutely aware of the darkening mood of the country as a whole.[52] Even so, although the standard accounts of the period readily accept that Harley was sincerely desirous of finding a peace formula in 1710, they tend to minimize the part played by him in the actual negotiations

---

[50] The figures are those operative at Eton. They are listed in Lord Ernle, *English Farming Past and Present* (3rd edn., London, 1922), p. 440. The effect of the soaring prices on the lower income groups were terrible. Daniel Baker believed that many poor people were "ready to famish". (Baker to Ralph Verney, Jan. 1710, *Verney Letters of the Eighteenth Century*, vol. I, p. 278.) So bad was the plight of the poor that the Queen felt compelled to take notice of it in her address to Parliament on 15 November 1709: "My Lords and Gentlemen; I think it proper to take notice to you that the great dearth and scarcity under which our neighbours abroad have suffered this year, begins to affect us in some measure at home, by the temptation of profit in carrying out too much of our corn while it bears so high a price in foreign parts. This occasions many complaints from the poor, for whose sake I earnestly recommend to you to take this growing evil into your consideration. . . ." (Cobbett, *op. cit.*, vol. VI, p. 802).

[51] Harley to Harcourt, 16 Oct. 1708 (copy), Longleat, Portland MSS., X, f. 53.

[52] See especially Harley to Newcastle, 22 Oct. 1708, N.U.L., Holles MSS., PW2, 95. The quotation is from Harley to Harcourt, 16 Oct. 1708 (copy), Longleat, Portland MSS., X, f. 53.

which culminated in the Utrecht settlement of 1713. In his masterly survey of Anne's reign, for example, the late G. M. Trevelyan stressed the contrast between the tardy progress of the early phase of the negotiations, when Harley was in sole charge, and the rapid strides made once St. John took a hand in the affair after March 1711. This contrast led Trevelyan to propound the opinion that it was St. John who was the real architect of peace, not Oxford, his nominal chief.[53]

It is naturally with diffidence that one ventures to question the verdict of so renowned an authority. Nevertheless, the evidence does seem to suggest that the Treasurer played a much more positive rôle in the peace negotiations than Dr. Trevelyan's account allows. In the first place it is important to note that the broad outlines of peace had already been settled between France and England before St. John was admitted to the negotiations in the spring of 1711. It had been agreed, for example, that Louis' grandson, Philip V, should remain King of Spain, that England should obtain substantial commercial advantages in the Mediterranean and the Spanish Indies, and that the extravagant concessions made to Holland in the notorious Whig Barrier Treaty of 1709 should be quietly abandoned.[54] Still more important—for Professor Trevelyan himself readily concedes the first point—is the fact that even after St. John took control of the negotiations in April 1711 Oxford remained, as the French had feared, very much at the head of affairs.[55] This becomes clear if we examine the Preliminary Articles of October 1711.

The October Preliminaries, which had been secretly negotiated between France and England in the summer and autumn of 1711, set out in detail the advantages to be enjoyed by England when a general European peace was eventually signed. These included the Asiento contract—the monopoly of supply-

[53] Trevelyan, *op. cit.*, vol. III, *passim*.
[54] "First Proposals of France", 22 April 1711, Cobbett, *op. cit.*, vol. VII, p. ciii.
[55] For French apprehensions see Torcy's memorandum dated 21 July 1711 (N.S.), Quai d'Orsay, Paris, Affaires etrangeres, Correspondance politique Angleterre, 233, ff. 43–7. This memorandum is of vital importance. In it (f. 44), Torcy states categorically that it was the express intention of Harley and his more favoured colleagues to exclude St. John entirely from the peace negotiations, and that it was only with the utmost reluctance that the premier allowed the Secretary to have some say after the latter had got wind of the talks in March 1711.

ing slaves to Spanish America; the restoration of the Hudson Bay Company's forts and territories; the acquisition of St. Kitts, Acadia and Newfoundland, of Gibraltar and Minorca; the granting of the most favoured nation treatment to English trade with the Spanish peninsula; and the dismantling of the fortifications of Dunkirk, the great nest of French privateering vessels that had for so long preyed upon English commerce. In addition to these detailed provisions, the Preliminaries also contained a section outlining in general terms the gains to be made by the other members of the Grand Alliance, plus a third document relating specifically to Savoy.[56]

From our point of view the great interest of the October Preliminaries lies in the fact that although they were in large measure negotiated by Secretary of State St. John, their real author was Oxford. Indeed, the Preliminaries did little more than carry into effect a series of proposals set out by the Treasurer in a paper drafted as far back as 16 June 1711. In this earlier document Oxford envisaged both the vast English gains—including the Asiento monopoly—embedded in the October agreement, and the outline settlement of the allies' claims. Even the special place enjoyed by Savoy in the Preliminary Articles was anticipated by the Treasurer.[57] How little rope St. John was given in the negotiations is clearly revealed by the letters which passed between the Queen and the Treasurer at this time. On 24 September, for example, Anne wrote to Oxford:

> I have this business of the peace so much at heart, that I cannot help giving you this trouble to ask if it may not be proper to order Mr. Secretary, in case he finds M. Mesnager very averse to the new proposition, not to insist upon it, and if you think it right I hope you will take care Mr. Secretary has such an order in my name, for I think there is nothing so much to be feared as the letting the Treaty go out of our hands.

One may compare the tone of this letter with that of a similar missive written a few weeks after the Preliminary Articles had been signed:

[56] The Preliminary Articles were signed on 27 Sep./8 Oct. 1711. They are printed *in extenso* in Cobbett, *op. cit.*, vol. VII, pp. cvii–cxiv.
[57] Instructions to Prior, 16 June 1711 (draft), B.M. Portland Loan, 10(17).

Not knowing whether Mr. Secretary has consulted you about the enclosed I send it for your approbation before I would copy it. Mr. St. John knows nothing of the little alteration there is made in the letter, therefore take no notice of it to him. He proposed the Secretary of the Embassy that is now at the Hague should carry this letter to the Emperor. I should be glad to know whether you think him a proper person to do it.[58]

Dr. Trevelyan was right to stress that St. John did much of the talking in 1711. But it is equally important to understand that the words the Secretary used were not always his own.

The final phase of peace negotiations opened at Utrecht in January 1712 and culminated some fifteen months later in the great peace settlement that bears the name of that Dutch city. As in the negotiation of the October Preliminaries so in these subsequent talks the evidence leaves one in little doubt that Oxford was the master and St. John the servant. In order to keep a close check on the movements of his Secretary the Treasurer was careful to conduct "by his own hand and [at] his own charge" a correspondence "in all the courts concerned in the negotiation". In particular he took special pains to keep secretly in regular touch with Torcy, the French foreign minister. [59] At the same time St. John was clearly expected to submit all important draft documents to his chief for vetting. The following undated letter from the Secretary illustrates nicely Oxford's commanding position:

I enclose the draft of a letter to the States together with theirs to the Queen. You will please to correct what may be amiss. It is a little more flourished than usual, but I hope on this occasion that may be allowable.[60]

[58] Anne to Oxford, 24 Sep. [1711], Longleat, Portland MSS., III, f. 46; same to same 6 Nov. [1711], ibid., f. 59.

[59] Oxford's "Account of Public Affairs", Cobbett, op. cit., vol. VI, appx. IV, p. ccxlvii; Gaultier to Torcy, 27 Jan. 1712 (N.S.), Quai d'Orsay, Paris, Affaires etrangeres, Correspondance politique, Angleterre, 237, ff. 29–30. A selection of Oxford's letters to Torcy may be found in the Baschet Transcripts in the Public Record Office. See P.R.O. 31/3/198 and 199, passim. For Oxford's correspondence with Buys, Heinsius and Van Huls see N.U.L., Harley MSS., PW2, HY, Foreign box.

[60] St. John to Oxford, [1712], B.M. Portland Loan 156(1). Cf. St. John's own confession: "his [Oxford's] concurrence was necessary to everything we did". Bolingbroke, "A Letter to Sir William Windham", The Works of Bolingbroke, vol. I, p. 16.

To render his grip even tighter the Treasurer kept a special file stocked with copies of St. John's diplomatic letters.[61]

Perhaps the incident which best sums up the relationship between the two ministers over the peace is the bitter altercation which ensued between them after the Secretary's special embassy to France in August 1712. St. John, now Lord Bolingbroke, had been sent across the Channel to speed the peace negotiations which had run into a number of difficulties.[62] Instead of negotiating quietly and then hastening back to England, the Secretary seized the opportunity of his stay in Paris to behave in the most extravagant Francophile manner. He was soon on Christian-name terms with the whole Torcy family, and before long was the toast of the town. Such was his popularity in the capital that when he attended a production of Corneille's *Le Cid* the entire audience rose to receive him and the performance was interrupted until he had taken his seat. Meanwhile, he had committed the crass blunder of acquiring as a mistress Madame de Tencin, an ex-nun who was in league with the French foreign minister, and he followed this up by unwisely attending the same performance at the Opera as the Pretender, thus kindling the hopes of Jacobite sympathisers.[63]

The various reports of the Secretary's antics which filtered back to England greatly disturbed Oxford. Shortly before Bolingbroke's departure for the continent, Torcy had put forward the proposal that England, France, Spain and Savoy should sign a separate peace, leaving the other Grand Alliance powers to fend for themselves. The Treasurer was adamantly opposed to any such move, considering it to be "so base, so knavish and so villainous a thing that everyone who served the Queen knew they must answer it with their heads". Bolingbroke

---

[61] B.M. Portland Loan, 309; N.U.L., Harley MSS., PW2, HY, box 6.

[62] Oxford seems to have despatched Bolingbroke to France on this occasion, in part at least, to restore the Secretary's self-esteem, which had been severely dented when the Queen conferred upon him a viscounty instead of the earldom he coveted. Our authority for this statement is Oxford himself: "This discontent [over the viscounty] continued until there happened an opportunity of sending him [Bolingbroke] to France; of which there was not much occasion: but it was hoped that this would have put him in good humour". Oxford's "Account of Public Affairs", Cobbett, *op. cit.*, vol. VI, appx. IV, p. ccxlvi.

[63] On Bolingbroke's French mission see T. Macknight, *The Life of Henry St. John, Viscount Bolingbroke* (London, 1863), pp. 298–307; and C. Petrie, *Bolingbroke* (London, 1937), pp. 210–7.

however, was known to sympathise with Torcy's proposal, and, indeed, he seems to have gone so far as to advise Anne to comply with the notion.[64] Hence the news of the Secretary's flamboyant behaviour in Paris seemed to confirm that he was willing to ditch the allies and link up with France. Accordingly, when Bolingbroke returned to England, Oxford at once took the peace negotiations out of his hands and passed them on to Secretary Dartmouth, a compliant Lord Treasurer's man. The boldness of the Treasurer's move caused considerable alarm in a number of quarters. Matthew Prior, for example, the English *chargé d'affaires* in Paris, feared that such a public display of ministerial division at so critical a juncture might easily drive out "to sea again" the peace which was then virtually "in the port".[65] There is also evidence to suggest that at home there was serious unrest in the Cabinet for the next month or so.[66] But Oxford remained undaunted. Bolingbroke had threatened to strike out on his own in the peace negotiations. He must therefore be disciplined. He must be taught who gave orders and who obeyed.

Thus, throughout the long and complex series of negotiations which began in 1710, and reached fruition in the Utrecht Settlement of 1713, Oxford played a dominant rôle. However, in a curious sense scholars have been right not to stress too heavily the Treasurer's part in the actual treaty-making, for the truth is that Oxford's most spectacular contribution to the peace came

---

[64] Torcy to Bolingbroke, 4 Aug. 1712 (N.S.), *Bol. Corr.*, vol. II, pp. 492–504; Cobbett, *op. cit.*, vol. VI, p. 1138; P. Vaillant (trans.), *Memoirs of the Marquis of Torcy . . . containing the History of the Negotiations from the Treaty of Ryswick to the Peace of Utrecht* (London, 1857), vol. II, pp. 347–8.

[65] Prior to Bolingbroke, 12 Sep. 1712 (N.S.), *Bol. Corr.*, vol. III, pp. 57–8.

[66] In mid-September Swift was trying valiantly "to keep people from breaking to pieces upon a hundred misunderstandings". (J. Swift, *Journal to Stella*, vol II, p. 556). But his efforts at conciliation failed, and the whole crisis came to a head in a series of heated Cabinet meetings at the close of the month, when Oxford at length prevailed over his adversary. (Kreienberg's reports of 26 Sep./7 Oct., 3/14 Oct. and 7/18 Oct., Staatsarchiv Hannover; L'Hermitage's report of 26 Sep./7 Oct., B.M. Additional MSS., 17,677, FFF, f. 361; Maynwaring to the Duchess of Marlborough, 29 Sep. 1712, Blenheim MSS., E. 27; W. Stratford to Edward Harley, 6 Oct, 1712, *H.M.C. Portland MSS.*, VII, p. 93). Thereupon Bolingbroke repaired in dudgeon to his country estate (Swift, *Journal to Stella*, vol. II, p. 565; Stratford to E. Harley, 6 Oct. 1712, *H.M.C. Portland MSS.*, VII, p. 93), Oxford succumbed to an "ugly fit of rheumatism" (Swift, *Journal to Stella*, vol. II, p.561; Gordon to Coke, 7 Oct. 1712, *H.M.C. Cowper MSS.*, III, p. 174), and poor Dartmouth, caught in the heavy cross-fire, tried vainly to resign (E. Lewis to Oxford, 6, 13 and 14 Oct. 1712, *H.M.C. Portland MSS.*, V, pp. 231–2 and 234–5; Anne to Oxford, 12 Oct. 1712, *H.M.C. Bath MSS.*, I, p. 22).

not at the conference table but in the House of Lords. After the beating they had taken in 1710 it seemed fairly certain that, sooner or later, the humbled Whig leaders would make a concerted effort to bring down the new administration. Moreover, it was clear that when the attack came it would in all probability be mounted in the Lords rather than in the Commons, for, as Harley observed in October 1710, it was in the Upper Chamber that the Whigs had "most of their strength" as well as "most of their able men".[67] In the first session of the new Parliament, however, the expected attack did not materialize. Despite some heavy skirmishing on a number of issues and particularly over the conduct of affairs in Spain, the Junto lords remained, throughout the session, relatively quiescent. Probably their restraint resulted from the fact that the new ministry had announced its determination, for the time being at least, to continue to pursue the Whig policy of all out continental war.[68] At any rate when, in the course of 1711, it became known that the ministry was secretly engaged in negotiating a peace with France, and that one of the assumptions underlying the talks was that Philip V should remain in possession of Spain, the Whig leaders quickly changed into higher gear. They determined, as soon as Parliament assembled in the autumn, to make "all the noise and bustle they could against the peace", and to oppose the ministers "in all their designs whatever they should be".[69] They thus initiated one of the most dramatic political contests of the entire reign.

The ministry was not slow to smell the danger in the air. As

[67] Harley's plan of administration, 30 Oct. 1710, *Miscellaneous State Papers from the Collection of the Earl of Hardwicke*, vol. II, p. 487. Cf. the verdict of a Whig spokesman: "The noble resolutions of the Lords have much revived my drooping spirits. They have long been our safety and I find will still save us, though upon the very precipice of ruin". Sir James Clavering to Lady Cowper, 22 Feb. 1711, Herts. R.O., Panshanger MSS., Cowper Family Books, I.

[68] Anne's speech to Parliament on 27 Nov. 1710 opened with the following words: "My Lords and Gentlemen; I have by calling this Parliament, made appear the confidence I place in the duty and affection of my subjects. And I meet you here with the greatest satisfaction; having no reason to doubt but that I shall find such returns as will add new life to our friends, and entirely disappoint the hopes of our enemies. To this end I shall recommend to you what is absolutely necessary for our common safety. The carrying on the war in all its parts, but particularly in Spain, with the utmost vigour, is the likeliest means, with God's blessing, to procure a safe and honourable peace for us and all our allies, whose support and interest I have truly at heart". Cobbett, *op. cit.*, vol. VI, p. 928.

[69] *Lockhart Papers*, vol. I, p. 411.

5*

early as August Shrewsbury had been apprehensive. "So many of our friends in the Lords' House being dead", he wrote to Oxford on 27 of that month, "and many more soured or at least become luke-warm by disappointments in their expectations, I apprehend matters in that House at least will meet with difficulties". Two months later the nature of the Whig plot was beginning to emerge in all its disturbing detail. On 1 November Sir Robert Davers wrote anxiously to the Treasurer from Rushbrooke:

> The reason I write to you now is to tell you that I believe the Whigs have mischief in their heads—that you know I believe. There was lately a great meeting of them at Lord Orford's to the number of seventeen, almost all Lords, Robin Walpole amongst them, and I find by words that dropped from some Lords of this country that they will be up the first day. Be on your guard.[70]

After this the warnings flowed in thick and fast.

Alerted in this way, Oxford did what he could to meet the threat. To gain time Parliament was put off by means of periodic prorogations until 7 December. Meanwhile, strenuous efforts were made to get as many government supporters as possible up to town for the vital opening day of the session. A letter to the Treasurer, written by William Bromley, and dated 3 December 1711, gives us a glimpse of the ministry's whips in action:

> Lord Denbigh will be here on Wednesday. He tells me he has sent to Lord Exeter, Lord Plymouth and Lord Conway to meet him. Lord Stawell will be in town before Friday. I hope I may conclude Lord Leigh is on the road.

Churchmen as well as laymen were reminded of their obligations. On 4 December 1711, Nathaniel, Lord Crewe, Bishop of Durham, wrote to Oxford:

---

[70] Shrewsbury to Oxford, 27 Aug. 1711, *H.M.C. Bath MSS.*, I, p. 207; Davers to Oxford, 1 Nov. 1711, *H.M.C. Portland MSS.*, V, p. 106.

The honour of your Lordship's commands last post should oblige me to a ready obedience, if old age and the depth of winter would allow my trying the experiment of such a hasty journey. If I know my own heart it is brim full of loyalty and fidelity to the Queen, of unfeigned sincerity for the Church, and of a steady adhering to the Constitution; all which, with concern I now perceive by your Lordship, will violently be pushed in matters of the greatest moment. And therefore, though I cannot so suddenly give my personal attendance in Parliament, yet that I may not seem, in such a critical juncture, to decline a service I have hitherto espoused with a more than ordinary zeal, I will presume to appear by proxy at the time desired; in order to which I have here enclosed a temporal one, with a space in it, for your Lordship, if you please, to insert the name of such a peer as you shall judge most proper.[71]

At the same time both Oxford and St. John did their best to mobilize public opinion. On 27 November Swift's devastating anti-Dutch pamphlet *The Conduct of the Allies* was published, and it ran through five editions before the end of the year. Defoe too was writing furiously. A month before Swift's tract appeared Defoe produced his *Reasons why this Nation ought to put a speedy end to this expensive War*. He followed this up in November and December with a number of other pamphlets, including *The Balance of Europe* and *Armageddon*.

Even so, in spite of the ministry's activity, as the weeks slipped by it became increasingly clear that the administration was losing ground. For one thing, the sixteen representative peers of Scotland, normally passive lobby-fodder for the government, were showing alarming signs of becoming restive. Disenchanted with the Union, peeved at what they regarded as their unnecessarily small share of government offices and perquisites, and, above all, mortified by the news that the Queen's stated intention to confer a British title upon the Duke of Hamilton was meeting with stiff opposition from a large section of the

---

[71] Bromley to Oxford, 3 Dec. 1711, B.M. Portland Loan, 128(3); Crewe to Oxford, 4 Dec. 1711, *H.M.C. Portland MSS.*, V. p. 121. See also Oxford's canvassing list dated 2 Dec. 1711, B.M. Portland Loan 10 (16).

English peerage, the sixteen chose to ignore Oxford's pressing appeals for their support at the opening of Parliament by "not making any haste"[72] to London. On top of this came other defections. By spreading rumours of an imminent Whig return to power, for instance, the Duke of Somerset succeeded in "spiriting up several depending lords".[73] The Junto lords also were busy nibbling at the ministry's structure. When Marlborough returned from the Continent they welcomed him with open arms. They also managed to drive a bargain with the Tory malcontent Nottingham. If Nottingham would engage to support their policy of "no peace without Spain" then they for their part promised to countenance an Occasional Conformity Bill.[74] Such was the audacity of the Whig leaders at this period that at one stage they even attempted to seduce the Treasurer himself.[75]

Oxford, fully alive to the situation, attempted valiantly to stop the drift. On 21 November, for example, he sought an interview with Marlborough who, for some time, had been absenting himself from Cabinet meetings.[76] Again, he endeavoured, both personally and through the good offices of Lord Poulett, to convince Nottingham of the attractiveness of the peace Preliminaries.[77] All his efforts, however, proved vain. Marlborough had resolved firmly and finally to cast his vote against the peace,[78] while Nottingham, "sour and fiercely

[72] Hamilton to Oxford, 13 Nov. 1711, H.M.C. Portland MSS., V, p. 109. The Scottish rebellion has been described in detail by Mr. Geoffrey Holmes. See G. S. Holmes, "The Hamilton Affair of 1711–1712; A Crisis in Anglo-Scottish Relations", English Historical Review, vol. LXXVII (1962), pp. 257–82.

[73] J. Swift, "The History of the Four Last Years of the Queen", Prose Works of Swift, vol. X, pp. 33–4.

[74] For the Whig bargain with Nottingham see H. Horwitz, Revolution Politicks: The Career of Daniel Finch, Second Earl of Nottingham 1647–1730 (Cambridge, 1968), pp. 230–2.

[75] See Halifax's letters to Harley of 9 Nov., 25 Nov., 2 Dec., and 6 Dec. 1711, H.M.C. Portland MSS., V. pp. 108, 115, 120 and 125; and those of 14 Nov. and 15 Nov. 1711, B.M. Portland Loan, 151(6).

[76] L'Hermitage's report, 23 Nov./4 Dec. 1711, B.M. Additional MSS., 17,677 EEE, f. 374. Oxford followed this up by getting the Queen to bring pressure on the General. Grafton. St. Albans, Dorset, Scarborough, Somers and Cowper were accorded the same treatment. Boyer, Annals, vol. X, p. 281.

[77] Nottingham to Oxford, 15 Oct, 1711, H.M.C. Portland MSS., V, p. 101. Poulett to Oxford, Nov. 1711, ibid., p. 119; Nottingham to Lady Nottingham, 16 Dec. 1711, Northants. R.O., Finch-Hatton MSS., 281.

[78] Marlborough to the Duchess of Marlborough, 22 Oct. 1711 (N.S.), Blenheim MSS., E.5.

wild", was equally unco-operative.[79] Even an eleventh hour attempt to placate the Scots lords by providing employment for at least some of their number in a newly established trade commission for Scotland proved largely ineffectual; Annandale, indeed, curtly turned down the post offered him as beneath his dignity.[80] In a last hectic fling the ministry turned to satire. On 6 December, the day before Parliament met, Swift, encouraged by the Treasurer, brought out his famous ballad on "an orator dismal of Nottinghamshire". The Tory *Post Boy* of the same day carried an advertisement in similar vein:

Whereas a very tall, thin, swarthy-complexioned man between sixty and seventy years of age, wearing a brown coat with little sleeves and long pockets, has lately withdrawn himself from his friends, being seduced by wicked persons to follow ill courses: these are to give notice that whoever shall discover him shall have ten shillings reward; or if he will voluntarily return he shall be kindly received by his friends, who will not reproach him for past follies, provided he give good assurances that for the future he will firmly adhere to the Church of England in which he was so carefully educated by his honest parents.[81]

But even here the government was outsmarted by the Junto. On the eve of the session the Whig *Daily Courant* printed prominently on its pages the Elector of Hanover's condemnation of "peace without Spain". Any peer who hoped to enjoy a political career after Anne's death was thereby served with a solemn warning.

Balked at every turn, the Treasurer could now do little more than steel himself for the inevitable onslaught. And when, on 7 December, the fateful hour at length struck his worst fears were realised. After the Queen's speech had been read and the customary address of thanks proposed, the Earl of Nottingham rose to his feet and delivered a passionate, hour-long harangue.

[79] Nottingham to Lady Nottingham, 16 Dec. 1711, Northants. R.O., Finch-Hatton MSS., 281. The quotation is from Poulett to Oxford, Nov. 1711, *H.M.C. Portland MSS.*, V, p. 119.

[80] Annandale to Oxford, 27 Nov. 1714, *ibid.*, pp. 116-7; Kinnoull to Oxford, 3 Dec, 1711, *ibid.*, p. 122.

[81] Boyer, *History of Queen Anne*, p. 525. For Swift's satire on Nottingham see H. Williams (ed.), *The Poems of Jonathan Swift* (Oxford, 1958), vol. I, pp. 141-5.

He concluded his remarks by moving an amendment to the address of thanks adding the crucial words "that no peace could be safe or honourable to Great Britain, or Europe, if Spain and the West Indies were allotted to any branch of the house of Bourbon". The government spokesmen responded to Nottingham's manoeuvre by taking the line that a debate on the Spanish issue would be inappropriate at that particular moment. The business before the House, they argued, was to thank the Queen, and to talk about Spain would be to wander down a side track. In any case, they continued, the making of peace was the prerogative of the Crown; it was not the concern of Parliament. Accordingly the ministry moved the previous question. When the votes were counted, however, it was found that the government had lost by the margin of a single vote. Thereupon the clause itself was carried by a majority of 64 to 52. At the news the Whigs went delirious. In the debate which followed Wharton was observed to put his hands round his neck in the form of a halter whenever any minister rose to speak, while "joy and vengeance sat visibly in every countenance of that party".[82] When, on the following day, ministerial supporters attempted to rescind Nottingham's amendment they were again defeated. The government's peace policy, indeed the administration's very existence, was thereby thrown in jeopardy.

As reports of the defeat spread outwards from Westminster Oxford's well-wishers were reduced to something near despair. It was not just the vote which alarmed people, but also the things which followed it. There was, for example, the ominous behaviour of the Queen. Upon leaving the Chamber, after listening to the debate incognito, Anne ostentatiously spurned the Duke of Shrewsbury and the Hereditary Lord Great Chamberlain, Lord Lindsey, and gave her arm instead to the Duke of Somerset "who was louder than any in the House for the clause against the peace".[83] Naturally, too, the Junto lords did all in their power to aggravate the situation. One of the chief

---

[82] Swift, "The History of the Four Last Years of the Queen", *Prose Works of Swift*, vol. X, p. 38. On the debate generally see Cobbett, *op. cit.*, vol. VI, pp. 1035–46, the accounts of Peter Wentworth (*Wentworth Papers, pp.* 222–3) and Burnet (Burnet, *op. cit.*, vol. VI, pp. 72–7), and Oxford's own embittered reflections (*Bol. Corr.*, vol. II, pp. 48–50).

[83] Swift, *Journal to Stella*, vol. II, p. 433.

reasons for the ministry's poor showing on 7 December had been the apparently deliberate failure of all but five of the Scottish representative peers to reach London in time to attend the crucial debate. On 20 December, in an attempt to perpetuate this division, the Whigs challenged the Duke of Hamilton's right to sit in the Lords by virtue of his British peerage.[84] From the Whig point of view the debate was an admirably staged affair since even a number of Tory peers were dubious about the constitutional propriety of Hamilton's grant, and, indeed, when, after eight hours of often heated argument, the House divided the Junto lords got home by fifty seven votes to fifty two. Hence, as Christmas approached, many of the ministry's most loyal friends began to entertain the thought that Oxford's days were strictly numbered. Swift caught the general mood when he informed Stella that, in his opinion, the administration was "certainly ruined".[85]

One of the Treasurer's most conspicuous qualities, however, was his political stamina. Others might be ready to throw in the sponge; he was not. Consequently, sometime in the second half of December he resolved to endeavour to persuade the Queen to take the dramatically bold, indeed, according to that amiable constitutional pedant, the Earl of Dartmouth, doubtfully legal step of creating no less than a dozen new government peers[86]— thereby restoring ministerial authority in the House. On 26 December Swift reported that Oxford had spent two hours with Anne and that Mrs. Masham was hopeful of the outcome. Next day the Treasurer scribbled down a list of the names of twenty one possible candidates for promotion to the peerage. Two days later Swift excitedly broke open the seal of his letter to Stella "to let you know that we are all safe",[87] and on the thirty-first the names of the twelve new lords were officially published in the London Gazette. When, on 2 January, the Lords reassembled it was clear that the crisis had passed. Despite the desertion of people like Thanet, Guernsey and Carteret a government motion for an adjournment was successfully carried.

[84] Holmes, "The Hamilton Affair", *loc. cit.*, p. 263 *et seq.*
[85] Swift, *Journal to Stella*, vol. II, p. 439.
[86] Burnet, *op. cit.*, vol. VI, p. 87, Dartmouth's note.
[87] Swift, *Journal to Stella*, vol. II, pp. 446–7, 449; Oxford's list, 27 Dec. 1711, B.M. Portland Loan, 10(16).

The ministerial victory of 2 January proved the great turning point in the peace struggle. From then on the opposition forces moved into rapid retreat. Both Marlborough and Somerset were peremptorily dismissed, and the General suffered the additional indignity, along with the Whig politician, Robert Walpole, of being accused in Parliament of financial corruption. For their part the Scots, after a somewhat pathetic attempt to organise a boycott of the Lords, came meekly to heel. But most significant of all was the reaction of the Junto Lords. Since the beginning of the reign they had been supreme in the Upper Chamber. Yet now, almost overnight, the steam and sparkle seemed to leave them. They still continued to force divisions whenever they could, and they were not without their minor successes. On 15 February, for example, they managed to get the Lords' approval for an address denouncing the French refusal to recognise the Queen's title.[88] But their opposition had lost its zest. When in September 1712, with all the ardour of the newly converted, Nottingham complained of the baleful effect Marlborough's projected flight abroad would have on opposition morale he received the tiredest of replies from the normally ebullient Sunderland:

> As to the present posture of our affairs they seem to be such that the quieter we are at present the better, for these people have by corruption, and one way or other, got such a majority in both Houses that till the nation open their eyes, which will never be till the peace is actually made and proclaimed, and then they will soon see the villainy and ruin of it though they are at present intoxicated with the expectation of it: till that is it seems to be running our heads against a wall to stir anything.[89]

---

[88] Nottingham to Lady Nottingham, 15 Feb. 1712, Northants. R.O., Finch-Hatton MSS., 281; same to same, 20 Feb. 1712, ibid.

[89] Sunderland to Nottingham, 26 Sep. 1712, Leicestershire R.O., Finch MSS., G.S., bundle 24. Lord Shaftesbury agreed with Sunderland's assessment of the situation: "We are now at the mercy of one single man [Oxford], who has all power in his hands, and every secret in his breast. How Providence may dispose that heart I know not. He has a head, indeed, but too able. Nor have we (in my opinion) a genius equal to oppose him. . . ." (Shaftesbury to Molesworth, 30 Aug. 1712, B. Rand (ed.), The Life, Unpublished Letters, and Philosophical Regimen of Anthony, Earl of Shaftesbury (London, 1900), p. 512).

All that Sunderland could offer on the positive side was that the opposition should be "upon the watch for any favourable accident that may happen". After the ministerial defeat on 7 December Wharton had told Oxford "by God, my Lord, if you can bear this, you are the strongest man in England".[90] In the interim the Treasurer had proved himself to be just that, and in their hearts the Junto lords knew it.

By 1712 it must have seemed to many that the Treasurer had at last reached political maturity. Ever since the disaster of 1708 his record had been impeccable. With considerable political finesse he had built up an impressive combination against the Marlborough–Whig administration, and then, piece by piece, he had taken the whole faction-ridden ministry apart. Once in power he had not only succeeded in taming the Bank, but he had also done much to help bring peace to Europe. To cap it all there was his parliamentary performance. Displaying both coolness and courage he had challenged the Junto lords, the toughest and most sophisticated party men of the period, in their strongest of strongholds, the Upper Chamber, and he had beaten them to their knees.[91] This was something which Godolphin had not only not done during his period of ascendancy, though sadly tried by Junto intransigence; it was a feat that he had not even dared to assay.

Once more, however, as with the story of Secretary Harley, there is a sting in the tail. If we look forward a year or so we find the political landscape completely altered. By 1714 the Junto lords were once again in full stride. In March and April of that year in particular they pummelled the ministry relentlessly on the succession question, raising issue after issue in the Upper House. Some of the votes were perilously close. On 5 April the government got home by a mere fourteen votes. Eight days later the Court majority sank to two. On this latter division Abel Boyer commented:

[90] R. Palmer to R. Verney, 11 Dec. 1711, *H.M.C. Verney MSS.*, p. 507.

[91] Daniel Defoe paid eloquent tribute to Junto toughness at this period. "I have not the fewest years over my head of any man that observes these things", he wrote in January 1712, "and I have seen many of these Court revolutions. But of all the outed parties that ever were seen, at least in the last 50 years, none ever pushed with so much fury at the government who have dismissed them as these have done. Nothing but downright taking of arms can be like this". (Defoe to Oxford, 10 Jan. 1712, *Defoe Letters*, p. 336).

This hard got victory of the Courtiers was by their antagonists treated as little better than a defeat. And it is certain that the Whig lords had that day carried their point were it not for the accidental loss of four votes: the Duke of Rutland being then at Newmarket with a proxy in his pocket; the Duke of Grafton being sent for home to his Duchess, then in travail with her first child; and the Earl of Gainsborough being taken so ill that morning that he was unable to sign his proxy. What was yet no less remarkable was that of sixteen bishops then in the House, two only (Rochester and Durham) voted with the Court; that the new Bishops of London and Bristol, who were thought blindly devoted to the ministry, sided with the Whigs, as did also the Earl of Anglesey. . . ."[92]

No wonder that Lord Bolingbroke should "hope never to see such another" session of Parliament.[93]

On its own the Whig recovery would have posed problems enough for the government, but matters were made much worse by the fact that the rise in Whig fortunes was accompanied by an alarming personal decline on the part of the premier. Oxford had never been a particularly lucid talker, but as his premiership wore on his speech became more and more opaque. Before the end of 1713 he had become all but incomprehensible. On 29 September Galke reported back to Hanover:

I am assured from all hands, especially by those who had business to transact with the Treasurer, that it is impossible to comprehend the answers he gives, much less to put them afterwards in writing. Besides, he frequently gives such as have no connexion with the proposals which were made to him. Again, when he takes me aside, and appears to speak with the

[92] Boyer, *History of Queen Anne*, p. 689. According to Peter Wentworth (*Wentworth Papers*, p. 368) voting was level –61/61– before proxies were counted. The debate arose out of the Queen's "dry answer" to the address of 8 April asking her to issue a reward for the apprehension of the Pretender. Viz: "It would be a real strengthening to the Succession in the House of Hanover as well as a support to my government that an end were put to these groundless fears and jealousies which have been so industriously promoted. I do not at this time see any occasion for such a proclamation. Whenever I judge it to be necessary, I shall give my orders for having one issued". (*Journals of the House of Lords*, XIX, p. 654). On the general parliamentary turmoil at this time see Cobbett, *op. cit.*, vol. VI, p. 1242 *et seq.*
[93] Bolingbroke to Shrewsbury, 13 April 1714, *Bol. Corr.*, vol. IV, p. 498.

utmost confidence to me, and to enter deep into business, he
leaves me, and bows to the right and to the left to those who
come in. All those in the room, who see such a farce, imagine
you have had an audience, and a favourable answer; and no
doubt but you to whom he spoke, knows that he said nothing
to you.

So marked was the deterioration that even the Queen felt con-
strained to take her Treasurer to task. "Now that I have a pen
in my hand", she wrote early in December, "I cannot help
desiring you again when you come next to speak plainly, lay
everything open and hide nothing, or else how is it possible I
can judge of anything".[94]

Moreover, unintelligibility was not the only symptom of
decay. The Treasurer also began to drink heavily, to stay up
later and later at night, and to neglect public business. Frequently he was not abroad before noon. Deeply disturbed by the
trend of events Auditor Harley wrote to his brother on 29 March
1714 exhorting him to pull himself together:

Permit me to hint that in the present situation the chief thing
to be intended is the obtaining an entire confidence with the
Queen by an insidious and punctual attendance, and often
expressing a resolution to do or hazard anything for her
service.

Frequent meetings with some Lords and Commons would
be of great service. In order to these it is necessary that you
should appropriate more time for the despatch of business, by
getting out earlier, and being freed from those who are only
the leeches of time. The leak that is sprung cannot be stopped
without pumping.[95]

By this time, however, Oxford had passed beyond the point of
no return. Indeed, realising that he had lost grip of the situation,
the premier began to talk seriously of resignation. In the end the
Queen herself was compelled to intervene. On 27 July, only five

[94] Galke to Robethon, 29 Sep. 1713 (N.S.), J. Macpherson (ed.), *Original Papers
containing the Secret History of Great Britain* (London, 1775), vol. II, p. 505; Anne to
Oxford, 8 Dec. 1713, Longleat, Portland MSS., III, f. 106.
[95] Auditor Harley to Oxford, 29 March 1714, *H.M.C. Portland MSS.*, V. p. 405.

days before she died, Anne finally took the staff of office away from her old friend. The Queen's explanation of her action provides us with a vivid description of Oxford's sad condition. She told the Lords

> that he neglected all business; that he was seldom to be understood; that when he did explain himself she could not depend upon the truth of what he said; that he never came to her at the time she appointed; that he often came drunk; that lastly, to crown all, he behaved himself towards her with ill manner, indecency and disrespect.[96]

All this was a far cry from 1712.

But what had brought about such a dramatic reversal of fortunes? Why had the Whigs recovered so completely? How can one explain Oxford's dreadful personal collapse? Was the premier perhaps still dogged in some way by his Country past? Or is the explanation simpler and less perplexing? In the next chapter an attempt is made to provide an answer to these questions.

---

[96] E. Lewis to Swift, 27 July 1714, *Swift Corr.*, vol. II, p. 199. For Oxford's thoughts of resignation see Oxford to Dartmouth, 25 Nov. 1713, Trevelyan, *op. cit.*, vol. III, pp. 260–1; Edward Harley's "Memoirs", *H.M.C. Portland MSS.*, V, p. 661; Harcourt to Oxford, 17 March 1714, *ibid.*, p. 400; Oxford to Harcourt, 19 March 1714, B.M. Portland Loan, 138(5); [Oxford] to [Anne], 9 June 1714 (draft), *ibid.*, 10(8); Oxford to Anne, 9 June 1714, Cobbett, *op. cit.*, vol. VI, pp. ccxliii–ccxliv.

7 Failure of a Prime Minister

HARLEY'S FALL IN 1708 has, over the years, proved a perplexing affair. Many contemporaries were at a loss to explain it, while, as we have seen, subsequent scholars have found a good deal in it upon which to disagree. On the other hand, the troubles which overtook the premier in 1714 seem, on the surface, more understandable. Both Oxford's personal collapse and the resurgence of the Whigs were, in a sense, natural events. The Treasurer's health had never been strong, and it was only to be expected that, with advancing years, plus the strains and the loneliness of supreme office, he would move into some sort of decline. Again, the powerful anti-Junto combination which Harley constructed in 1710 was by its very nature a temporary thing. All that held together its disparate elements was a common hatred of the five tyrannizing lords. It was inevitable, once the Junto regime had been overthrown, that, sooner or later, self opinionated men like Argyll and Somerset, who were basically Whig in outlook, would fall foul of the new rulers and drift over to swell the ranks of the opposition. Nevertheless, although the situation in 1714 undoubtedly has about it a certain air of inescapability, the scene would not have been anywhere near as bleak and dispiriting had it been merely the product of passing years. Oxford's most severe bout of illness, it is instructive to note, occurred in the summer and autumn of 1713.[1] By the beginning of 1714 he was well on the way to

---

[1] On 25 July 1713 Bolingbroke told Shrewsbury: "The Treasurer is again extremely ill, and I doubt his health is so shattered by frequent returns of illness, as to be little depended upon" (Bolingbroke to Shrewsbury, 25 July 1713, *Bol. Corr.*, vol. IV, p. 207). In a letter to John Drummond of the same date he diagnosed Oxford's malady as "a severe fit of gravel, an inflammation in his eyes, and a falling of the same, or some other humour, into his knees" (*Ibid.*, p. 208). For other references to the illness see Bolingbroke to Prior, 25 July 1713, *ibid.*, p. 205; Bolingbroke to Richmond, 30 July 1713, *ibid.*, p. 211; Bolingbroke to Strafford, 7 Aug. 1713, *ibid.*, p. 232; Anne to Oxford, 5, 20 and 21 July 1713, *H.M.C. Bath MSS.*, I,

recovery. Similarly the moderate Whig alliance had begun to look very sick long before the darkness came. Newcastle, for example, perhaps the premier's most important Whig supporter, was in his grave by July 1711, months before the Treasurer's hour of greatest triumph. Somerset had deserted even earlier.[2] Unquestionably the passage of time created severe problems for the government, but as the events above indicate these problems were by no means insurmountable. The dialectic of the situation ensured that Harley would have a rough passage during the course of his premiership. It does not, however, explain why he failed to weather the storm. For this we have to look elsewhere, at the internal history of the Tory Party rather than at the Whig resurgence or at Oxford's personal disintegration.

We have already noted that one of the reasons for the Whig triumph in the great peace debate in the Lords on 7 December 1711 was the Junto's success in securing the support of the Tory Earl of Nottingham. Nottingham's link-up with the opposition Whigs, however, was only one of a number of important Tory desertions from the government in the years after 1710. In fact, even before Dismal's much publicised change of allegiance one of these splits had already occurred. On 8 December 1710 Peter Wentworth wrote to his brother, Lord Raby, warning him that "a great many" of the rank and file Tories in the Commons were "resolved to proceed in methods of their own".[3] A month or so later this grumbling unrest at last came to a head with the founding of the October Club.[4]

---

pp. 235–6; Shrewsbury to Oxford, 1/11 Aug. 1713, ibid., p. 237; Lady Bolingbroke to Oxford, 9 Aug, 1713, *H.M.C. Portland MSS.*, V, p. 321. There is evidence to suggest that as late as October the Treasurer was still far from well. (Anne to Oxford, 6 Oct. 1713, *H.M.C. Bath MSS.*, I, p. 239; Shrewsbury to Oxford, 9 Oct. 1713, *ibid.*, p. 240; Elizabeth to Abigail Harley, 10 Oct. 1713, B.M. Portland Loan 67(3)).

[2] Peter Wentworth to Lord Raby, 26 Sep. 1710, *Wentworth Papers*, pp. 143–5. Cf. Swift's account, Swift, "The History of the Four Last Years of the Queen", *Prose Works of Swift*, vol. X, pp. 31–4. Newcastle died on 15 July as a result of a fall from his horse while out stag hunting.

[3] Wentworth to Raby, 8 Dec. 1710, *Wentworth Papers*, p. 161.

[4] The earliest references to the Club date from February 1711. E.g. Tullie House, Carlisle, Bishop Nicolson's MS. Diary, 6 Feb. 1711; Swift, *Journal to Stella*, vol. I, p. 194 (18 Feb. 1711); Francis Legh to Peter Legh, 20 Feb. 1711, Lady Newton (ed.), *Lyme Letters*, 1660–1760 (London, 1925), p. 303.

The October Club, so called "because the strongest beer is brewed in the month of October",[5] consisted of some 150 Tory squires who met regularly at the Bell Tavern in King Street, Westminster, to sup ale and discuss parliamentary tactics. Before long this "set of high, hot, out of temper politicians"[6] was successfully carrying divisions against the Court as well as against the Whigs. By the spring of 1711 the situation in the Commons had become so serious that the whole of the ministry's financial programme seemed on the point of grinding to a halt. "The nearer I look upon things", observed Swift gloomily, "the worse I like them. I believe the confederacy will soon break to pieces; and our factions at home increase. The ministry is upon a very narrow bottom, and stands like an isthmus between the Whigs on one side and the violent Tories on the other. They are able seamen, but the tempest is too great, the ship too rotten, and the crew all against them".[7] Indeed, it was only the most fortunate of accidents which saved the day. On 8 March 1711 Antoine de Guiscard, formerly Abbé de la Bourlie, was summoned before a meeting of the Committee of the Council to be examined on a charge of treason. As the Frenchman prepared to leave after the interrogation he suddenly produced a knife, leapt forward, and stabbed Harley twice in the chest. Happily 8 March was the anniversary of the Queen's accession, and to celebrate the occasion the premier was wearing his best blue and silver waistcoat. This garment, heavily embroidered with flowers, absorbed much of the force of Guiscard's onslaught and, together with his jacket and stomacher, prevented the blows from being fatal.[8] Nevertheless, Harley's wound was sufficiently bad to keep him out of politics for over six weeks.

As news of the attempted assassination spread a huge wave of sympathy for the stricken minister gathered and spilt out

---

[5] Robethon to the Elector of Hanover, 21 March 1711, Churchill, *op. cit.*, vol. 2, p. 800.

[6] D. Defoe, *The Secret History of the White Staff* (London, 1714), p. 22.

[7] Swift, *Journal to Stella*, vol. I, p. 206.

[8] On the significance of Harley's waistcoat see Harley to Abigail Harley, 22 March 1711, *H.M.C. Portland MSS.*, V, pp. 668–70. The fullest account of the affair is that given by Auditor Harley in his "Memoirs", B.M. Lansdowne MSS., 885, ff. 30–9.

over the countryside.[9] The Queen herself was so overwhelmed with grief and anxiety that she became physically ill, and at five o'clock on the morning of Saturday 10 March four of her doctors had to be hastily summoned to attend at the royal bedside. Even Harley's enemies began to melt. On 27 March, after informing his brother of the loss of the Leather Tax in the Lower House, Peter Wentworth observed that "several politicians that could not endure Mr. Harley say they see now there's no man the Court employs has address enough to manage the House of Commons but him; if he had been well he would either have had intelligence of what was intended and so have endeavoured to have brought them to the House in a better temper, or at least when there would have put it off for a fitter opportunity". Such was the revulsion in Harley's favour that by mid April the Junto lords of all people were offering the premier pledges of their loyalty and support. Swift probably accurately summed up the feelings of most patriotic Englishmen when he penned his celebrated "Lines to Mr. Harley's Surgeon":

> On Britain Europe's safety lies,
> And Britain's lost if Harley dies,
> Harley depends upon your skill,
> Think what you save or what you kill.[10]

Hence, when, in May, Harley returned in triumph to the Commons to announce his South Sea scheme, the October men found their belligerence ebbing away. Caught up in the general euphoria, they at last came to heel and allowed supply to go through the Lower Chamber.[11] Even so it had been a close call.

---

[9] E.g. W. Alwood to Harley, 19 March 1711, B.M. Portland Loan, 125(4). This letter which speaks of Harley's "deliverance from the Popish rage which picked you out as the minister from whom it met with the chief obstruction" as "a national blessing" is typical of the many messages of sympathy the premier received at this time from people of all walks of life.

[10] Kreienberg's report 13/24 March 1711, Staatsarchiv Hannover; Wentworth to Raby, 27 March 1711, Wentworth Papers, pp. 189–90; Poulett to Harley, 18 April 1711, H.M.C. Portland MSS., IV, p. 674; Halifax to Harley, 18 April 1711, ibid., p. 675; Edward Harley's "Memoirs", ibid., V. p. 655; Poems of Swift, vol. I, p. 140.

[11] L'Hermitage's report, 4/15 May 1711, B.M. Additional MSS., 17,677 EEE, f. 193; Swift "History of the Four Last Years of the Queen", Prose Works of Swift, vol. X, p. 120.

Moreover, although the great days of Octoberist activity were now unquestionably at an end, both the Club and the October spirit lived on giving the government cause for concern for the rest of the reign.

For the ministry both the defection of Nottingham and the October Club revolt were painful body blows. Still more damaging was the fissure which opened up between Harley and his chief lieutenant Secretary of State Henry St. John. There had long been rumours of unrest between the two men,[12] but the first really serious evidence of division occurred at the time of the Guiscard affair. For some while a plan to send a military expedition to attack the French possessions in Canada had been under discussion in the Cabinet. Harley was known to be severely critical of the scheme. However, the whole project, with its dashing prospect of imperial dominion, appealed strongly to St. John's mercurial temperament. Accordingly when Harley was laid low by Guiscard's attack the Secretary hurriedly seized the opportunity of his chief's absence to press forward with the scheme. Alarmed, Harley did what he could from his sick bed to reassert control by sending Rochester with his "dying request" that the scheme be abandoned. But all was to no avail.[13] The Secretary now had the bit firmly between his teeth and nothing could hold him back. The expedition was rapidly equipped, and early in May it set sail under the joint command of Rear-Admiral Sir Hovenden Walker and Brigadier Jack Hill, Abigail's brother. The ill feeling that all this engendered was greatly enhanced by the fact that a number of St. John's followers spread the tale that Guiscard's knife had been intended for their master, not for Harley.[14] This attempt on the part of the St. John group to gain the glory of the assassination attempt while at the same time profiting by the premier's enforced inactivity was adding insult to injury with a vengeance.

[12] E.g. [Harley] to [Mansell], 30 Sep. 1709, N.L.W., Penrice and Margam MSS., L. 648.
[13] Edward Harley's "Memoirs", *H.M.C. Portland MSS.*, V. p. 655; Rochester to Harley, 18 April 1711, *ibid.*, IV, p. 675; St. John to Harley, 19 April 1711, *ibid.*, p. 675.
[14] Edward Harley's "Memoirs", *H.M.C. Portland MSS.*, V. p. 654; Swift, "Memoirs relating to that Change in the Queen's Ministry in 1710", *Prose Works of Swift*, vol, V, p. 389; "An Enquiry into the Behaviour of the Queen's Last Ministry", *ibid.*, pp. 440–1.

Thus when Harley returned to the political scene at the end of April relations between the two chief ministers were by no means at their most cordial, and in the months which followed things went from bad to worse. By August 1711 the division between the two men was common knowledge. On the twenty seventh Swift reported:

The Whigs whisper that our new ministry differ among themselves and they begin to talk out Mr. Secretary. They have some reason for their whispers, although I thought it was a great secret. I do not much like the posture of things; I always apprehended that any falling out would ruin them, and so I have told them several times. The Whigs are mighty full of hopes at present; and whatever is the matter all kinds of stocks fall.

The news of the failure of the Quebec expedition which reached England in the autumn added another source of discord. Oxford, "just as merry as usual", was clearly untroubled by the disaster. St. John, on the other hand, "much mortified" by the failure of his pet project, did not scruple to ascribe the miscarriage to the Treasurer's lukewarmness. Then in April 1712 the Secretary quarrelled openly with the staunch Oxford man, Richard Savage, Earl Rivers.[15] A few months later came the disastrous incident of his elevation to the peerage. The Secretary confidently expected an earldom for his part in negotiating the peace settlement; indeed he had specifically asked Oxford for such an honour. Consequently when in July he was fobbed off with a mere viscounty his rage against his chief reached boiling point. "I own to you", he confided to his friend Strafford on the twenty third, "that I felt more indignation than ever in my life I had done; and the only consideration which kept me from running to extremes was that . . . any appearance of a breach between myself and the Lord Treasurer would give our common enemies spirit. To friendship, therefore, and the public good . . . I sacrificed my private resentment, and remain clothed with as

---

[15] Swift, *Journal to Stella*, vol. I, p. 346, vol. II, p. 378; Rivers to Oxford, 7 April 1712, *H.M.C. Portland MSS.*, V, p. 162.

little of the Queen's favour as she could contrive to bestow".[16] The following October Bolingbroke's pride took another terrible blow when six new Knights of the Garter were created and he was passed over in favour of such nonentities as Poulett, Beaufort and the Whig Duke of Kent. So deeply did the Secretary resent this second insult that his anger still burned undiminished a year later.[17] All hope of a real *rapprochement* between the two men was now at an end. From this point on one can discern only brief periods of reconciliation between them.

What made the quarrel with Bolingbroke so especially serious was the fact that the Secretary did not remain content to criticise the ministry as the October Club had done, or even to join forces with the opposition like Nottingham. His aim was nothing less than to wrest the leadership of the government from Oxford by blackening the Treasurer in the eyes of the ministry's supporters.[18] One reason why he pushed the appointment of Jack Hill to the joint command of the Quebec expedition, for example, was that he hoped thereby to win the applause of Abigail. He also took pains to ensure that the royal favourite profited financially from the venture.[19] Even more blatant was the Secretary's courtship of the Queen in 1714. In this last difficult year of the reign Oxford tried to treat the successive crises which confronted the government in a statesmanlike manner— even if this involved taking an unpopular line. Bolingbroke, however, thought only of playing to the gallery, When, for instance, in April, Baron Schütz, the Hanoverian agent in London, urged on by the Junto, and pressed by that "merry old woman that has but one tooth in her head",[20] the octogenarian Dowager Electress Sophia, presented himself before Chancellor Harcourt and requested that the young Electoral Prince be

[16] St. John to Oxford, [28 June 1712?], *ibid.*, p. 194; Bolingbroke to Strafford, 23 July 1712, *Bol. Corr.*, vol. II, pp. 484–5. Cf. St. John to Oxford, 3 July 1712, *H.M.C. Portland MSS.*, V, p. 198.

[17] Boyer, *History of Queen Anne*, p. 605; Oxford's "Account of Public Affairs", *H.M.C. Portland MSS.*, V, p. 465; Duchess of Marlborough to Lady Cowper, 2 Oct. 1713, Herts R.O., Panshanger MSS., Cowper Family Books, I.

[18] In Lockhart's words the Secretary "affected daily to be more and more popular [with the Tories], and aimed at nothing less than being prime minister of state". *Lockhart Papers*, vol. I, p. 412.

[19] On the financial side of the venture see Oxford's "Account of Public Affairs", *H.M.C. Portland MSS.*, V. p. 465; Edward Harley's "Memoirs", *ibid.*, p. 655.

[20] Lord Stawell to Lord Dartmouth, N.D., W.S.L. Dartmouth MSS., D. 1778. V. 1089.

summoned to take his seat in Parliament in virtue of his English title as Duke of Cambridge, the two men reacted entirely differently. Oxford saw that the request must be complied with even though it afronted Anne, who had a horror of seeing any member of the Hanoverian family in England during her lifetime. Bolingbroke on the other hand, oblivious to wider issues, seized the opportunity to ingratiate himself with the Queen by delivering a hectoring attack upon Schütz in the Cabinet.[21]

One further Tory defection deserves mention—the revolt of the Whimsical or Hanoverian Tories. Ever since the conclusion of the October Preliminaries in 1711 a number of Tory M.P.s. had looked with suspicion upon what they regarded as the growing friendship between Louis XIV's regime and the Oxford ministry. In June 1713 this current of unease was given tangible form when some 80 Tory members joined with the Whigs in the Lower Chamber to reject the Commercial Treaty with France negotiated by Bolingbroke as part and parcel of the Utrecht settlement.[22] It is true, of course, that a good deal of the Tory disquiet over the issue can be traced to purely economic factors. Perhaps through over hastiness, Bolingbroke had succeeded in producing an agreement which seemed to many to be harmful rather than advantageous to English trade, and it is clear that in casting their votes against the Bill men like Peter Shakerley, the member for Chester, and the four London M.P.s were acting under pressure from mercantile interests in their constituencies.[23] Nevertheless there is no question that many of

---

[21] For a general account of the affair see W. Michael, *England Under George I: The Beginnings of the Hanoverian Dynasty* (London, 1936), pp. 29–32. On the divergent attitudes of Bolingbroke and Oxford see also Harcourt's "Account about Mr. Schütz", B.M. Portland Loan, 138(5), and Edward Harley's "Memoirs", *H.M.C. Portland MSS.*, V, p. 662.

[22] Justinian Isham's estimate that "Sir Thomas Hanmer and about 80 of our friends" voted against the Commerce Bill (Justinian Isham to his father Justinian Isham, Northants. R.O., Isham Corr., 2325), is borne out by the division list printed in the anonymous tract *A Letter from a Member of the H[ouse] of C[ommons] to his Friend in the Country relating to the Bill of Commerce* (London, 1713), which lists 79 Tories among those who opposed the Bill. This pamphlet is also important for another reason: it indicates that there had been unrest among the Tory rank and file over the government's attitude to France for some time. It does this by drawing a distinction between 44 of the Tory rebels, "which were hardly ever known to struggle from us but this once", and the remaining 35, described by the author as "whimsicals"—i.e. Tories who had opposed the ministry on a number of previous occasions.

[23] Trevelyan, *op. cit.*, vol. III, p. 257.

the Tory rebels were opposed to the commercial settlement at least in part because they saw it as a symbol of dangerous Francophile and even Jacobite tendencies in the government. As the months passed this fear of Jacobitism grew apace. Consequently, when, from March 1714 onwards, the Whig leaders forced a number of divisions on the succession issue which were unconnected with commerce they continued to receive valuable support from this Whimsical wing of the Tories.[24]

By the end of the reign, then, the Tory Party was riven by discord and division, and it was this great series of cracks in the ministerial amalgam which lay at the root of the despairing situation in 1714. The Whigs, for instance, were only able to hammer the government so hard in the parliamentary crisis of March and April because they received invaluable support from Nottingham and the Hanoverian Tories. Moreover, for the Junto this Tory help was not just a question of counting heads. It also had a psychological aspect, an aspect which was eagerly exploited by the five lords with all their old panache. In debate after debate, so as to emphasize the sad disarray of the ministry, the Whig leaders kept as far as possible in the background and pushed forward the rebels to do the talking. Hence, when, on 5 April, during a debate on the state of the nation, the Lords moved on to consider the dangers besetting the Protestant succession, it was not Wharton or Somers who stole the limelight, but the Whimsical Tory Anglesey. Upon hearing the Earl of Ferrers smoothly declare that the Hanoverian cause was perfectly safe in the hands of the Oxford ministry, Anglesey "got up in great warmth and said he was surprised, after what had appeared in the House, that any Lord could make such a motion". He then launched into a fiery speech in which he "ripped up the peace" and expatiated on the manifold perils threatening the Protestant interest.[25] This spectacle of Tory slaying Tory, repeated over and over again in the closing phase of the reign, gave a new lease of life to the opposition. The Junto sparkle, which had faded badly after the Whig defeat over the

<hr/>

[24] The fortunes of the Whimsicals are traced in detail in the correspondence in B.M. Stowe MSS., 225–7.

[25] Percival Letterbook, Sir John Percival to his brother, 8 April 1714, B.M. Additional MSS., 47,087 (unfoliated). Cf. Bathurst to Strafford, 6 April 1714, *Wentworth Papers*, pp. 362–5.

peace, now returned in all its former glory. Correspondingly, the zest and confidence of the ministry sagged visibly.

Just as the Whig revival derived its edge from rebel support in this way, so too Oxford's personal troubles were intimately linked with the Tory disunity. In the early eighteenth century the premiership was almost by definition a lonely eminence. For Oxford, however, both the isolation and strain of his position were increased many times by the successive rebellions he had to face. By the end of the reign so many of the Treasurer's nominal supporters had moved into semi-opposition that Oxford could trust nobody but himself and a small circle of friends.[26] This meant that he was often compelled to handle even the most trivial tasks personally for fear of being stabbed in the back. At the Treasury things were not so bad as here the premier was able to fill a number of the important minor offices with members of his own family. In particular his son-in-law, George Hay, Viscount Dupplin, was appointed as one of the four Tellers of Receipt in July 1711, while early in 1713 Thomas Foley joined Edward Harley as Auditor of the Imprest.[27] But elsewhere it was a jungle. Bolingbroke himself, in attempting to diagnose the ills of the ministry, saw where the trouble lay. "You are forced", he wrote to Oxford, "to execute more than you should and cannot therefore supervise. You are pulling at the beam when you should be in the box whipping and reining in". Dr. Radcliffe, the eminent physician, also apparently understood the symptoms. Lockhart records how the worthy doctor, when summoned to attend Oxford during one of his bouts of illness, "prescribed to him to read a certain portion of the Old Testament, which, after the doctor was gone, he [Oxford] found was the advice given to Moses by his father-in-law, to choose a certain number of wise men to assist him in the administration of affairs".[28] The trouble was, of course, as Bolingbroke well knew, the Treasurer had not elected to govern without "wise men" but had had it "forced" upon him, and this

---

[26] The Treasurer, averred Lockhart, had "fewer personal friends . . . than any minister that ever sat at the helm of affairs". *Lockhart Papers*, vol. I, p. 369. Cf. Shaftesbury to Furley, 18 Oct. 1712 (N.S.), Rand, *Life of Shaftesbury*, p. 519.

[27] 23 July 1711, *Calendar of Treasury Books*, vol. XXV, p. 379; 22 Jan. 1713, *ibid.*, vol. XXVII, p. 89.

[28] Bolingbroke to Oxford, 27 July 1713, *H.M.C. Portland MSS.*, V, p. 311; *Lockhart Papers*, vol. I, p. 369.

involuntary isolation contributed in full measure to his personal decline in the dying months of the reign.

However, the premier's descent into besotted indolence was not entirely a question of cracking under the strain. The succession of Tory rebellions contributed in another and equally significant way to Oxford's "impotent, womanish behaviour"[29] in 1714. As defection followed defection one avenue of movement after another began to close down to the Treasurer, so that by the final phase of the reign his opportunities for action were severely circumscribed. As the Queen, for example, wooed by Bolingbroke, drifted away from him, he was less and less able to persuade her to adopt his policies. Similarly, as his command over the Tory legions weakened, the list of things he could assay in Parliament dwindled rapidly. It is most instructive to note that in certain areas and on certain occasions Oxford remained as active and effective as he had ever been. In February 1714, for instance, he despatched Thomas Harley to Hanover with a most subtly framed series of instructions which reveal all his old diplomatic skill.[30] Again, when, two months later, the Junto launched an attack in the Lords on the administration's policy of paying small bribes to the highland clans, Oxford rose and delivered a brilliant speech that completely transformed the debate. As a result what had begun as an attempt to sink the government ended in a vote of confidence in the Treasurer.[31] But most remarkable of all was the premier's unwavering performance at the Treasury, which, as we have seen, was safely staffed with his intimate relations. Abel Boyer has left us a description of one especially resourceful move that occurred in September 1713:

An advertisement had been inserted in the *London Gazette* whereby it was proposed to raise three hundred thousand

[29] E. Lewis to Swift, 24 July 1714, *Swift Corr.*, vol. II, p. 194.

[30] Thomas Harley's instructions, 11 Feb. 1714, B.M. Additional MSS., 40,621, ff. 169–70. Thomas was to point out that the succession was secured by Act of Parliament, the declarations of the Queen and the oaths of her statesmen, and to ask what additional securities were required. If any were suggested he was empowered to say that the Queen would actively promote such proposals which were consistent with her safety and with the law. On top of this Harley was authorised to promise payment of the arrears of the Hanoverian troops and to offer a pension to the Electress Sophia (Oxford to Thomas Harley, March 1714, *ibid.*, ff. 177–80).

[31] Bathurst to Strafford, 20 April 1714, *Wentworth Papers*, pp. 373–4.

pounds . . . by way of loan on the security of South Sea stock . . . Not above seventy thousand pounds were subscribed into this loan in six or seven weeks, which made many believe it would never be filled up. But upon an order issued out on the ninth of September by the Lord Treasurer importing that whoever should subscribe one hundred pounds to the said loan should be entitled to buy ten tickets of ten pounds each in the household lottery of five hundred thousand pounds, there was the next day such a crowd of subscribers . . . that more than the said three hundred thousand pounds were subscribed. Hereupon the Lord Treasurer, improving the opportunity and the eagerness of the money adventurers, enlarged the loan to five hundred thousand pounds, which in a few days was filled up, as was at the same time the lottery of the like sum: so that by this means the Lord Treasurer raised a million sterling in two or three days, which did much advance his credit and reputation.[32]

A glance at the pages of the Treasury books shows that this particular incident was no fluke. To the end the premier remained firm and meticulous in his control of finance. All these examples indicate that one can easily exaggerate Oxford's physical crumbling in his last year of power. Where his way was not blocked off by lack of support he could still perform with applause. Paradoxical though it may seem the Treasurer was under employed as well as overworked. His inaction and hard drinking were as much the result of frustration as of excessive strain.

By now enough has been said to indicate that both Oxford's personal afflictions and also the revival in Whig fortunes at the close of the reign derived their real force from the numerous cleavages in the government camp. Hence, in order fully to understand the Treasurer's slide from the commanding heights of 1711–12 it is imperative to explain why these various fissures opened up. Here it must be admitted that each defection is to some extent a story on its own. Nottingham's protest, for example, was in part sheer frustrated ambition. In 1704 Dismal had resigned the fruits of office for the Tory cause. Accordingly

[32] Boyer, *History of Queen Anne*, p. 650.

he expected lavish reward in 1710. When this was not forthcoming his anger was extreme. On the other hand, the Oxford–
Bolingbroke clash had about it much more the air of a conflict of
personalities. Temperamentally the two men were at opposite
poles, the Secretary youthful, quick-witted, urbane, ambitious,
the Treasurer plodding, moralistic and old beyond his years.
Again, the October Club rebellion was, in some measure at
least, a back-bench revolt against the centre, Countrymen
versus Courtiers. On this point the report of the Dutch agent,
L'Hermitage, on the formation of the Tory March Club in 1712
is revealing. "All the Club's members", he wrote, "were in the
October Club . . . They left it because a minister of state [Henry
St. John] joined it and came to be elected President of it, and
they do not wish to be governed by the Court".[33] Even so, although each separate movement had its own distinctive characteristics, the rebellions resembled one another far more than
they differed. All the revolts were linked together by a common
theme—their party character. Without this common aspect a
number of the movements may never have got under way. Certainly none of them would have taken the extreme turn which
they did.

To appreciate the nature of this underlying party theme it is
essential to glance briefly at Oxford's attitude to party during
the course of his premiership. Despite the fact that in 1710
Harley had been swept in on a great tide of Tory triumph, his
attitude to party seems to have altered very little from what it
had been during his spell as Secretary of State. The Harleyite
pamphlet *Faults on Both Sides*,[34] for instance, which appeared in
1710, and may perhaps with some justice be regarded as the
new premier's manifesto, set out in unblushing terms all the old,
familiar themes. In it the evils of party rule from the Commonwealth onwards were laid bare and castigated. "From the beginning of our contests to this very time", the author asserted,
"party leaders have inflamed the people with talk of the public
good till the heads and leaders of either side could get themselves into the saddle, and then they have driven on their own

---

[33] L'Hermitage's report, 1 April 1712, G. S. Holmes and W. A. Speck (eds.),
The Divided Society: Parties and Politics in England, 1694–1716 (London, 1967), p. 151.
Cf. Wentworth to Strafford, 8 April 1712, *Wentworth Papers*, pp. 283–4.
[34] *Faults on Both Sides* is reprinted in *Somers Tracts*, vol. XII, pp. 678–707.

6

interests". This "poisoning our constitution" which had so long
bled the nation, he insisted, must now stop, and he pledged that
for the future Anne was "firmly resolved against all extremes".
"She will", he continued, "bear equal regard to men that behave themselves well of either side, and desires that the names
of parties and factions may be buried in oblivion". To drive
home the point he warned that any Tories admitted to the
ministry would be expected to "come into moderate measures".
"When any of them act otherwise", he concluded, "they will be
laid by".

That the blueprint sketched in *Faults on Both Sides* was intended seriously is clearly shown if we examine Harley's efforts
at ministry building in the autumn of 1710. He went to inordinate lengths to dissuade Whigs like Walpole and Cowper from
leaving the government. Indeed, his pursuit of Cowper amounted to little short of persecution. Both personally and through
Newcastle's aide, Robert Monckton, Harley bombarded the
Whig Lord Chancellor almost daily with entreaties to stay in
office. To convince Cowper of his sincerity the new premier
persuaded the Attorney General, Sir James Montagu, to vacate
his post in return for a pension and bestowed the honour
on Harcourt, the obvious Tory candidate for the Great
Seal. When on 22 September Cowper tried to resign Anne,
prompted by Harley, handed back the seals no less than five
times.[35]

In the event Harley's efforts to win over Cowper, Boyle[36] and
Walpole proved unavailing. Even so, the actual Cabinet that
did emerge in 1710 was still surprisingly non-partisan in

[35] E. C. Hawtrey (ed.), *The Private Diary of William, first Earl Cowper, Lord
Chancellor of England* (Eton, 1833), *sub* September 1710. For Harcourt's replacement
of Montagu see Montagu to Harley, 17 Sep. 1710, *H.M.C. Portland MSS.*, IV, p.
595; Marlborough to the Duchess of Marlborough, 4 Oct. 1710 (N.S.), Blenheim
MSS., E5. On Walpole: W. Coxe, *Memoirs of the Life and Administration of Sir Robert
Walpole, Earl of Orford* (London, 1816), vol. I, pp. 57–9.
[36] A letter from Harley in the Chatsworth archive reveals how anxious the
premier was to secure Boyle's co-operation at this time: "It has been either your
fault, or mine, that we have not of late talked more freely together. I broke the
ground last night, though it cost me a whole night's want of sleep. Yet I received some
comfort this morning [when] the Queen was pleased to tell me that you were
easier. I beg I may have another opportunity to discourse [with] you before you
determine yourself; and I flatter myself I can make all your objections vanish".
Harley to Boyle, 11 Aug. 1710, Chatsworth MSS., Devonshire Family Papers,
102.2.

character. St. John, it is true, secured a Secretaryship of State, and his friend Granville was made Secretary-at-War. But, on the other hand, Newcastle, to Harley's infinite satisfaction, retained the Privy Seal, while Shrewsbury, as Lord Chamberlain, used his immense prestige to damp party animosity. Queensberry, too, continued as third Secretary, and through him the government held the allegiance of the Scottish Presbyterians. Harcourt's acquisition of the Great Seal was balanced by the retention of Somerset as Master of the Horse and by the appointment of the Whig Admiral Sir John Leake to the chair of the new Admiralty Board. Nottingham was pointedly omitted, and the only members of the Tory old guard who got high office were Buckingham as Lord Steward and the Lord Lieutenant of Ireland, Ormonde. Admittedly Rochester, the Queen's uncle, became Lord President, but this particular leopard had radically changed his spots since tacker days, and from 1710 until his death the following year he acted as a loyal Harleyite, behaving, in St. John's estimation, with "more temper and moderation than he had ever showed in his life".[37]

If one turns from the major to the minor office holders the picture presented is the same. At this lower end of the scale large numbers of Whigs were retained. Sir John Holland and Lord Cholmondeley, for example, kept their posts as Comptroller and Treasurer of the Queen's Household. Other Whigs reprieved included the Postmaster General Sir Thomas Frankland, his Irish counterpart Isaac Manley, Richard Steele, Commissioner of the Stamp Office, and Swift's friend Sir Matthew Dudley. That all this was not just forgetfulness on Harley's part was clearly shown in the last week of September when the veteran Whig spokesman John Smith was appointed a Teller of the Exchequer.[38] On the local level, too, the new premier stubbornly resisted a purge. The only major changes we hear of

[37] St. John to Drummond, 10 Nov. 1710, *Bol. Corr.*, vol. I, p. 18. On hearing the news of Rochester's death Archbishop King wrote: "The death of the Earl of Rochester is a great blow to all good men . . . I was of the opinion that he contributed much to keep things steady". (King to Swift, 15 May 1711, *Swift Corr.*, vol. I, p. 262). The major office holders in 1710 are listed in Trevelyan, *op. cit.*, vol. III, pp. 322–3.

[38] Swift, *Journal to Stella*, vol. I, pp. 11–12, 44; vol. II, p. 434; Wentworth to Raby, 26 Sep. 1710, *Wentworth Papers*, p. 144.

in the counties are the appointments of Beaufort and Hamilton to the Lieutenancies of Hampshire and Lancashire, the replacement of Godolphin by Rochester in Cornwall, and the nomination of the Tory soldier General John Webb to the Governorship of the Isle of Wight. In addition, the London Lieutenancy was refashioned—but this was a specific attempt on Harley's part to prevent the election of the dangerously unco-operative Heathcote as Lord Mayor.[39] In any case, all these changes were more than offset in Tory eyes by the stunning announcement that none other than Lord Cowper had been designated Lord Lieutenant of Hertfordshire.[40] Even the Whig hack Oldmixon was forced to concede Harley's moderation, though, characteristically, he ascribed the premier's indulgence towards his opponents to the "small number of men there was in his party who had heads fit for business".[41]

This middle-of-the-way mentality which characterised Harley's attitude in 1710 remained with him to the very end of the reign. At first he brushed aside Tory criticisms with the not unreasonable excuse that both the delicate state of government finances and the paramount necessity of bringing peace to Europe enjoined caution. However, even after credit had been restored and peace safely signed and sealed, he clung limpetlike to the same course. As George Lockhart bitterly observed: "everybody now expected my Lord Oxford, even for his own sake, would reform what he had so frequently and solemnly undertaken; but his Lordship jogged on in the same old way."[42] It is true, as Mr. Holmes has pointed out, that by the beginning of 1714 only thirteen Whig peers survived among the sixty nine Queen's servants in the House of Lords.[43] But this gradual erosion of the Court Whig element had been accomplished despite the Treasurer rather than because of him. Oxford's continuing antipathy to Tory dominance is plainly revealed by the

<hr />

[39] Boyer, *History of Queen Anne*, pp. 476–7; Oldmixon, *op. cit.*, p. 451. There seems to have been general surprise that the London Lieutenancy was not changed sooner. See *Wentworth Papers*, p. 140.

[40] Bromley to Harley, 12 Aug. 1710, *H.M.C. Portland MSS.*, IV, p. 563; Ralph Freeman to Harley, 13 Aug. 1710, *ibid.*, pp. 563–4; Stratford to Edward "Lord" Harley, 13 Aug. 1710, *ibid.*, VII, p. 11.

[41] Oldmixon, *op. cit.*, p. 450.

[42] *Lockhart Papers*, vol. I, p. 438. Cf. Bolingbroke, "A letter to Sir William Windham", *The Works of Bolingbroke*, vol. I, p. 22.

[43] Holmes, *British Politics in the Age of Anne*, pp. 402, 436–9.

stand he took in the great Tory *cause célèbre* of the 1714 session of Parliament, the Schism Act agitation. So quintessentially Tory was the Schism Act, which aimed at closing Nonconformist schools, that it succeeded in temporarily winning back to the government banner such staunch Whimsicals as Hanmer and Anglesey.[44] However, Oxford was clearly completely out of sympathy with the measure. When, for example, it was proposed in the Lords that a Presbyterian deputation be heard against the Bill it was observed that all the Treasurer's friends supported the motion and that the great man himself pointedly left the Chamber early to avoid the vote. In the Commons Auditor Harley actually spoke and voted against the Bill itself, while when the final debate came on in the Upper Chamber the premier "sat dumb and swelling with a discontent that visibly spoke his affections to the Bill".[45] Far from agreeing with the advocates of Tory Power, Oxford was, in his last months in office, busily engaged in attempting to negotiate a *rapprochement* with the Whigs in order to save England from "the brink of ruin".[46]

It was this dogged refusal on the part of the premier to become a purely Tory leader, even though the Church Party had won a crushing victory at the polls, which provided the common theme for all the anti-government revolts we have listed. The October Club, for instance, was not just a collection of backbenchers. It was also, and primarily, a group of zealous Tories. Among its members were such lusty old tackers as Sir John Packington and Sir Robert Davers, as well as out and out Jacobites like George Lockhart and William Shippen. The prime concern of these men was not to promote place bills, but to shake the ministry out of its moderation. Their aim, averred

[44] One Tory who did not return to the fold was Nottingham. Indeed, he even went so far as to deliver a speech against the Bill, concluding in admirable Whig fashion "by alluding to a passage in the Acts when St. Paul was in danger of shipwreck, that unless men stay together in the ship we must all perish". (N.N. to N.N., 3 June 1714, Somers MSS., Surrey R.O., Acc. 775, 02/60).

[45] Boyer, *History of Queen Anne*, p. 705; *Lockhart Papers*, vol. I, p. 462; L'Hermitage's report, 1/12 June 1714, B.M. Additional MSS., 17, 677 HHH, f. 238; Bolingbroke, *Considerations on the Secret History of the White Staff* (London, 1715), pp. 22-3.

[46] Cowper to Oxford, 30 March, 1 April 1714, B.M. Portland Loan, 132(3); same to same, 14 May 1714, *H.M.C. Portland MSS.*, IV, p. 440; Halifax to Oxford, 8 May, 13 May, 29 May 1714, *ibid.*, pp. 437, 438, 451; Oxford to Cowper, 12 May, 30 May 1714, Herts. R.O., Panshanger MSS., box 33. The quotation is from Halifax to Oxford, 21 April 1714, B.M. Portland Loan, 151(8).

Swift, was to "drive things on to extremes, to call the old ministry to account, and get off five or six heads".[47]

In a similar way, St. John's quarrel with his chief was far more than a personal difference.

> I am afraid [he confessed in his *Letter to Sir William Windham*] that we came to Court in the same dispositions as all parties have done; that the principal spring of our actions was to have the government of the state in our hands; that our principal views were the conservation of this power, great employments to ourselves, and great opportunities of rewarding those who had helped to raise us, and of hurting those who stood in opposition to us . . . The view therefore of those amongst us who thought in this manner, was to improve the Queen's favour, to break the body of the Whigs, and to render their supports useless to them, to fill the employments of the king-dom down to the meanest with Tories.[48]

In setting up as Oxford's rival the Secretary was endeavouring to replace a milk and water administration with true party government. As he explained to George Clarke of the Admiralty Board in 1713, his aim was "a clear Tory scheme".[49] In 1704 St. John had left the Tories not so much because of any dis-enchantment with Tory ideals but rather because he was dis-gusted with the old guard Tory leadership.[50] He saw that, in

---

[47] Swift, *Journal to Stella*, vol. I, p. 195; cf. Wentworth to Raby, 20 Feb. 1711. *Wentworth Papers*, p. 180. The leaders of the Club are listed in Oldmixon, *op. cit.*, p. 482.

[48] Bolingbroke, "A Letter to Sir William Windham", *The Works of Bolingbroke*, vol. I, pp. 8–9. Cf. St. John's statement in June 1710 that he was resolved "to neglect nothing in my power which may contribute towards making the Church interest the prevailing one". St. John to Trumbull, 2 June 1710, Berks. R.O., Trumbull Additional MSS., 133, 39/2.

[49] Bolingbroke to Clarke, 19 Dec. 1713, B.M. Egerton MSS., 2,618, f. 214.

[50] Bundle 33 of the Trumbull Additional MSS. in the Berkshire Record Office contains an important series of letters from St. John to Trumbull. These papers clearly establish St. John's political outlook in the early part of Anne's reign. See especially letter 27 (2 May 1704) where the future Secretary of State draws a pointed contrast between Nottingham's attempts to bully Anne and Burghley's patience with Queen Elizabeth, and letter 28 (9 May 1704) in which he describes Jersey and Nottingham as the heads of a hectoring "cabal", unrepresentative of the Tory Party as a whole. Letter 29 (16 May 1704) is also revealing. Here St. John characterises the 1704 ministerial reshuffle as a change in "persons" not "things". The new regime, the letter proclaims, is essentially the same as the old; like its predecessor it is "far from being in a Whig interest". It is interesting to note that

obstructing the war effort, men like Rochester and Nottingham were not only cutting their own throats, but also discrediting the Tory movement as a whole. By 1711, however, the war had, to all intents and purposes, been won. Moreover with a huge parliamentary majority at their command the Tories seemed to have the future in their hands. It was now Oxford who was the nigger in the woodpile with his pointless moderation.

As with St John and the October Club, so with Nottingham the party factor was crucial. Even before Harley's return to power in 1710 Nottingham had shown himself to be deeply suspicious of the ex-Secretary's schemes on party grounds. Once the Herefordshire man was firmly in the saddle, and the true extent of his "trimming measures"[51] was plain for all to see, Dismal's language lost all restraint. Lord Dartmouth has left us with a revealing description of a meeting which took place in February 1711 between himself, Harley, Shrewsbury, Poulett and Secretary St. John on the one hand, and Nottingham on the other. Dartmouth recalled how Nottingham

> desired to know what we designed to do, for as yet, he said, we had done nothing. I said, I believed at the conclusion of the last session he would have thought the dissolving the Parliament, and turning out all the Whig ministers something. He said that was nothing, if we did not make it impracticable for them ever to rise again. The Duke of Shrewsbury desired to know by what means that should be accomplished. Lord Nottingham said, unless we prosecute them, he should think we protected them; for it was plain they had brought things to such a pass that they could neither make peace nor war: and we were doing their work for them. I desired to know who he would have prosecuted: he said Lord

---

Harley's view of the significance of the 1704 changes was fundamentally different from this. "The Queen", he told Marlborough, "hath wisely and happily delivered herself of a party, and I believe she will not easily put herself again into the power of another party whatsoever" (Harley to Marlborough, 29 June/10 July 1705, Blenheim MSS., A 1–25). Perhaps in both cases the wish was to some extent father to the thought.

[51] "The last night some of us met with the Speaker and came to a resolution ... to expose that mask of moderation by which we have so much suffered and the trimming measures we fear, and this in the boldest, lively colours". J. Ward to Nottingham, 3 April 1711, Leicestershire R.O., Finch MSS., G.S., bundle 24.

Sunderland for one, and he was sure I could find matter enough in his office, if I pleased: I said, that should be some other body's business not mine; and I knew the Queen would never be brought into such measures. He got up, and as he went out, said if we did not act in concert with the Whigs, we should soon find the effects of our good-nature. And from that day was most indefatigable in persecuting the Queen and all her servants, with all the art that he was master of.

As if all this were not enough to make his attitude to "a medley-administration" clear, a month or so later the old Tory war horse sat down and committed the grounds of his opposition to the government to paper:

There are some propositions so plain and evident that I need only mention them.
1. that a coalition scheme is impracticable.
2. that the attempt of it cannot be with a good design because whatever tends to the interest of our Constitution in Church and State will be more faithfully pursued by friends than enemies, and because
3. that reason and experience show that such a scheme must end in Whiggism, and therefore it may be presumed that 'tis designed to do so, and the rather because he [Harley] who projected the last union of parties is the only person who can now carry on the like measures.

In 1704 Nottingham had resigned because Anne refused to purge her ministry entirely of Whigs. His behaviour shows that in 1711 he was still essentially the same kind of political animal. In Lord Poulett's words he was still "party sense in person".[52]

The final split in government ranks—the Hanoverian rebellion—may also be related to the party issue. The great irony of the Whimsical revolt, which gave such a fillip to the Whig revival, is that it might in happier circumstances so easily have been avoided. Most Tories were not confirmed Jacobites.

---

[52] Burnet, *op. cit.*, vol. VI, p. 37, Dartmouth's note; Memorandum in Nottingham's hand, Leicestershire R.O., Finch MSS., P.P., 150; Poulett to Harley, 4 May 1711, *H.M.C. Portland MSS.*, IV, p. 684. For the date of the meeting described by Dartmouth see Oxford's "Account of Public Affairs", *ibid.*, vol. V, p. 464.

They simply had not come to "any very settled resolution" about the succession.[53] All that was required to turn them in the direction of Hanover was firm leadership. In theory Oxford was the ideal person to give this lead. He had the talent. He was also strongly committed to the Hanoverian cause. Admittedly the premier had had his dealings with St. Germain. But, as Berwick saw, these had never amounted to anything more than "fair words".[54] Where Hanover was concerned, on the other hand, Oxford acted as well as spoke. He defeated an attempt to repeal the Union with Scotland,[55] for example, he insisted on the issue of the Duke of Cambridge's writ, he was in favour of paying the arrears of the Hanoverian troops,[56] and he obtained the issue of a proclamation against the Pretender.[57] A glance at the Treasurer's private papers shows clearly where his real sympathies lay. One memorandum in Oxford's hand, dated May 11 1714, specifically sets out the arguments for and against the Pretender as he saw them. It is divided into two columns. The first column, headed "Arguments for Hanover", runs as follows:

1. Security of our religion which cannot be under a Papist.
2. Securing our ancient rights which cannot be under one bred up in French maxims, and who comes with the intention to revive his father's quarrels.
3. Hazards of the Queen's health
4. Designs of any in power against the succession.

The second column—"Arguments for the Pretender" is left completely blank.[58] Yet, despite the fact that he was so eminently

[53] Bolingbroke, "Letter to Sir William Windham", *The Works of Bolingbroke*, vol. I, p. 10.
[54] *Berwick to James III*, 2 Oct. 1713, *H.M.C. Stuart MSS.*, I, p. 277.
[55] Cobbett, *op. cit.*, vol. VI, pp. 1216–20; *Lockhart Papers*, vol I, pp. 425–36; L'Hermitage's report, 2/13 June 1713, B.M. Additional MSS., 17,677 GGG, ff. 202–4.
[56] Oxford to Thomas Harley, March 1714, B.M. Additional MSS., 40,621, ff. 177–80; Kreienberg's report, 14/25 May 1714, B.M. Stowe MSS., 227, f. 46; Bolingbroke to Strafford, 18 May 1714, *Bol. Corr.*, vol. IV, p. 531; Strafford to Edward "Lord" Harley, 3 June 1714, *H.M.C. Portland MSS.*, VII, p. 185; *Lockhart Papers*, vol. I, pp. 467–70.
[57] Galke's report, 25 June/6 July 1714, Macpherson, *Original Papers*, vol. II, pp. 630–1; Kreienberg's report, 25 June/6 July 1714, *ibid.*, pp. 631–2.
[58] B.M. Portland Loan, 10(8). Cf. Oxford to Thomas Harley, March 1714, B.M. Additional MSS., 40, 621, ff. 177–80; same to same, 13 April 1714, *ibid.*, ff. 210–4 Oxford to Auditor Harley, 24 March 1716, B.M. Portland Loan, 70(10).

qualified to give the necessary lead, the premier failed to do so, and what doomed him to failure was his unwavering political moderation. Deeply mortified by the great man's stubborn refusal to countenance party government, the great bulk of the Tory Party would no longer respond to his call. Indeed by this time even Anne had ceased to listen to her old friend. A draft of a letter intended for the Queen's eye, but in the event not sent, gives us a moving glimpse of the terrible extent of the Treasurer's isolation and ineffectiveness:

> Madam,
>   Godolphin is out, Harley is out. Who will [you] trust after that? Who has any credit to lose?
>   In order to keep your affairs quiet I have retired myself. I do not quarrel. I do not set people to approach you. Nobody will believe you act by yourself.
>   You manage so as to be for neither Hanover nor the Pretender. Nobody would join in their scheme.
>   Has Hanover any credit but what your conduct gives them?[59]

The spirit was indeed willing, but the flesh was woefully weak. In these circumstances the best Oxford could do was to sit tight and hope thereby to block the pathway of the anti-Hanoverians and the quasi-Jacobites. As Bolingbroke cryptically put it the premier's policy became one of marking time so that he could "deliver us up, bound as it were hand and foot, to our adversaries".[60] But for the Whimsicals such prevarication was insufficient. Despairing of a more positive lead from the government side they joined forces with the Junto.

In 1708 Harley had been brought low by his non-party zeal. In 1714 his sad condition owed much of its poignancy to the same factor. Moreover, Oxford's antipathy to party rule at this later date took its rise from the same source as it had done previously—his continuing desire for pure and national government, his ineradicable Country psychology. True, in 1710 there

---

[59] [Oxford] to [Anne], 9 June 1714, B.M. Portland Loan, 10(8).
[60] Bolingbroke, "Letter to Sir William Windham", *The Works of Bolingbroke*, vol. I, p. 24.

were strong prudential reasons for resisting Tory pressure. The Bank was extremely touchy. There was, too, the danger that a wholesale Whig purge might panic the Dutch into concluding a separate peace with France. But even after these particular problems had been ironed out the Treasurer's attachment to his trimming measures continued unabated. The real reason for his undying hatred of party is clearly shown in his quarrel with Bolingbroke. To Oxford the Secretary represented all that was worst in party politics. He seemed to be using the party band-waggon simply to advance his own career and line his own pockets. Accordingly, when, in the dying weeks of the reign, the Whigs launched a full-scale parliamentary attack on Boling-broke's friend and financial adviser Arthur Moore—and, by implication, upon Bolingbroke himself—accusing him of bribery and corruption, they received the whole-hearted co-operation of Oxford and his entourage. Auditor Harley, for example, concerted tactics with the rising Whig leader Lord Townshend, while the Treasurer himself openly rallied to the Junto in the Lords.[61] Alarmed by the turn of events, Anne was compelled to prorogue Parliament on 9 July in order to save her Secretary. But even then Oxford was not done. On 27 July, at a specially summoned Cabinet meeting, he rose and delivered a blistering attack upon Bolingbroke across the Queen's semi-recumbent body, denouncing the Secretary in classic Country fashion for avarice, shady dealing, and insatiable ambition. It was the last great act of his premiership. That evening the Treasurer was dismissed.[62]

Thus it is impossible to regard Harley's career as Secretary of State as simply his political adolescence, part of the process of growing up. Many good courtiers were often angered by corruption, malpractice and unconstitutional behaviour. But Harley's concern with these things was obsessive. Whenever it

---

[61] MS. notes, partly in Auditor Harley's hand, headed "To the Rt. Honourable the Lord Viscount Townshend", Brampton Bryan MSS, unbundled political papers; Erasmus Lewis to Swift, 6 July 1714, *Swift Corr.*, vol. II, pp. 168–9; *Journals of the House of Lords*, XIX, p. 746. Cf. Oxford's anger at the Secretary's profiteering at the time of the Quebec expedition (Oxford's "Account of Public Affairs", *H.M.C. Portland MSS.*, V, p. 465), and his vigilance at the Treasury (E.g. *Calendar of Treasury Books*, vol. XXV, p. 532 (20 Oct. 1711); *ibid.*, vol. XXVI, p. 398 (8 Aug. 1712); *ibid.*, vol. XXVII, p. 51 (2 Oct. 1713).
[62] Defoe, *Secret History of the White Staff*, pp. 53–61.

became a choice between efficient government and the purity of his soul he uncompromisingly chose the latter. In a revealing letter, penned in October 1705, Harley told Sir Robert Davers: "I have the same principles I came into the House of Commons with; I never have willingly nor never will change them".[63] Notwithstanding his sparkling achievements as Secretary and subsequently at the Treasury, honest Robin remained to the end a countryman at heart, a purist, a man of the provinces rather than the centre, concerned above all else with "good husbandry".[64] But why was this so? What made the pull of his Country past so powerful? Why, when given so much opportunity and so admirably equipped, did he fail so signally to adjust to his role as a courtier? Even more puzzling, since such a position was obviously so alien to his basic impulses, what induced him to become involved with the Court at all? Why did he not remain permanently a ministry wrecker, a perpetual back-bencher? A closer look at the Herefordshire man's background and personality will, it is hoped, provide the answers to these questions.

[63] Harley to Davers, 16 Oct. 1705, *H.M.C. Portland MSS.*, IV, p. 261.
[64] On the day the Queen gave him the Treasurer's staff Oxford wrote to Marlborough saying that his chief concern in his new post would be to attend to everything that would promote "good husbandry" (Oxford to Marlborough, 29 May/9 June 1711, Blenheim MSS., B11–19). In describing the actual working of the Oxford regime John Arbuthnot preferred domestic rather than agrarian imagery: "Now and then, you would see him [Oxford] in the kitchen, weighing the beef and butter, paying ready money that the maids might not run a tick at the market, and the butchers (by bribing them) sell damaged and light meat. Another time, he would slip into the cellar and gauge the casks". According to Arbuthnot all this cheeseparing arose from the Treasurer's sworn determination to rescue England "from the claws of harpies and blood-suckers" (Arbuthnot, "John Bull still in his senses", G. A. Aitken (ed.), *Later Stuart Tracts* (Westminster, 1903), pp. 345–6). Cf Dartmouth's verdict. He characterised Oxford as one who "loved the constitution" and his administration as "four years cessation of plunder" (Burnet, *op. cit.*, vol. VI, p. 45, Dartmouth's note.)

8 Puritan Politician

AT HALF PAST seven on the morning of Sunday 1 August 1714 Queen Anne at length went to her eternal rest. "I believe", wrote Dr. Arbuthnot, "sleep was never more welcome to a weary traveller than death was to her".[1] Anne's passing effectively ended Oxford's political career. Toryism, as Thomas Barber observed, was now "an out of fashion thing",[2] and Oxford, who had so ably presided over the great Tory resurgence of 1710, found himself an object of particular disfavour. Just how low the former premier's stock had sunk was shown in the general election held in the spring of 1715. At New Radnor his nominee Lord Harley was soundly beaten. In the county election it was the same sorry tale. At Leominster Auditor Harley scraped home by a mere 19 votes, and even this narrow victory was "quite contrary" to what was expected, and was accordingly greeted with unalloyed rejoicing by the Harley clan.[3] But electoral defeat was a mere pin-prick compared with what happened once the new assembly met. In June 1715 Oxford, along with Bolingbroke and Ormonde, was impeached for "high treason and other crimes and misdemeanours", and for two years, while his case was pending, he was kept a prisoner in the Tower.[4] The hour of reckoning had well and truly struck.

George I's accession, then, meant political death for Oxford.

---

[1] Arbuthnot to Swift, 12 Aug. 1714, *Swift Corr.*, vol. II, p. 232.

[2] Thomas Barber to Peter Legh, 16 Aug. 1714, John Rylands Library, Legh of Lyme MSS., box 49.

[3] Oxford to Lord Harley, 1 Feb., 6 Feb. 1715, *H.M.C. Portland MSS.*, V, pp. 505, 506; Abigail Harley to Lord Harley, 4 Feb. 1715, *ibid.*, pp. 505–6; Edward Harley's "Memoirs", *ibid.*, p. 663. What made the electoral beating particularly galling was the fact that the Harleys had canvassed with considerable care. See, for example, the election papers in Brampton Bryan MSS., bundle 6, packet 4.

[4] Cobbett, *op. cit.*, vol. VII, p. 67. On Oxford's imprisonment see Auditor Harley's embittered account, Edward Harley's "Memoirs", *H.M.C. Portland MSS.*, V, pp. 665–9, and the selections from Oxford's letters to various members of his family, *ibid.*, pp. 529–32.

Admittedly, after his release from prison in July 1717 things were a little less dismal. For one thing he was able to make a spirited return to the Lords. In January 1719, for example, he "spoke very handsomely" in favour of adding to the Church Bill a clause aimed at preventing the growth of socinianism. Shortly after, he threw his weight into the scales against the Peerage Bill.[5] But there was never any real chance of a come-back, for even though the treason charges against him had been swept aside, he remained a marked man. He was still, for instance, forbidden to attend Court, or even to come within the presence of the King.[6] Moreover, the few men rash enough to show sympathy for his predicament quickly found themselves in trouble, as Henry Carey, clerk to Lincoln's Inn chapel, learnt to his cost. On the Sunday after Oxford's impeachment was dropped Carey was imprudent enough to select for the chapel service psalm 124—"the Church blesseth God for a miraculous deliverance". Within a week he had lost his job and been branded as "a person disaffected to the government".[7]

Oxford's reaction to this total eclipse was both stoical and level-headed. He was not the man to wallow in self pity. Nor did he intend to fight the inevitable. Anne was scarcely in her grave before, reading the signs aright, he announced his "fixed resolution to retire".[8] In the autumn of 1719 he finally carried his resolve into effect. Instead of journeying up to London for the opening of the parliamentary session he elected to remain in Herefordshire, pottering about his bowling green, browsing

[5] Edward Harley (jnr.) to Abigail Harley, 13 Jan. 1719, *ibid.*, p. 576; letters from various Scottish peers, *ibid.*, pp. 578–82; Ruglen to Oxford, 5 May 1719, B.M. Portland Loan, 163(10) misc. 79.

[6] Oxford to the Bishop of Salisbury, 20 March 1718, 29 April 1719, *H.M.C. Portland MSS.*, V, pp. 559, 582.

[7] Carey to Oxford, endorsed 1717/18, *ibid.*, pp. 552–3. Psalm 124 runs:
    If it had not been the Lord who was on our side, now may Israel say;
    2. If it had not been the Lord who was on our side, when men rose up against us:
    3. Then they had swallowed us up quick, when their wrath was kindled against us:
    4. Then the waters had overwhelmed us, the stream had gone over our soul:
    5. Then the proud waters had gone over our soul.
    6. Blessed be the Lord, who hath not given us a prey to their teeth.
    7. Our soul is escaped as a bird out of the snare of the fowlers: the snare is broken, and we are escaped.
    8. Our help is in the name of the Lord, who made heaven and earth.

[8] Oxford to Auditor Harley, 13 Feb. 1717, Herefordshire R.O., Harley Papers, C.64.

through his books, and generally savouring the pleasures of rural life.[9] When, the following year, his friends, terrified by the South Sea crisis, pressed him earnestly to come to town, he brushed aside their entreaties with the excuse that his health was too frail to stand the long coach journey to the capital.[10] He had made the great break and there was no looking back. From now onwards, as the years slipped by, his links with Westminster snapped one by one. But age, too, crept on. By 1723 it was clear that he was sinking steadily. Increasingly his letters took on a valetudinarian tone. On the last day of the year he wrote a particularly moving note to his brother Edward:

> The conclusion of the old year puts me in mind of the thanks I owe your dearest father and all at Eywood for the many instances of affection and tenderness I have received from you all there in the course of your several lives, and as I bless God, the author of this happiness, so I return my most grateful thanks to all of you.[11]

Barely five months later, on 21 May 1724, he died while on a brief visit to London. He was in his sixty third year. "There is a great man now fallen in Israel", wrote Dr. Gastrell, the worthy bishop of Chester, "and he died full of honour though not of days".[12]

Unlike Marlborough the soldier, Harley the politician was given no hero's funeral. His body was carried back to Brampton Bryan and buried with the minimum of fuss among the bones of his ancestors.[13] It was a curiously appropriate end, for, essentially, Harley was a very ordinary man. A glance at agriculture illustrates this. Much of Harley's energy and thinking was absorbed in the pursuits of the typical landed squire. Even his political correspondence is shot through with agrarian

[9] For Oxford's failure to appear in London at all during the 1719–20 session see especially Bromley to Oxford, 5 July 1720, *H.M.C. Portland MSS.*, V, p. 600.

[10] E.g. Stratford to Oxford, 24 Dec. 1720, *ibid.*, p. 611; Lord Harley to Oxford, 17 Jan. 1721, *ibid.*, p. 613.

[11] Oxford to Auditor Harley, 31 Dec. 1723, Herefordshire R.O., Harley Papers, C.64.

[12] Gastrell to Auditor Harley, 24 May 1724, Brampton Bryan MSS., bundle 117.

[13] In his will Oxford specifically directed that his funeral should be conducted "without pomp". See the copy of his will in Brampton Bryan MSS., unbundled family papers.

undertones. In the autumn of 1709, for example, we find him exchanging doleful stories about flood damage and the lateness of the harvest with his parliamentary crony Sir Thomas Mansell. Again, in 1703, the eye of the countryman flashes out from the heart of London. "We have had a very uncertain summer", he wrote to his sister Abigail in July of that year, "which hath much affected all the rich meadows on the Thames, yet the farmers near the town wish for scarcity to increase the price of their grain". The observation is sandwiched between an account of events in Scotland and descriptions of the military situation on the continent. Long before this, however, Harley's habit of juxtaposing political and agrarian matters had become something of a by-word among his fellow politicians. "Your making excuses for your entertaining letters has a great deal of the country fashion in it", wrote Henry Boyle in 1696. "I have already told you how much you are a country gentleman, and therefore I won't expose my ignorance in writing about the harvest which is so good that nothing but the skill and integrity of the managers you speak of could reduce the people to want and necessity in the midst of so much plenty".[14]

Harley, indeed, seems to have been typical of the improving landlords so characteristic of later Stuart England. The latest experimental crops, for instance, were avidly taken up at Brampton Bryan. In 1691 we find Harley combing London for Dutch flax, while at the time of his death in 1724 no less than fifteen acres of land were under turnips. Clover was also extensively grown. In addition strenuous efforts were made to preserve the fertility of the soil and to increase productivity by means of regular liming and manuring. It was careful management of this sort which enabled Harley to increase the size of the sheep flock on the home farm from 413 in 1718 to 615 in 1724. Moreover, agrarian improvement was accompanied by an attempt to consolidate and expand Harley's holdings. In 1688, for example, we find him negotiating the purchase of the Lordship of Downton—an estate of some 740 acres. Again, in 1705, he bought the Coxall estate from the Earl of Arundel for a

---

[14] Mansell to Harley, 26 Sep. 1709, *H.M.C. Portland MSS.*, IV, p. 527; Harley to Abigail Harley, 6 July 1703, *ibid.*, p. 64; [Boyle] to Harley, 14 Sep. 1696, *ibid.*, III, pp. 578–9.

figure somewhere in the region of £4,000. It is a story which was being enacted many times over throughout the length and breadth of England.[15].

Harley's agrarian interests form only one example of his ordinariness. There are many others. His social aspirations, for instance, were typical of his age and class. The pride he displayed in his absurdly vague connection with the Vere family demonstrates nicely the importance he attached to social *éclat*. The extravagant wording of his patent of nobility, reciting at length his invaluable services to Queen and country is a further indication of his delight in social success.[16] Like most landed men of his standing too Harley was anxious to marry his children well. And here also his efforts met with much success. In 1709 he succeeding in netting George Hay, Viscount Dupplin, for his younger daughter Abigail,[17] while his favourite child Elizabeth landed an even bigger fish. On 16 December 1712 Elizabeth took in marriage Peregrine Hyde Osborne, Marquess of Carmarthen, the grandson of Charles II's Danby. Unfortunately both unions were darkened by unhappiness. Hay's profligacy eventually drove Abigail to seek refuge in her brother's house; and poor Elizabeth, to Oxford's great grief, died in childbed on 20 November 1713.[18] No such fate, however, blighted the life of Harley's son and heir Edward. For Edward the Treasurer secured the greatest prize of all—the beautiful,

[15] Harley to Elizabeth Harley, 11 April 1691, B.M. Portland Loan, 164(7); MS. Inventory of the Earl of Oxford's Goods in 1724, Hereford City Library; Accounts of the Brampton Demesne, 1716, 1717, 1722 and 1724, Brampton Bryan MSS., bundle 2; Bailiff's Memorandum, 15 Jan. 1720, *ibid.*, unbundled estate papers; Harley's correspondence with Richard More, B.M. Portland Loan 151(11); Letters of Henry Jeffreyes, 1703–5, *ibid.*, 148(2). Further agrarian information may be found among the various farm indentures, leases and agreements in the Brampton Bryan MSS.

[16] For the high flown preamble to Harley's patent see T. Osborne (ed.), *The Harleian Miscellany* (London 1744–6), vol. I, pp. 1–2. Although Harley adopted the title of Oxford his sole connection with the family was the fact that his great-grandmother's sister had married Lord Vere of Tilbury, son of a younger son of the fifth Vere Earl of Oxford. Even his friend Swift censured him for making too much of the link. Swift, "An Enquiry into the Behaviour of the Queen's Last Ministry", *Prose Works of Swift*, vol. V, p. 431.

[17] The attraction of Dupplin as a prospective son-in-law is clearly indicated by the Duchess of Marlborough's behaviour. Upon hearing the news of his betrothal to Abigail she lost all control and "stamped and roared like a bedlam". [Harley] to [Mansell], 30 Sep. 1709, N.L.W., Penrice and Margam MSS., L.648.

[18] On Abigail's disastrous match see Erasmus Lewis to Swift, 30 June 1737, *Swift Corr.*, vol. VI, p. 31; and *H.M.C. Portland MSS.*, VII, *passim.* Swift to Oxford, 21 Nov. 1713, *Swift Corr.*, vol. II, pp. 86–8 for Elizabeth's untimely death.

red-headed Henrietta Cavendish Holles, only child of the fabulously wealthy John Holles, Duke of Newcastle. The brilliance of the capture is indicated by the fact that at one stage rumours were abroad of Henrietta's impending betrothal to the Electoral Prince of Hanover, the future George II. Bolingbroke, embittered by his rival's success, cynically described the match as "the ultimate end" of the Oxford administration. This, of course, was gross exaggeration. Nevertheless, the fact remains that ever since 1703 Harley had been cultivating Newcastle's friendship and studiously ministering to his wishes. As Swift averred the matter had "been privately managing this long time", and when the negotiations finally bore fruit Harley brimmed over with satisfaction in a manner typical of his class.[19]

One further illustration of Harley's unexceptional nature may perhaps be permitted. His social aspirations and his agrarian pursuits mark him out as the quintessence of ordinariness. So too does his homely character. One can easily be misled by Harley's spectacular political success. Underneath he remained a shy, fumbling figure. Personal friendship and family accord were enormously important to him. His first marriage to Elizabeth, daughter of Thomas Foley the Worcestershire iron-master, was an especially intimate affair. Absence from her always released an ocean of affection. In 1688, for example, he wrote:

Should I have written all that my thoughts with truest affection have been entertained with towards my dearest heart since our parting, I should have wanted a secretary with a hundred hands continually to have accompanied me, and you would have stood in need of more eyes than are in a peacock's train to have despatched the reading.

And again in 1691:

I wish you did know or remember how solitary and desolate

<hr />

[19] For the projected alliance with George see Bonnell to Newcastle, N.D., *H.M.C. Portland MSS.*, II, p. 193. See also Bolingbroke to Swift, 21 Dec. 1721, *Swift Corr.*, vol. III, p. 113; and Swift, *Journal to Stella*, vol. II, p. 407.

I am without you. I trust what time we shall be asunder God will preserve us and show us mercy that we may meet again in comfort.

Harley clearly relied very heavily upon Elizabeth, and her death from smallpox on 30 November 1691 was a terrible blow.[20]

Many other facets of Harley's private life touch a similar homely note. Sarah Middleton, for example, his second wife, was an incurable domestic mouse. The ladies of Queen Anne's Court never tired of poking fun at her unfashionable ways. To them she was "an old housekeeper" who "knew no lord but the Lord Jehovah". The contrast with the pushing, politically conscious Sarah Churchill is almost total. Again Harley's convivial evenings with Swift and the Tory literary set had an almost child-like innocence about them. On 11 October 1711 Swift depicted a typical scene for Stella:

> I dined today with Lord Treasurer. Thursdays are now his days when his choice company comes, but we are too much multiplied. George Granville sent his excuses upon being ill; I hear he apprehends the apoplexy, which would grieve me much. Lord Treasurer called Prior nothing but Monsieur Baudrier, which was the feigned name of the Frenchman that writ his journey to Paris. They pretend to suspect me; so I talk freely of it, and put them out of their play. Lord Treasurer calls me now Dr. Martin, because Martin is a sort of swallow, and so is a Swift. When he and I came last Monday from Windsor, we were reading all the signs on the road. He is a pure trifler; tell the bishop of Clogher so. I made him make two lines in verse for the Bell and Dragon, and they were rare bad ones.

Add to all this Harley's love of good wine—in August 1707 alone he bought over a hundred gallons of French claret—and

[20] Harley's letters to Elizabeth are in B.M. Portland Loan, 164. The two letters quoted are dated 13 June 1688 and 7 March 1691. For the "devouring griefs" occasioned by Elizabeth's death see Harley to Sir Edward Harley, 10 Dec. 1691, and subsequent letters. *Ibid.*, 79.

top it with his discriminating fondness for books and manuscripts—his voluminous library included the collections of such
men as Foxe the martyrologist and the celebrated antiquary Sir
Simon D'Ewes—and the picture rounds out nicely. The scene is
affable, slow-moving, unruffled, remarkable only for being un-
remarkable. It requires something of a wrench to realise that the
sphere in which this cumbrous, homely, rather shy man
operated daily was the rough and tumble of Westminster.[21]

Basically, then, Queen Anne's Treasurer was a very ordinary
person. But, in view of this, how do we explain his extraordinary political impact? What group of circumstances determined that he should enjoy such a remarkable parliamentary
career? The answer seems to be that although Harley was in so
many ways so mundane he nevertheless boasted two quite
exceptional qualities. One of these characteristics we have already examined in some detail in the course of our narrative—
Harley's political flair. His penchant for intrigue was un-
deniable. His mastery of the details of Commons' business was
unchallenged. His multi-coloured contacts—among the gentry,
with the merchant interest, among bishops and Presbyterians,
with Scotsmen and Quakers—were of incalculable value. His
grasp of public relations was at times uncanny. But over and
above this range of political talents there was another outstanding ingredient in Harley's political make-up, and it is this
second factor which explains the peculiar shape of his career,
why he remained a countryman to the end, and yet, at the same
time, was not averse to accepting office at Court. From first to
last Harley's life was riddled with Puritanism.

One of the problems in studying Harley is that much of his
career is threaded with false trails. His link with the Puritan
tradition is no exception. Here the major blind alley is presented
by his relations with the official Nonconformist hierarchy of his
day. These frequently left much to be desired. Harley got along
amicably enough with the pacific Quakers and with dissenting

---

[21] *Wentworth Papers*, pp. 218 and 263; Swift, *Journal to Stella*, vol. II, pp. 381–2.
Harley's wine bills are at B.M. Portland Loan, 155. For his book collecting activities
see especially Humphrey Wanley's Diary, B.M. Lansdowne MSS, 171–2; *Remarks
and Collections of Thomas Hearne*, vol. I, p. 163, vol. III, p. 1; Wanley's description of
Oxford's library, 27 July 1715, *H.M.C. Portland MSS.*, V, pp. 514–6; Tullie House,
Carlisle, Bishop Nicolson's MS. Diary, 11 Nov. 1705; and the relevant papers in
B.M. Portland Loan, 126(1), 134(5), 160(3), 161, 262 and 356.

outsiders like Defoe and John Shower, the Presbyterian minister of Old Jewry.[22] But when it came to more central figures like the quarrelsome Nonconformist leader Daniel Williams relations were far cooler. Williams, indeed, seems to have entertained an immovable distrust of Harley, and although the Herefordshire man made a number of spirited attempts to wean both Williams and his fellow Nonconformists from their allegiance to the Junto he was conspicuously unsuccessful. In 1710, for instance, Harley offered Williams £1,000 to make good the damage done to meeting houses during the Sacheverell riots, while a year later, when his popularity was at its zenith as a result of Guiscard's attempt on his life, he renewed his bid for Nonconformist support. Both overtures, however, were coldly received, and in 1712 we find Lord Harley bitterly complaining of the continued intransigence of the Dissenters, and the fact that they had "fasted and prayed against peace . . . and made a collection for printing all the virulent pamphlets that have been wrote against the Queen and this ministry in two volumes".[23] Dissenting distrust of Harley is all the more impressive when we remember that the Nonconformists were subjected to frequent shabby treatment by their Junto allies. The let down over the Occasional Conformity Bill in 1711 is only one example of Whig bad faith. Many more could be cited. The Reverend Daniel Burgess, for instance, had ample cause for complaint. On 28 February 1710 Burgess was warned that his meeting house was scheduled for attack by the mob the following night. Accordingly he applied to the Whigs for aid. A guard was promised for seven o'clock in the evening, but it failed to appear and

[22] For Harley's relations with Shower see especially Shower to Harley, 27 Oct. 1705, *H.M.C. Portland MSS.*, IV, p. 268; same to same, 20 Dec. 1711, B.M. Portland Loan, 305; and Oxford to Shower, 21 Dec. 1711, *ibid.*, 160. Harley's correspondence with William Penn illuminates his link with the Quakers. See *H.M.C. Portland MSS.*, III–V, *passim*. It is interesting to note that on Swift's first visit to Harley's London house to discuss in detail his proposals about the Irish Church he found the Herefordshire man at dinner with Penn. Swift, *Journal to Stella*, vol. I, p. 45. Another dissenting group with whom Harley was *au fait* was the Irish Presbyterian minority. See Francis Iredell's letters to Oxford from 1712–14, B.M. Portland Loan, 148(1).

[23] Williams to Harley, 4 Aug. 1710, B.M. Portland Loan, 160; Harley to Williams, 5 Aug. 1710 (copy), Herefordshire R.O., Harley Papers, C. 64. For evidence of the renewed overtures of 1711 see Swift's seductive appeal in *Examiner* no. 37 and Defoe's subtly worded *Eleven Opinions about Mr. Harley* (London, 1711). The quotation is from Lord Harley to [Auditor Harley?], 7 Oct. 1712, Brampton Bryan MSS., bundle 117.

the chapel was pulled to pieces by the infuriated populace.[24]

In the light of all this it is tempting to conclude that Harley's link with the Puritan tradition was of minimal importance. It would, however, be entirely erroneous to do so. A mere glance at his correspondence should suggest caution. Many of Harley's letters are laced with biblical phraseology. "The God of all grace, Father of mercy, and Giver of every good and perfect gift", he wrote to his wife in 1689, "give us thankful hearts and to live obedient lives before Him". A quarter of a century later his language was still as colourful. "I have no other refuge", he confided to his sister Abigail in March 1715, "than to fly to Him, with entire submission to the Divine Will, in this time when I am amongst those who are set on fire, whose teeth are spears and arrows, and their tongues a sharp sword". The opening of his political tract 'Plain English', written in 1708, reads like a page from the Hebrew Prophets:

> I said days should speak and multitudes of years should teach wisdom; but great men are not always wise, neither do the aged understand judgment. Therefore I said hearken to me, I also will show my opinion, I will not accept any man's person, neither will I give flattering titles unto man, but my words shall be of the uprighteousness of my heart, and my lips shall utter knowledge clearly.

Cromwell himself would have felt at home reading this.[25]

Moreover, language is only one pointer. There are many others. At his own expense, for instance, Harley helped to sponsor the printing of 8,000 copies of the 1678 edition of the Bible in Welsh for distribution among the poor people of Wales and the March.[26] He poured continual scorn on the gambling

---

[24] Abigail Harley to Edward Harley, 4 March 1710, *H.M.C. Portland MSS.*, IV, pp. 553–4. For a good account of the Dissenters' loyalty to the Whig cause see P. M. Scholes, "Parliament and the Protestant Dissenters, 1702–1719" (M.A. Thesis, University of London, 1962).

[25] Harley to Elizabeth Harley, 8 June 1689, B.M. Portland Loan, 164(3); Harley to Abigail Harley, 8 March 1715, *ibid.*, 67(5); "Plain English to All who are Honest or would be so if they knew how", *ibid.*, 10(1).

[26] David Jones to Harley, 10 Sep. 1688, 23 March 1689, B.M. Portland Loan, 148(3); John Hall to Harley, 18 May 1689, *ibid.*, 138(1); same to same, 28 May 1689, *H.M.C. Portland MSS.*, III, p. 438; Richard Davis to Harley, 17 Aug. 1689, B.M. Portland Loan, 133(6); Harley to Sir Edward Harley, 22 Dec. 1691, *ibid.*, 79(2); Sir Edward Harley to Robert Harley, 16 Feb. 1692, *ibid.*, 141(6).

fraternity at White's Chocolate House. He frequently jotted down erudite scriptural arguments in spare corners of his manuscripts and papers. Even his London porter was "a Scotch fanatic".[27] The truth is, in fact, that from earliest childhood Harley had been subjected to sustained Puritan indoctrination by his Presbyterian father. His first tutor, a man named Blagrave, was a dabbler in Fifth Monarchism. From Blagrave he was passed on to the care of Samuel Birch of Shilton in Oxfordshire, a former Roundhead officer and one of the ministers ejected in 1662. Thence he travelled up to London to attend the Haymarket Dissenting Academy, an establishment run by the Huguenot refugee Henri Foubert. Finally, in 1682 he entered the Middle Temple, that breeding ground of active Puritanism.[28] And an even more powerful influence than Harley's schooling was his actual home. The entire Harley household rose every morning at six and began the day with a corporate meeting for prayer and meditation. The evening concluded in similar fashion. This regime seems to have persisted right up to Sir Edward's death in 1700; he even insisted on its continuance when he himself was absent in London.[29]

Thus Harley's whole background and upbringing was blood red Puritan; and, not surprisingly, it left an indelible impression upon his personality. Indeed his character was as closely shaped by the Puritan tradition as were the personalities of those Nonconformist divines with whom he was so frequently at odds. His courage is an excellent illustration of this. In times of stress and

[27] J. Swift, "An Essay on Modern Education", *Prose Works of Swift*, vol. XI, p. 53 (White's); Swift, *Journal to Stella, passim* (Harley's porter).

[28] For Blagrave see *H.M.C. Portland MSS.*, III, pp. 312, 328 and 321; and Blagrave's letters in B.M. Portland Loan 126. His interest in Fifth Monarchism is revealed in a letter dated 18 Feb. 1688. For Birch: J. Foster (ed.), *Alumni Oxonienses* (Oxford, 1887–92), vol. I, p. 126; *H.M.C. Portland MSS.*, III, pp. 324–61, *passim*; Harcourt to Harley, 1677, B.M. Portland Loan, 138(5). For Foubert: *H.M.C. Portland MSS.*, III, pp. 366–74, *passim*, IV, p. 614, and V, pp. 142, 175 and 204; Robert Harley to Edward Harley, 22 Aug, 1684, B.M. Portland Loan, 70(9). Harley's certificate of admission to the Middle Temple, dated 18 March 1682, is in *ibid.*, 162(7).

[29] Elizabeth Harley to Robert Harley, 9 May 1689, B.M. Portland Loan, 144(1); Sir Edward Harley to Abigail Harley, 21 June 1690, *ibid.*, 66(2); Sir Edward Harley to Robert Harley, 9 Feb. 1692, *ibid.*, 141(6); same to same, 1 May 1692, *ibid.*, 142(9); Edward Harley to Sir Edward Harley, 14 March 1693, *H.M.C. Portland MSS.*, III, p. 514; Abigail Harley to Robert Harley, 26 Jan. 1700, B.M. Portland Loan, 139(7).

crisis Harley repeatedly displayed incredible bravery. In 1708, for example, when the Whigs, baying for their old enemy's blood, attempted to implicate him in William Greg's treason, his nonchalance amazed Francis Atterbury. "Your brother's head is upon the block", exclaimed the bewildered High Churchman to Edward Harley, "and yet he seems to have no concern about it". Antoine de Guiscard's attempt on Harley's life on 8 March 1711 produced a similar reaction. The Treasurer's Cabinet colleagues were panic stricken, but he himself remained icy calm. So marked was Harley's bravery on occasions like this that it drew considerable comment from contemporaries. Swift thought his friend "the most fearless man alive", while in 1715 Sir Thomas Cave felt he could with safety lay a bottle of red port with Daniel Baker that whatever other ex-ministers might do the former Treasurer would remain in England and confront his enemies face to face. This celebrated courage of Harley was a direct outcome of his Puritan character. The thing which made him so fearless was his rock-like faith, his unshakable conviction that he was numbered among the chosen. He explicitly admitted that it was his trust in God which sustained him during the Greg affair. In a similar way he confessed that his confidence in "the providence of the Almighty" enabled him to face impeachment with equanimity after Queen Anne's death. He knew that whatever storms might rage the Lord of Hosts would not neglect His own. "The ark", as he told his father in 1691, "was as stable in the promise of God as the temple built upon the mountains".[30]

A second way in which Harley's Puritan background shaped his life may be seen in the nature of his links with other members of his family. Throughout the seventeenth century the Harleys exuded a quite peculiar close-knit, clannish aura. Harley's younger brother Edward, for example, in some ways the most deeply Puritan member of the entire family, deliberately sacri-

---

[30] *H.M.C. Portland MSS.*, V, p. 648 (Atterbury's remark); Burnet *op. cit.*, vol. VI, p. 39, Dartmouth's note; *Examiner*, no. 33; St. John to Drummond, 13 March 1711, *Bol. Corr.*, vol. I, pp. 102–3;—Harley to Abigail Harley, 22 March 1711, *H.M.C. Portland MSS.*, IV, pp. 668–70; Swift, *Journal to Stella*, vol. I, p. 206; Cave to Fermanagh, 18 June 1715, *Verney Letters of the Eighteenth Century*, vol. I, p. 339; *H.M.C. Portland MSS.*, V, pp. 648 and 663 (Harley's statements about his courage); Robert Harley to Sir Edward Harley, 15 Dec. 1691, B.M. Portland Loan, 79(2).

ficed his chances of a front line political career in order to smooth
his brother's pathway in every way he could.[31] Harley's success
never ceased to delight him. The fact, for instance, that his
"dear relation" had been "so eminently useful" in reducing the
size of the army after the Treaty of Ryswick filled him with
"thankfulness". Again in his memoirs—themselves a piece
of family piety—Edward celebrated "the dispensations of
the Almighty to my most entirely beloved brother". He took
care also to praise "divine goodness" for providing them
with such "excellent parents who from our infancy instructed
and initiated us in all the principles of sincere piety and
virtue".[32]

Edward's feelings are paralleled by the sentiments of other
members of the family. Robert Harley's own letters often assume
a similar clannish tone. So too do those of his sister Abigail.
Abigail, for instance, was transported with joy at the news that
William Greg had refused to gratify the Junto by smearing her
brother with the stigma of treason. She expressed the fervent
hope that the mercy which God had extended to Harley
would "never be forgotten by any member of the family".
"I trust", she continued, "the same goodness will follow
him all the days of his life". Her concern was fully reciprocated by her brother. On 5 April 1715 he wrote, in a typical
letter:

> I desire my sister Harley may know my prayers are daily for
> her; and I hope God will multiply to her and hers all the
> kindness she and my brother have shown to me and mine. My
> dearest sister cannot doubt from your own mind that we are
> not so near in blood and birth as we are in tenderest affection,

---

[31] Edward was especially helpful in watching over his brother's estates at Brampton. As Robert put it on one occasion: "the entire confidence [I have] in your
affection and conduct makes anything about my own concerns in the country
needless" (Robert Harley to Edward Harley, 10 March 1694, B.M. Portland Loan,
70(9)). But often Edward's stage management of his brother's career went far
beyond agricultural matters. It was Edward, for instance, who negotiated Robert's
second marriage. (Edward Harley to Sir Edward Harley, 25 July, 28 July, 4 Aug.,
1 Sep., 8 Sep., 10 Sep. 1694, *H.M.C. Portland MSS.*, III, pp. 552–5; Robert Harley
to Sir Edward Harley, 18 Aug., 8 Sep., 18 Sep., 1694, *ibid.*, pp. 553–7).

[32] Edward Harley to Sir Edward Harley, 10 Jan. 1699, *H.M.C. Portland MSS.*,
III, p. 601; Edward Harley's "Memoirs", *ibid.*, V, pp. 641–69. See generally
Edward's letters in B.M. Portland Loan, 143.

and I assure myself our prayers for each other ascend to our God every day.

"The only strife that ever was between us", he averred in a later missive, "was which should love each other best. My trouble has been that you put it out of my power to equal you in the expression of tenderness".[33]

Like Harley's courage this sense of family solidarity was Puritan in origin. Traditionally Christianity had been largely antipathetic to sex. Celibacy was regarded as the ideal Christian way of life; marriage was a concession to weaker brethren. The attitude is neatly captured in Chrysostom's description of woman as a "desirable calamity".[34] Puritanism, however, departed from this traditional view. In the various Puritan manuals on personal conduct published during the course of the seventeenth century—books like Dod and Cleaver's *A Godlie Forme of Householde Government*, Lewis Bayly's *Practice of Piety*, and William Perkins' numerous tracts—a new emphasis gradually emerged. Increasingly wedlock came to be looked upon with favour. Perkins indeed categorically affirmed that in his view marriage was "a state in itself far more excellent than the condition of single life", and he was echoed in this opinion by Richard Rogers in his *Seven Treatises*, by Milton in *Paradise Lost*, and by a host of others. One of the main reasons for this increasing stress on the desirability of matrimony was that the Puritans saw the purpose of wedlock as much more than merely biological. Marriage symbolised the founding of a family, and to the Puritans family life was the source of companionship, of understanding, of love and compassion, and of social unity. The Puritan family was intended to be a microcosm of the community at large of which they dreamed, a "little Commonwealth", or a "little Church" in which regular devotional duties could be performed, and where the arts of godly living, so necessary to the good society in general, could be learnt and practised. Hence, the Harleys' emphasis on family was a typical Puritan

---

[33] Abigail Harley to Edward "Lord" Harley, 9 Dec. 1708, *H.M.C. Portland MSS.*, IV, p. 514; Robert Harley to Abigail Harley, 5 April 1715, B.M. Portland Loan, 67(5); same to same, 20 Dec. 1719, *ibid.*

[34] W. E. H. Lecky, *History of the Rise and Influence of the Spirit of Rationalism in Europe* (London, 1897), vol. I, p. 78.

emphasis. Indeed, old Sir Edward's household, revolving as it did around its daily prayer meetings, was the Puritan preacher's ideal in a nutshell.[35]

Both Harley's courage, then, and his sense of family reveal how deep and lasting was the influence of his Puritan upbringing. Other facets of his character could be marshalled to show the same thing—his undemonstrative nature, for example, or his secretiveness, the reflex of the persecuted. Enough has been said, however, to illustrate the point. What it is important for us to note is that it was this Puritan strain in Harley's personality which, more than anything, determined that he should remain at heart a countryman to the very end of his career. It is easy, of course, to divine a link between Harley's Puritanism and his desire for clean government and frugal administration, his dislike of the sort of profiteering in which St. John so liberally indulged. But the influence of the Herefordshire man's religious outlook upon his Country stance was much more powerful and pervasive than this simple linkage suggests. As we have seen, at the core of Harley's political stand was his desire for a truly national government, his opposition to all forms of political monopoly. At times, especially in William's reign, this ideal expressed itself in suspicion of the Crown, while on other occasions, particularly under Anne, it took the form of antipathy to party. But always the aim was to keep government responsive to the needs of the political nation as a whole, to prevent any one man or group of men engrossing a preponderance of power. As with Harley's desire for honesty at Court this more embracing wish for open government was, in part at least, an obvious and straightforward country gentry reaction. The frame of mind it suggests is typical of the mentality of the provincial, London-fearing squirearchy. Nevertheless, although it owed much to

---

[35] W. Perkins, *Works* (London, 1612–13), vol. III, p. 671; R. Rogers, *Seven Treatises* (London, 1630), p. 233; J. Milton, *Paradise Lost*, IV, l. 744 *et seq.* The idea of the family as a "little Church" or a "little Commonwealth" was a commonplace among seventeenth-century Puritan writers. A typical instance is William Gouge. For Gouge a family was "a little Church and a little Commonwealth whereby trial may be made of such as are fit for any place of authority or of subjection in Church or Commonwealth". A family, he reiterates, "is a school wherein the first principles and grounds of government and subjection are learned". W. Gouge, "Of Domestical Duties", *Works* (London, 1626–7), vol. I, p. 10. Cf. generally C. Hill, "The Spiritualization of the Household", *Society and Puritanism in Pre-Revolution England* (London, 1964), pp. 443–81.

Harley's class background, it was also, like his wish for clean government, in a very real sense an outcome of his Puritan up-bringing; and it was precisely because of this that it proved, along with his hatred of racketeering and dishonesty, to be utterly ineradicable long after Harley had left the back benches.

At first sight the group of Puritan preachers to whom "the beloved disciple" Sir Robert Harley and his neighbour Hum-phrey Walcot extended their patronage in the fourth and fifth decades of the seventeenth century seem a curiously disparate collection of men. Thomas Froysell, vicar of Clun, and the rector of Brampton Bryan, Stanley Gower, were fairly orthodox Presbyterians, content to work for reformation within the Church. On the other hand the Brownist Walter Cradock was one of the founders of Welsh Independency, while Vavasour Powell and the mystic Morgan Llwyd were fired by Fifth Monarchist teachings.[36] However, although they differed so markedly on such matters as church government, in one very interesting respect they seem to have spoken with a single voice. Not one of them appears to have been a characteristic fire and brimstone preacher. On the contrary, they were all capable at times of an amazing display of tolerance. Froysell's treatment of backsliders as children demanding tenderness and understand-ing rather than sinners in need of whipping is a remarkable in-stance of this. In similar vein the poet Llwyd appealed for understanding among the sects:

> Men's faces, voices differ much
> saints are not all one size
> flowers in one garden vary too
> let none monopolize.

Cradock agreed with the sentiment. "Presbytery and Independ-ency", he wrote, "are not two religions but one religion to the godly, honest heart; it is only a little ruffling of the fringe".[37]

This essentially tolerant theme, already beginning to appear

[36] A perceptive analysis of Puritanism at Brampton Bryan in the time of Sir Robert is G. F. Nuttall, *The Welsh Saints,* 1640–60.

[37] T. Froysell, *The Beloved Disciple,* p. 91 *et seq.*; T. E. Ellis (ed.), *Gweithiau Morgan Llwyd o Wynedd* (Bangor, 1899), p. 24; W. Cradock, *Gospel Liberty* (London, 1648), p. 135.

at Brampton Bryan in Sir Robert's day, was taken up and developed by the Harleys' later spiritual mentor Richard Baxter. Baxter had been given his first job by Richard Foley in 1638, and he became a lifelong friend of the Harley and Foley families. Sir Edward Harley admired Baxter deeply, and the feeling was fully reciprocated.[38] The Harleys often attended Baxter's chapel when they went up to London, and when the old man died in December 1691 Edward Harley, the future Auditor, was selected as one of the executors of his will.[39] All his life Baxter was consumed with "a burning desire after the peace and unity of the churches".[40] In his tracts and sermons he repeatedly stressed the importance of forbearance, charity, and mutual forgiveness. His crusade against Antinomianism was inspired by the doctrine's cruel condemnation of the non-elect to irredeemable damnation. In 1660 he refused Clarendon's offer of the bishopric of Hereford because the Anglican Church claimed a monopoly of truth. He declined to associate himself with the "separating rigour" of Independency on the same grounds. Throughout he remained "a middle way man", attacking intolerance and spiritual tyranny wherever it appeared, determined always to promote unity and understanding.[41]

The connection between Harley's desire for national government and his Puritan upbringing will now be apparent. Harley's political outlook was in large measure a secularisation of his

[38] When Baxter died Sir Edward wrote of his great grief for "the loss of incomparable Mr. Baxter". Sir Edward Harley to Robert Harley, 14 Dec. 1691, B.M. Portland Loan, 142(6). In his autobiography Baxter spoke of Sir Edward as "a sober and truly religious man, the worthy son of a most pious father, Sir Robert Harley". M. Sylvester (ed.), *Reliquiae Baxterianae* (London, 1696), I, pp. 59–60.

[39] *Reliquiae Baxterianae*, I, p. 13; Sir Edward Harley to Robert Harley, 20 Aug. 1680, B.M. Portland Loan, 140(1); same to same, 28 Dec. 1680, *ibid.*, 140(2); same to same, 18 Nov. 1690, *ibid.*, 140(9); Abigail Harley to Sir Edward Harley, 14 Sep. 1689, *H.M.C. Portland MSS.*, III, p. 440; Edward Harley's "Memoirs", *ibid.*, V, p. 643; Robert Harley to Sir Edward Harley, 8 Dec. 1691, *ibid.*, III, p. 484; Edward Harley to Sir Edward Harley, 10 Dec., 19 Dec. 1691, *ibid.*, p. 485.

[40] Baxter to Durie, 5 Feb. 1653, Dr. Williams's Library MSS., 59. 6.94.

[41] Three recent essays with excellent things to say on Baxter's religious position are: G. F. Nuttall, "The First Nonconformists" in G. F. Nuttall and O. Chadwick (eds.), *From Uniformity to Unity, 1662–1962* (London, 1962), pp. 149–87; R. Thomas, *Daniel Williams, Presbyterian Bishop* (London, 1964); and R. D. Whitehorn, "Richard Baxter, Meer Nonconformist" in G. F. Nuttall and others, *The Beginnings of Nonconformity* (London, 1964), pp. 61–77. For a description of Baxter as "a middle way man . . . neither fish nor flesh nor good red herring" see Calamy, *Historical Account of My Own Life*, vol. I, p. 308.

spiritual inheritance. In countering royal tyranny and in opposing party monopoly he too was posing as "a middle way man"; he was advocating in Parliament what Baxter was calling for in the Church. This translation of ideas from the sphere of theology to the sphere of politics was eased by the fact that many of the most celebrated parliamentary battles of Harley's day had distinct religious overtones. The Act of Toleration, for example, was as integral a part of the Revolution settlement as the Bill of Rights. Similarly the Schism Act was an expression of religious hatred as well as a bid for political monopoly. The pathway was rendered still smoother by the conduct of Harley's father and grandfather. They too had been in the habit of behaving politically in the same manner as they behaved theologically. Sir Robert, for instance, opposed the dictatorship of the Cromwellian army as well as the demands of the Laudians. Sir Edward strove for "the healing of breaches among the sons of Zion"[42] as well as for moderate royalism. Indeed, before the Restoration it was scarcely possible to think of religion and politics as separate compartments. When the King claimed to be the Vicar of God, and royal opponents considered themselves Christ's hand-picked storm troopers, politics and religion were to all intents and purposes one and the same thing. Only later on in the seventeenth century did it become possible to split life into its component parts, and to live in what Sir Thomas Browne termed "divided and distinguished worlds".[43] Even then it was fatefully easy to slip back into old ways of thinking as the popularity of theories of Providential Divine Right in the 1690's demonstrates.[44] For Harley this was especially so since to him God was scarcely less immanent and embracing than He had been for the great saints of Cromwell's day. Illness, for example, was not regarded by the Herefordshire man as a straightforward physical malfunctioning. Sickness was a "cross" from above, a "chastisement" from God, a "fatherly correction".[45] Similarly,

[42] Sir Edward Harley to Edward Harley, 1694, B.M. Portland Loan, 70(7).
[43] Quoted in B. Willey, *The Seventeenth Century Background* (London, 1934), p. 23. Cf. generally A. McInnes, "The Shifting Centre", *The Listener*, vol. LXXIII, no. 1875 (1965), pp. 333–7.
[44] G. M. Straka, "The Final Phase of Divine Right Theory in England, 1688–1702", *English Historical Review*, vol. LXXVII (1962), pp. 638–58.
[45] E.g. Robert Harley to Sir Edward Harley, 2 Jan. 1692, B.M. Portland Loan 79(2); Robert Harley to Edward Harley, 9 June 1717, *ibid.*, 70(9).

sudden or unexpected death was not just a regrettable accident. It was a divinely ordained reminder that the joys of "this lower world" are hollow and impermanent, that we are only "pilgrims and strangers" in our earthly habitation, that our eyes should be set always upon "those regions of light, life and love, those pure and unmixed joys, delight without satiety or end, so great that human understanding we now think boundless cannot comprehend".[46] Indeed, even the weather was not without its portents, for God "maketh the clouds His chariot, and rideth upon the wings of the wind".[47] Hence it is not difficult to see how Harley's religious inheritance was able to invade and colour his political viewpoint.

Harley's Country mentality, then, was as much a part of his religious outlook as of his place in society, and because of this it lived on even after he had ceased to be a back-bencher. In a similar way it was Harley's Puritan upbringing which enabled him—indeed compelled him—to accept office at Court even though he remained in all essentials a countryman. Harley had no particular liking for office. He rejected the post of Secretary of State at least twice in William's reign.[48] When first elected to the Speaker's chair he went so far as to draw up a petition to the King to excuse him.[49] It took a whole month of browbeating from Marlborough and Godolphin before he would agree to enter the Cabinet in 1704.[50] But his Puritan beliefs made him see politics not as a career, but as a "calling" or a "holy profession".[51] Harley believed that he had been divinely ordained to be a politician, and that, consequently, it was his duty to walk in his appointed station "as becomes a child of God in the midst of a crooked and perverse generation".[52] Hence, if office were

[46] Harley to Elizabeth Harley, 30 July 1690, *ibid.*, 164(5) (referring to the death of their short-lived second son Robin) ; Harley to Sir Edward Harley, 31 Dec. 1691, *ibid.*, 79(2) (referring to the death of Elizabeth).
[47] Robert Harley to Sir Edward Harley, 4 Feb. 1692, *ibid.*, 79(2).
[48] Harley, "Large Account: Revolution and Succession", *ibid.*, 165, misc. 97, f. 3 ; Auditor Harley's "Memoirs", B.M. Lansdowne MSS., 885, f. 16.
[49] A copy of the petition may be found in B.M. Portland Loan, 161.
[50] A. McInnes, "The Appointment of Harley in 1704", *The Historical Journal*, vol. XI, (1968), pp. 255–71.
[51] Harley to Sir Edward Harley, 23 July 1689, *H.M.C. Portland MSS.*, III, p. 438. Cf. Sir Edward's letters to Harley in B.M. Portland Loan, 140–142, especially those dated 15 Nov. 1690, 5 Dec. 1690, 30 Dec. 1690, 25 Feb. 1691, 10 March 1691, 22 Dec. 1691, and 22 Jan. 1692.
[52] Harley to Sir Edward Harley, 23 Jan. 1692, B.M. Portland Loan, 79(2).

vigorously thrust upon him then, whatever his personal inclinations might be, he must in the end accept the proferred dignity, for, since God ruled the universe, the offer must clearly be the will of heaven. The Lord, as Harley wrote to his brother in 1714, "chooses what is best for us . . . I beg only to know my duty, and then strength from above to perform it". It was this reasoning which made it impossible for Harley to reject the Treasurer's staff in 1711. On the day of the appointment his daughter Elizabeth wrote to Abigail Harley explaining his action:

> This morning the Queen gave my father the White Staff. God has in a wonderful manner owned and preserved him, so I hope will make him a great instrument of promoting His glory. I believe nothing but that prospect could have prevailed with him to take so great a trust.[53]

It was this same belief, too, that he had been selected as "an instrument of glory" which made Harley accept other "ensnaring" offices, for, as his father once reminded him, a "calling", once understood, could not be "shifted" since it was "the ordinance of God".[54]

Thus, paradoxically, Harley's Puritanism contributed not only to his Country mentality, and hence to his downfall in 1708 and 1714, but also to his willingness to accept office at Court. Indeed it did far more than this. Harley's notion of "calling" gave both to him and to his administration a depth, a sense of responsibility and public spiritedness that was utterly lacking in the work of men like St. John. Many of Harley's associates saw this and warmed to him visibly—Rochester, for example, Bromley, and Dartmouth. Indeed, such was Dartmouth's admiration of Harley's probity that he named one of his six sons Robert, in part at least, to honour the great Treasurer.[55] In the course of our study we have been concerned to show how Harley's religious outlook contributed to his political weakness. It is only proper in conclusion to stress that it contributed also,

---

[53] Harley to Edward Harley, 21 Nov. 1714, *ibid.*, 70(9); Elizabeth Harley to Abigail Harley, 29 May 1711, *ibid.*, 67(3).
[54] Sir Edward Harley to Edward Harley, *ibid.*, 70(7); Mary Foley to Robert Harley, 16 Jan. 1702, *ibid.*, 135(5).
[55] Bingley to Dartmouth, N.D., W.S.L., Dartmouth MSS., D. 1778. V. 811.

and immeasurably, to his political strength. His Puritanism laid him low in 1708 and 1714. But it helped too to make him, for all his faults and failings, a figure of real stature, perhaps the greatest politician of his day.

Appendices

Bibliography

1. MANUSCRIPT SOURCES

A. NATIONAL REPOSITORIES

1. *Public Record Office.*
   State Papers
      Series 34—Domestic.
         Vols 4–9. Letters and Papers, 1704–8.
      Series 41—Military.
         3. Secretary-at-War's Out-Letters, 1702–11.
         34. Letters from Office of Ordnance Board to Secretaries of State, 1702–14.
      Series 42—Naval.
         7. Secretary of State's In-Letters from Lords of the Admiralty, 1703–8.
         67. Secretary of State's In-Letters from Naval Commanders, 1700–10.
      Series 44—Entrybooks.
         77. Criminal, 1704–15.
         150. Ecclesiastical, 1688–1729.
         151. Ecclesiastical, 1690–1727.
         171. Military, 1702–6, Hedges.
         172. Military, 1704–9, Harley and Boyle.
         173. Military, 1706–14, Sunderland, Boyle, Dartmouth and Bromley.
         353. Warrants and Passes, 1704–10, Hedges and Sunderland.
         354. Warrants and Passes, 1074–8, Harley and Boyle.
      Series 45—Various.
         7–8. Precedent Books, 1677–1780.
      Series 67—Ireland, Entrybooks.
         3. Secretary's Letter Book, 1702–11.
   Admiralty Papers.
      Series 1—In-Letters.
         4,090–1 Secretary of State's Letters to Admiralty, 1704–8.

Series 2—Out-Letters.
     365. Lord's Letters to Secretaries of State, 1702–8.
War Office Papers.
    Series 4—Secretary-at-War, Out-Letter Entrybooks.
       3–5. St. John, 1704–7.
        6. St. John and Cardonnel, 1707–8.
Gifts and Deposits.
    Series 24—Shaftesbury Papers.
      20–2. Letters to and from the 3rd Earl of Shaftesbury. Many of these papers have been printed, but some useful material still remains. Of particular interest are the letters of Sir John Cropley.
Transcripts
    Series 3—Baschet Papers.
      196–202. Papers dealing with Anglo-French relations. Some letters from Oxford.

2. *British Museum.*
Additional MSS.
      4,253 Miscellaneous Letters 1693–1758. Several to Robert Harley.
      5,834. Memoirs of the Harley Family.
      7,059. Stepney Papers.
      7,077. Stepney Papers.
      7,121. Miscellaneous Letters, 1693–1706.
      10,403. Two Treatises on the Union by William Paterson.
      15,866. Letters of Robert Harley to James Dayrolle.
      17,677 RR-HHH. Dutch Dispatches. L'Hermitage's reports are particularly informative.
      28,052–5. Godolphin Papers.
      30,000 E. Transcripts of Dispatches of F. Bonnet.
      34,355. Letters to William Blathwayt.
      34,521. Miscellaneous Letters—including some correspondence of the Junto lords.
      40,621. Correspondence of Thomas and Robert Harley
      47,087. Percival Letterbook.

Egerton MSS.
  2,618. Miscellaneous Letters and Papers, 1556–1753.
Harleian MSS.
  1,545. Sixteenth Century Pedigree of the Harley Family.
  6,846. Papers relating to Parliament.
Lansdowne MSS.
  171–2. Humphrey Wanley's Diary.
  773. Letters of Charles Davenant to Henry Davenant.
  829. Miscellaneous Letters and Papers.
  885. MS. copy of Auditor Harley's "Memoirs". Fuller in some respects than the version printed in *H.M.C. Portland MSS.*, V.
Stowe MSS.
  225–7. Reports of Bothmar, Galke and Schütz to Hanover. Selectively printed by Macpherson.
  597. Notes on the Harley Family.
Portland Loan (Loan 29).
  The Harley Papers. Only a small portion of this vast collection has been calendared by the Historical Manuscripts Commission. The great bulk of the deposit relates to the career of Robert Harley. At its core is an immense series of letters addressed to Robert Harley, to his father, and to other members of the family. In addition, however, there is much other material of significance, such as Harley's Cabinet minutes (box 9) and his "Large Account: Revolution and Succession" (box 165). Taken as a whole the collection proved far and away the most important single source for this study.

3. *National Library of Wales.*
  Bettisfield MSS.
    Papers of Sir Thomas Hanmer.
  Chirk Castle MSS.
    Papers of Sir Richard Myddleton.
  Penrice and Margam MSS.
    Papers of Sir Thomas Mansell, 1st. Baron Mansell. Includes a number of letters from Harley.

B. UNIVERSITY LIBRARIES

1. *All Souls College, Oxford.*
    MSS. 158a. and b.
    "An Abstract of the Debates, Orders, and Resolutions In the House of Commons, which are not printed in their Votes. Collected by N[arcissus] L[uttrell] during his attendance therein as a Member". Volume I of this journal (158a) runs from 6 Nov. 1691 to 4 Nov. 1692, and volume II (158b) from 4 Nov. 1692 to 7 Nov. 1693. The accounts given of the Commons' debates are extremely detailed—in many cases much more detailed than the printed version of Anchitel Grey. The journal brings out more clearly than any other source the fact that the most significant division in the Commons after the autumn of 1691 was between Court and Country rather than between Whig and Tory.
2. *Bodleian Library, Oxford.*
    Additional MSS.
        A.191. Letters to Gilbert Burnet, 1680–1713.
        A.269. Letters of Edmund Gibson to William Nicolson.
    Ballard MSS.
        6. Letters of Edmund Gibson.
        7. Letters of Smalridge and Kennett to Arthur Charlett.
        31. Letters of William Bishop to Arthur Charlett.
        38. Includes some papers of William Bromley.
    Carte MSS.
        125. Miscellaneous Letters and Papers.
        130. Miscellaneous Letters and Papers—including some important letters from Robert Price to the Duke of Beaufort.
    Rawlinson MSS.
        A.245. Memoranda of Anthony Hammond, including a crude Diary.
        D.965. Memoranda and Notes by Anthony Hammond for the year 1706.

3. *Cambridge University Library.*

Additional MSS.

7,093. Anonymous Parliamentary Diary, 1705–6.

Throws valuable light on Harley's attitude to the Country section of the Regency Bill.

Cholmondeley (Houghton) MSS.

The Walpole Papers. Disappointingly thin for this period.

4. *Nottingham University Library*

Harley MSS (PW2, HY).

A small but important collection of papers covering the whole span of Harley's career. Contains, among other things, Harley's "Advice to a Son", and a quantity of letters relating to the peace negotiations.

Holles MSS. (PW2).

Papers of the Duke of Newcastle.

Portland MSS (PWA).

Papers of William Bentinck, 1st. Earl of Portland. Large numbers of these were printed by N. Japikse, but many important letters remain unprinted.

C. COUNTY RECORD OFFICES

1. *Berkshire R.O.*

Downshire MSS; Trumbull MSS; Trumbull Additional MSS.

Papers of Sir William Trumbull. Extensively calendared by the Historical Manuscripts Commission. Some useful matter remains, however, including Trumbull's Diary, and a series of letters from Henry St. John.

2. *Herefordshire R..O*

The Harley Papers, C. 64.

Photographic copies of unbundled political papers at Brampton Bryan. Chiefly letters to Auditor Harley and his wife.

3. *Hertfordshire R.O.*

Panshanger MSS.

The Cowper Papers. A substantial collection, including

Sir David Hamilton's Diary, and letters to Lord and Lady Cowper.

4. *Leicestershire R.O.*

Finch MSS.

Papers of Daniel Finch, 2nd Earl of Nottingham. Partially calendared by the Historical Manuscripts Commission. A number of uncalendared items remain which shed valuable light on Nottingham's breach with the Oxford ministry.

5. *Northamptonshire R.O.*

Finch-Hatton MSS.

Contain some revealing letters from Nottingham to his wife.

Isham MSS.

Papers of Sir Justinian Isham.

6. *Surrey R.O.*

Somers MSS.

Letters and Papers of Lord Somers. Very few of political import.

D. OTHER LIBRARIES·

1. *Hereford City Library,*

Harley letters.

Transcripts of Letters relating to the Harley Family in the Seventeenth Century from the originals at Brampton Bryan.

MS. Inventory of the Earl of Oxford's Goods, 1724. Throws light on farming practices at Brampton Bryan.

2. *John Rylands Library, Manchester.*

Legh of Lyme MSS.

Papers of Peter Legh, some of which touch on Parliamentary affairs.

3. *William Salt Library, Stafford.*

Dartmouth MSS.

Papers of Lord Dartmouth. Include Dartmouth's Cabinet minutes, and a quantity of political correspondence, chiefly undated, not calendared by the Historical Manuscripts Commission.

Kaye MSS.

MS. Diary of Sir Arthur Kaye. Sheds light on the Country Tory opposition to the Oxford ministry which found expression, first in the October Club, and subsequently the March Club.

4. *Tullie House, Carlisle,*

Bishop Nicolson's MS. Diary.

Contains a number of important and detailed accounts of debates in the Upper Chamber. Particularly valuable for the 1702–6 period.

5. *Dr. Williams's Library, London.*

MSS. 59. 1–6.

Richard Baxter's Correspondence. A useful supplement to Baxter's printed works—throwing valuable light on his personality and religious position.

Roger Morrice's Entering Book.

A detailed account of dissenting activities from the late 1670s to the early 1690s by an ejected Presbyterian minister. Contains occasional matter of wider political interest.

E. COLLECTIONS IN PRIVATE CUSTODY

1. *Blenheim Palace, Woodstock.*

Blenheim MSS.

The Marlborough Papers. Much of this massive collection has been printed by Coxe and other historians. But useful material still remains unpublished. The collection contains a considerable number of unprinted letters from Harley to Marlborough for the years 1704–8, but, unfortunately, many of these are very formal in character.

2. *Brampton Bryan Hall, Herefordshire.*

Brampton Bryan MSS.

Some 150 bundles of papers relating to the Harley family. Most of these MSS. are estate papers, but they also include items of political interest.

3. *Chatsworth, Derbyshire.*

Devonshire House Notebook.

In the hand of the 1st Marquess of Halifax. Contains

considerable hitherto unknown information on English
politics for the years 1687–91.

Devonshire Family Papers.

Mainly private correspondence—but also some papers
of political significance, including four letters from
Robert Harley to Henry Boyle.

4. *Longleat House, Wiltshire.*

Portland MSS.

Extensively printed by the Historical Manuscripts Commission. However, there are still items of vital importance as yet unpublished, including an entire volume of
letters (Portland Misc. MSS) from Godolphin to Harley.

F.   FOREIGN REPOSITORIES

1. *Staatsarchiv, Hannover.*

Cal. Br. 24 England.

99, 107a, 113a. Kreienberg's reports to Hanover. Particularly useful for the Cabinet crisis of September 1712.

2. *Quai d'Orsay, Paris (Archives du ministère des Affaires étrangères).*

Correspondance politique Angleterre.

231–58.   Copies of many of these papers may be found
in the Baschet Transcripts in the Public Record Office.
Much of value, however, particularly regarding the
peace negotiations, remains. The papers have only been
very selectively used in the present study.

II.   PRINTED WORKS CITED

A.   PRIMARY MATERIAL

1. *Official Documents.*

Acts of the Parliaments of Scotland, 1593–1707, edited by
T. Thomson and C. Innes. London, 1814–75. Vols.
XI–XII.

*Calendar of State Papers, Domestic Series, of the Reign of Charles I,
Preserved in Her Majesty's Public Record Office,* edited by

J. Bruce and W. D. Hamilton. London, 1858–97. Vol. for 1625–6.

Calendar of State Papers, Domestic Series, 1649–60, Preserved in Her Majesty's Public Record Office, edited by M. A. E. Green. London, 1875–86. Vol. for 1649–50.

Calendar of State Papers, Domestic Series, of the Reign of William III, Preserved in the Public Record Office, edited by W. J. Hardy and E. Bateson. London, 1908–37. Vol. for 1697.

Calendar of State Papers, Domestic Series, of the Reign of Anne, Preserved in the Public Record Office, edited by R. P. Mahaffy. London, 1916–24. 2 vols.

Calendar of Treasury Books, Preserved in the Public Record Office edited by W. A. Shaw and others. London, 1931–55. Vols. IX–XXVIII.

Journals of the House of Commons. Vols. VII–XVIII.

Journals of the House of Lords. Vol. XIX.

2. *Reports of the Historical Manuscripts Commission.*

Report on the MSS. of Capt. J. F. Bagot. 10th. Report, Appendix, Part IV. London, 1885.

Report on the MSS. of the Marquis of Bath, at Longleat. London, 1904–8. Vols. I–III.

Report on the MSS. of the Duke of Buccleuch, Montagu House, Whitehall. London, 1903. Vol. II.

Report on the MSS. of Earl Cowper, at Melbourne. 12th Report, Appendix, Part III. London, 1889. Vol. III.

Report on the MSS. of the Earl of Denbigh. 7th Report, Appendix. London, 1879.

Report on the MSS. of the Marquis of Downshire, at Easthampstead. London, 1924. Vol. I, Part II.

Report on the MSS. of the Earl of Egmont. London, 1909. Vol. II, Part II.

Report on the MSS. of the House of Lords. 12th. and later Reports. London, 1889–1962. Vols. 2–11.

Report on the MSS. of the Duke of Marlborough. 8th Report, Appendix, Part I. London, 1881.

Report on the MSS. of the Duke of Portland. 13th, and later Reports. London, 1893–1931. Vols. II–X.

Report on the Stuart Papers belonging to His Majesty the King, preserved at Windsor Castle. London, 1902. Vol. I.

Report on the MSS. of Sir Harry Verney Bt. 7th Report, Appendix. London, 1879.

3. *Other Original Correspondence and Diaries.*

The Letters of Joseph Addison, edited by Walter Graham. Oxford, 1941.

Correspondence of George Baillie of Jerviswood, 1702–1708, edited by the Earl of Minto for the Bannatyne Club. Edinburgh, 1842.

Reliquiae Baxterianae, edited by M. Sylvester. London, 1696.

State Papers and Letters Adressed to William Carstares . . . during the Reign of King William and Queen Anne, edited by J. McCormick. Edinburgh, 1774.

Memoirs of Sir John Clerk of Pennicuik, edited by J. M. Gray for the Roxburghe Club. London, 1895.

The Private Diary of William, First Earl Cowper, Lord Chancellor of England, edited by E. C. Hawtrey for the Roxburghe Club. Eton, 1833.

The Letters of Daniel Defoe, edited by G. H. Healey. Oxford, 1955.

The Diary of John Evelyn, edited by E. S. de Beer. London, 1955. 6 vols.

"Letters on Godolphin's Dismissal in 1710", edited by C. Buck and G. Davies, *Huntington Library Quarterly,* III. 1939–40, pp. 225–42.

Correspondence of the Family of Hatton, edited by E. M. Thompson for the Camden Society. London, 1878.

Remarks and Collections of Thomas Hearne, edited by C. E. Doble, D. W. Rannie, and H. E. Salter for the Oxford History Society. Oxford, 1885–1918. Vols. I–IV.

The Diary of John Hervey, First Earl of Bristol, with Extracts from his Book of Expenses, 1688–1742. Wells, 1894.

The Letter Books of John Hervey, First Earl of Bristol. Wells, 1894.

The Lexington Papers, or, some Account of the Courts of London and Vienna at the conclusion of the Seventeenth Century . . . , edited by the Hon. H. Manners-Sutton. London, 1851.

Original Letters of Locke, Algernon Sidney, and Anthony Lord Shaftesbury, Author of the 'Characteristics', edited by T. Forster. London, 1830.

A Brief Historical Relation of State Affairs . . . , by Narcissus Luttrell. Oxford, 1857. 6 vols.

Lyme Letters, 1660–1760, edited by Lady Newton. London, 1925.

A Selection from the Papers of the Earls of Marchmont . . . illustrative of Events from 1685 to 1750, edited by G. H. Rose. London, 1831. Vol. III.

Private Correspondence of Sarah, Duchess of Marlborough, illustrative of the Court and Times of Queen Anne. London, 1838. 2 vols.

Catalogue of the Autograph Letters . . . formed by Alfred Morrison, edited by A. W. Thibaudeau. London, 1883–92. Vol. V.

The Norris Papers, edited by T. Heywood for the Chetham Society. Manchester, 1846.

Letters of Humphrey Prideaux, sometime Dean of Norwich, to John Ellis, sometime Under-Secretary of State, 1674–1722, edited by E. M. Thompson for the Camden Society. London, 1875.

Letters and Correspondence, Public and Private, of Henry St. John, Lord Viscount Bolingbroke, during the time he was Secretary of State to Queen Anne, edited by G. Parke. London, 1798. 4 vols.

Letters Relating to Scotland in the Reign of Queen Anne by James Ogilvy, Earl of Seafield and others, edited by P. H. Brown. Edinburgh, 1915.

The Life, Unpublished Letters, and Philosophical Regimen of Anthony Earl of Shaftesbury, edited by B. Rand. London, 1900.

The Correspondence of Jonathan Swift, edited by F. Elrington Ball. London, 1910–14. 6 vols.

Swift, J., *Journal to Stella*, edited by H. Williams. Oxford, 1946. 2 vols.

Private and Original Correspondence of Charles Talbot, Duke of Shrewsbury, edited by W. Coxe. London, 1821.

Verney Letters . . . of the Eighteenth Century from the MSS. at Claydon House, edited by Margaret Maria, Lady Verney. London, 1930. Vol. I.

Letters Illustrative of the Reign of William III from 1696 to 1708 Addressed to the Duke of Shrewsbury, by James Vernon Esq.,

Secretary of State, edited by G. P. R. James. London, 1841. 3 vols.

The Wentworth Papers, 1705–39, edited by J. J. Cartwright. London, 1883.

Letters of William III and Louis XIV and of their Ministers . . . 1697–1700, edited by Paul Grimblot. London, 1848. 2 vols.

4. *Contemporary Pamphlets, Sermons, Tracts and Poems.*

Addison, J., *The Freeholder*. Glasgow, 1752.

Bayly, L., *Practice of Piety*. London, 1862.

Cradock, W., *Gospel Libertie*. London, 1648.

Davenant, C., *An Essay upon I the Balance of Power, II the Right of Making War, Peace and Alliances, III Universal Monarchy*. London, 1701.

——, *The True Picture of a Modern Whig*. London, 1701.

Defoe, D., *Armageddon: or the Necessity of Carrying on the war if such a Peace cannot be obtained as may render Europe safe, and trade secure*. London, 1711.

——, *The Balance of Europe* . . . London, 1706.

——, *Caledonia. A Poem in Honour of Scotland and the Scots Nation*. Edinburgh, 1706.

——, *Eleven Opinions about Mr. Harley*. London, 1711.

——, *An Essay at Removing National Prejudices* . . . *Part I*, London, 1706.

——, *An Essay at Removing National Prejudices* . . . *Part II*, London (?), 1706.

——, *An Essay at Removing National Prejudices* . . . *Part III*. London (?), 1706.

——, *An Essay upon Loans* . . . London, 1710.

——, *An Essay upon Publick Credit* . . . London, 1710.

——, *A Fourth Essay at Removing National Prejudices* . . . Edinburgh, 1706.

——, *A Fifth Essay at Removing National Prejudices* . . . Edinburgh, 1707.

——, *Reasons why this Nation ought to put a Speedy End to this Expensive War*. London, 1711.

——, *The Secret History of the White Staff*. London, 1714.

——, *The Shortest Way with Dissenters*. London, 1702.

Drake J., *Memorial of the Church of England*. London, 1705.

Dod, J., and Cleaver, R., *A Godlie Forme of Householde Government*. London, 1612.

Froysell, T., *The Beloved Disciple*. London, 1658.

Gouge, W., *The Works*. London, 1626.

H——, P., *An Impartial View of the Two Late Parliaments*. London, 1711.

Gweithiau Morgan Llwyd o Wynedd, edited by T. E. Ellis. Bangor, 1899.

Milton, J., *Paradise Lost*.

Paterson, W., *An Enquiry in the Reasonableness of an Union with Scotland*. London, 1706.

Perkins, W., *The Workes*. London, 1612–13. 3 vols.

Rogers, R., *Seven Treatises*. London, 1630.

St. John, H., Viscount Bolingbroke, *Considerations on the Secret History of the White Staff*. London, 1715.

A Collection of scarce and valuable Tracts selected from . . . the Royal, Cotton, Sion and other Libraries, particularly that of the late Lord Somers, edited by W. Scott. London, 1809–15. Vols. X–XII.

Later Stuart Tracts, edited by G. A. Aitken. Westminster, 1903.

Jonathan Swift: Miscellaneous and Autobiographical Pieces, Fragments and Marginalia, edited by H. Davis. Oxford, 1962.

The Poems of Jonathan Swift, edited by H. Williams. Oxford, 1958. 3 vols.

The Prose Works of Jonathan Swift, edited by Temple Scott. London, 1901. 12 vols.

Toland, G., *The Art of Governing by Parties*. London, 1701.

Walsh, W., "The Golden Age Restored", *The Works of the Most Celebrated Minor Poets*. London, 1749.

Anon, *The Age of Wonders*. London, 1710.

——, *A Letter from a Member of the H[ouse] of C[ommons] to his Friend in the Country relating to the Bill of Commerce*. London, 1713.

5. *Accounts and Memoirs Written by Contemporaries after the Event*.

Boyer, A., *The History of Queen Anne* . . . . London, 1735.

——, *The Reign of King William III*. London, 1702–3. 3 vols.

Memoirs of Thomas Bruce, Second Earl of Ailesbury, written by himself, edited by W. E. Buckley for the Roxburghe Club. Westminster, 1890. Vol. II.

Burnet, G., *History of My Own Time.* Oxford, 1823. 6 vols.

Calamy, E., *Historical Account of My Own Life.* London, 1829. 2 vols.

"Lord Coningsby's Account of the State of Political Parties during the Reign of Queen Anne", edited by Sir Henry Ellis, *Archaeologia,* Vol. XXXVIII, 1860, pp. 1–18.

Defoe, D., *The History of the Union of Great Britain.* London, 1787.

Kennett, W., *The Wisdom of Looking Backward.* London, 1715.

The Lockhart Papers : *containing Memoirs and Commentaries upon the Affaires of Scotland from 1702 to 1715,* edited by A. Aufrere. London, 1817. Vol. I.

The Memoirs of Edmund Ludlow, edited by C. H. Firth. Oxford, 1894. 2 vols.

Memoirs of the Secret Service of John Macky during the Reigns of King William, Queen Anne and King George I, London, 1733.

Memoirs of Sarah, Duchess of Marlborough, edited by W. King. London, 1930.

The Conduct of the Earl of Nottingham, edited by W. A. Aitken New Haven, 1941.

Oldmixon, J., *The History of England during the Reigns of King William and Queen Mary, Queen Anne, King George I.* London, 1735.

Memoirs of the Marquis of Torcy . . . containing the History of the Negotiations from the Treaty of Ryswick to the Peace of Utrecht. London, 1857.

6. *Compilations—chiefly of Original Documents and Other Original Papers.*

   A Complete Collection of State Trials, compiled by T. B. Howell. London, 1816. Vol. XIV.

   The Divided Society : *Parties and Politics in England, 1694–1716,* edited by G. S. Holmes and W. A. Speck.

   The Harleian Miscellany, edited by T. Osborne. London, 1744–6. Vol. I.

The History of the Reign of Queen Anne digested in Annals, compiled by Abel Boyer. London, 1703–10. 8 vols.

Miscellaneous State Papers from 1501 to 1726 from the Collection of the Earl of Hardwicke, edited by Philip Yorke. London, 1778. Vol. II.

Original Papers containing the Secret History of Great Britain, edited by J. Macpherson. London, 1775. Vol. II.

The Parliamentary History of England, compiled by W. Cobbett. London, 1806–12. Vols. V–VII.

The Political State of Great Britain, compiled by Abel Boyer. London, 1711–15. 5 vols. (A continuation of the *Annals*).

State Papers and Correspondence Illustrative of the Society and Political State of Europe, edited by J. M. Kemble. London, 1857.

B. SECONDARY AUTHORITIES

1. *Books.*

Baxter, S. B., *The Development of the Treasury, 1660–1702*. London, 1957.

Beeching, H. C., *Francis Atterbury*. London, 1909.

Browning, A., *Thomas Osborne, Earl of Danby*. Glasgow, 1944–51. 3 vols.

Burton, J. H., *The History of Scotland*. Edinburgh, 1905. Vol. VIII.

Campbell, J., *Lives of the Chancellors and Keepers of the Great Seal of England*. London, 1846. Vol. IV.

Churchill, W. S., *Marlborough, His Life and Times*. London, 1947. 2 vols.

Clapham, J., *The Bank of England*. London, 1945.

Collins, A., *Historical Collection of Cavendish, Holles, Vere, Harley and Ogle*. London, 1752.

Coxe, W., *Memoirs of John, Duke of Marlborough, with His Original Correspondence*. London, 1820. 6 vols.

——, *Memoirs of the Life and Administration of Sir Robert Walpole, Earl of Orford*. London, 1816. 4 vols.

Davies, G., *Essays on the Later Stuarts*. San Marino, 1958.

Dottin, P., *Daniel Defoe et ses Romans*. Paris, 1924.

Ernle, Lord, *English Farming Past and Present*. 3rd edn., London, 1922.

Feiling, K. G., *History of the Tory Party, 1640–1714*. Oxford, 1924.

Foster, J., ed., *Alumni Oxoniensis*. Oxford, 1887–92. Vol. 1.

Fraser, P., *The Intelligence of the Secretaries of State and their Monopoly of Licensed News, 1660–88*. Cambridge, 1956.

Hart, J., *Viscount Bolingbroke, Tory Humanist*. London, 1965.

Hill, C., *Society and Puritanism in Pre-Revolution England*. London, 1964.

Holmes, G., *British Politics in the Age of Anne*. London, 1967.

Horsfield, J. K., *British Monetary Experiments, 1650–1710*. London, 1960.

Horwitz, H., *Revolution Politicks: The Career of Daniel Finch, 2nd Earl of Nottingham 1647–1730*. Cambridge. 1968.

Kenyon, J. P., *Robert Spencer, Earl of Sunderland*. London, 1958.

Klopp, O., *Der Fall des Hauses Stuart*. Wien, 1875–88. Vol. X.

Lang, A., *History of Scotland*. Edinburgh, 1907. Vol. IV.

Leadam, I. S., *The History of England from the Accession of Anne to the Death of George II*. London, 1912.

Lecky, W. E. H., *History of the Rise and Influence of the Spirit of Rationalism in Europe*. London, 1897. 2 vols.

Macknight, T., *The Life of Henry St. John, Viscount Bolingbroke*. London, 1863.

Michael, W., *England Under George I: The Beginnings of the Hanoverian Dynasty*. London, 1936.

Minto, W., *Daniel Defoe*. London, 1879.

Moore, J. R., *Daniel Defoe, Citizen of the Modern World*. Chicago, 1958.

Namier, L. B., *Crossroads of Power*. London, 1962.

Nicholson, T. C., and Turberville. A. S., *Charles Talbot, Duke of Shrewsbury*. Cambridge, 1930.

Noorden, C. von, *Europaische Geschichte im achtzehnten Jahrhundert*. Düsseldorf, 1870–82. Vol. III.

Notestein, W., *English Folk*. London, 1938.

Nuttall, G. F., *The Welsh Saints, 1640–60*. Cardiff, 1957.

——, and Chadwick, O., eds., *From Uniformity to Unity, 1662–1962*. London, 1962.

——, and Others, *The Beginning of Nonconformity*. London, 1964.

Petrie, C., *Bolingbroke*. London, 1937.

Plumb, J. H., *The Growth of Political Stability in England, 1675–1725*. London, 1967.

Ranke, L. von, *A History of England Principally in the Seventeenth Century*. Oxford, 1875. Vols. V and VI.

Richards, T., *Piwritaniaeth a Pholitics, 1689–1719*. Wrecsam, 1927.

Rogers, J. E. T., *A History of Agriculture and Prices in England*. Oxford, 1866–1902. 7 vols.

Scott, W. R., *The Constitution and Finance of English, Scottish and Irish Joint Stock Companies to 1720*. Cambridge 1910–12. 3 vols.

Scudi, A. T., *The Sacheverell Affair*. New York, 1939.

Sharp, T., *The Life of John Sharp, D.D., Lord Archbishop of York*. London, 1825. 2 vols.

Somerville, D. H., *The King of Hearts*. London, 1962.

Story, R., *William Carstares*. London, 1874.

Thomas, R., *Daniel Williams, Presbyterian Bishop*. London. 1964.

Thomson, M. A., *The Secretaries of State, 1681–1782*. Oxford 1932.

Trevelyan, G. M., *England Under Queen Anne*. London, 1930–4.

Turberville, A. S., *The House of Lords in the Eighteenth Century*. Oxford, 1927.

Walcott, R. R., *English Politics in the Early Eighteenth Century*. Oxford, 1956.

Ward, W. R., *The English Land Tax in the Eighteenth Century*. London, 1953.

Willey, B., *The Seventeenth Century Background*. London, 1934.

Williams, W. R., *The History of the Great Sessions in Wales 1542–1830, together with the Lives of the Welsh Judges*. Brecknock, 1899.

2. *Articles.*

Ansell, P. M., "Harley's Parliamentary Management", *Bulletin of the Institute of Historical Research*, Vol. XXXIV. 1961.

Banks, R. W., "An Account of the Siege of Brampton Bryan Castle", *Archaeologia Cambrensis*, 3rd series, Vol. X. 1864.

Bennett, G. V., "Robert Harley, the Godolphin Ministry, and the Bishoprics Crisis of 1707", *English Historical Review*, Vol. LXXXII. 1967.

Browning, A., and Milne, D. J., "An Exclusion Bill Division List", *Bulletin of the Institute of Historical Research*, Vol. XXIII. 1950.

Davies, G., "The Fall of Harley in 1708", *English Historical Review*, Vol. LXVI. 1951.

Davies, O. R. F., "The Wealth and Influence of John Holles, Duke of Newcastle, 1694–1711", *Renaissance and Modern Studies*, Vol. IX. 1965.

Habakkuk, H. J., "English Landownership, 1680–1740". *Economic History Review*, Vol. X. 1939–40.

Holmes, G. S., "The Attack on 'The Influence of the Crown' 1702–16", *Bulletin of the Institute of Historical Research*, Vol. XXXIX. 1966.

——, "The Hamilton Affair of 1711–1712: A Crisis in Anglo Scottish Relations", *English Historical Review*, Vol. LXXVII. 1962.

——, and Speck, W. A., "The Fall of Harley in 1708 Reconsidered", *English Historical Review*, Vol. LXXX. 1965.

Johnson, B. L. C., "The Foley Partnerships: the Iron Industry at the End of the Charcoal Era", *Economic History Review*, 2nd series, Vol. IV. 1951–2.

Lees, R. M., "Parliament and the Proposal for a Council of Trade, 1695–6", *English Historical Review*, Vol. LIV. 1939.

McInnes, A., "The Appointment of Harley in 1704", *Historical Journal*, Vol. XI. 1968.

——, "The Political Ideas of Robert Harley", *History*, Vol. L. 1965.

——, "The Shifting Centre", *Listener*, Vol. LXXIII, no. 1875. 1965.

Speck, W. A., "The Choice of a Speaker in 1705", *Bulletin of the Institute of Historical Research*, Vol. XXXVII. 1964.

Sperling, J. G., "The Division of 25 May 1711 on an Amendment to the South Sea Bill : A Note on the Reality of Parties in the Age of Anne", *Historical Journal*, Vol. IV. 1961.

Straka, G. M., "The Final Phase of Divine Right Theory in England, 1688–1702", *English Historical Review*, Vol. LXXVII. 1962.

Touche, J. D. la, "Brampton Bryan Castle : Its Sieges and Demolition", *Transactions of the Woolhope Club*. 1882.

3. *Unpublished Theses.*

Ellis, E. L., "The Whig Junto in Relation to the Development of Party Politics and Party Organization from its Inception to 1714". D. Phil., Oxford University, 1962.

——, "The Whig Party, 1702–8". M.A., University of Wales, 1949.

McInnes, A., "Robert Harley, Secretary of State". M.A., University of Wales, 1961.

Ming-Hsun, L., "The Great Recoinage". Ph. D., London University, 1940.

Scholes, P. M., "Parliament and the Protestant Dissenters, 1702–1719". M.A., London University, 1962.

Speck, W. A., "The House of Commons, 1702–14 : A Study in Political Organization". D. Phil., Oxford University, 1965.

Index